MARKETING HIGHER EDUCATION

This book provides a comprehensive and accessible guide to marketing Higher Education institutions, discussing how universities are service providers and how education is a service, both of which need to be defined and marketed together.

Unlike the current offering available on the subject, this book provides a uniquely applied approach, linking the theory of marketing practice to the Higher Education sector through real life case studies and examples. Each topic is covered in depth, including marketing segmentation, pricing, location, brand management, internationalization, and expansion. Overarchingly, the book considers how to develop and promote the university as a product and as a brand. Two case studies from real life universities in a broad range of locations are provided at the end of each chapter, alongside questions to aid understanding and application.

Holistic and practical, *Marketing Higher Education* is an ideal guide for academics and students studying services marketing, Higher Education management and leadership, and marketing in the public sector. It will also be an invaluable resource for professionals working in Higher Education administration looking to develop their skills and understanding of marketing and brand building.

Paul Sergius Koku, PhD, is a Fulbrighter and Tenured Full Professor at the College of Business at Florida Atlantic University, USA.

MARKETING HIGHER EDUCATION

Understanding How to Build and Promote the University Brand

Paul Sergius Koku

Routledge
Taylor & Francis Group

LONDON AND NEW YORK

Cover image: ArtistGNDphotography

First published 2023
by Routledge
4 Park Square, Milton Park, Abingdon, Oxon OX14 4RN

and by Routledge
605 Third Avenue, New York, NY 10158

Routledge is an imprint of the Taylor & Francis Group, an informa business

British Library Cataloguing-in-Publication Data
A catalogue record for this book is available from the British Library

Library of Congress Cataloging-in-Publication Data
Names: Koku, Paul Sergius, 1955– author.
Title: Marketing higher education : understanding how to build and promote the university brand / Paul Sergius Koku.
Description: Abingdon, Oxon ; New York, NY : Routledge, 2023. |
Includes bibliographical references and index.
Identifiers: LCCN 2022003168 (print) | LCCN 2022003169 (ebook) |
ISBN 9780367749170 (hardback) | ISBN 9780367749194 (paperback) |
ISBN 9781003160267 (ebook)
Subjects: LCSH: Universities and colleges–Marketing. |
Education, Higher–Marketing. | Branding (Marketing)
Classification: LCC LB2342.82 .K65 2023 (print) |
LCC LB2342.82 (ebook) | DDC 378.1/01–dc23/eng/20220317
LC record available at https://lccn.loc.gov/2022003168
LC ebook record available at https://lccn.loc.gov/2022003169

ISBN: 978-0-367-74917-0 (hbk)
ISBN: 978-0-367-74919-4 (pbk)
ISBN: 978-1-003-16026-7 (ebk)

DOI: 10.4324/9781003160267

Typeset in Bembo
by Newgen Publishing UK

To my late parents, and RVK.

CONTENTS

STATEMENT OF AIMS

The definition of marketing as a business activity has evolved over the years to reflect the current thinking as the world's economy expands and new activities are developed. Marketing was defined in the early twentieth century as:

> The process of transferring goods through commercial channels from producer to consumer.
>
> *(Brown, 1925, p. 3; see Brunswick, 2014)*

About three decades ago, a premier academic marketing association, the American Marketing Association (AMA), defined marketing as:

> The process of planning and executing the conception, pricing, planning and distribution of ideas, good, and services to create exchanges that satisfy individual and organizational objectives.

A thoughtful European scholar in the field of marketing, around the same time, stated that:

> Marketing is to establish, develop and commercialise long-term customer relationships so that objectives are met. This is done by a mutual exchange and keeping of promises.
>
> *(Gronroos, 1989, p. 57)*

However, the AMA's current definition of marketing introduced in 2013 states that

> Marketing is the activity, set of institution, and processes for creating, communicating, delivering, and exchanging offerings that have value for customers, clients, partners, and society at large.
>
> *(AMA, July 2013)*

One should not be surprised if a new definition is proffered a decade from now. However, the point to note in the current definition of marketing is its inclusion of "value creation." Marketing as a value creating activity/process relates or should relate to everything that is offered for sale, or for exchange in the marketplace (this concept will be more clearly explained later in the text). Contemporary marketing activities include services such as politics (political marketing), family planning, and religion (religion marketing) to mention just a few. It also includes higher education and the "producers" of higher education – universities and other tertiary institutions. Notwithstanding the fact that universities in the United States alone collectively spent $1.265 billion dollars on advertising in 2016 (Brock, 2017), to the best of our knowledge, there is no book to date on the marketing of universities. This book fills this gap. It discusses how marketing relates to higher education, specifically universities and how it is practiced, or should be practiced. This book is an ideal compendium for university administrators (deans, department chairs, admission officers, recruitment officers, and enrollment managers) who wish to familiarize themselves with the "lay of the land" with respect to university marketing. To the extent that understanding how to market a university has now become indispensable to potential university administrators, this book is also suitable as a textbook on "current topics" and "contemporary issues" in education for students in Educational Administration & Leadership programs. This book can also be used for graduate "special topics" course in services marketing. To make it a suitable textbook, it includes questions and two cases (that are relevant to the issues discussed) at the end of each chapter.

References

American Marketing Association (AMA) (2013). Definition of Marketing. www.ama.org/AboutAMA/Pages/Definition-of-Marketing.aspx.

Brock, B. (2017). College Advertising at All-Time High. Marketing Group, October 5. https://emgonline.com/2017/10/college-advertising-at-all-time-high/. Retrieved on April 10, 2020.

Brown, E. (1925). *Marketing*. New York: Harper and Brothers.

Brunswick, G. (2014). A Chronology of the Definition of Marketing. *Journal of Business & Economics Research* 12 (2), 105–113.

Grönroos, C. (1989). Defining Marketing: A Market-Oriented Approach. *European Journal of Marketing*, 23 (1), 52–60.

ABOUT THE AUTHOR

Professor Paul Sergius Koku is a Fulbrighter and Tenured Full Professor in the College of Business in Florida Atlantic University. He works on interdisciplinary issues including but not limited to issues on poverty eradication, services marketing, interface between finance and marketing, corporate governance, information asymmetry, issues in education, boycotts, and social activism. He comments on boycott activities in the national and international media, and has authored and co-authored three books. His papers have appeared in several peer-reviewed journals and as book chapters. Professor Koku holds a BA (summa cum Laude) with concentration in Finance from the University of the Virgin Islands. He also holds MBA (Marketing) from Oregon State University, MBA (Finance), MA (Applied Economics), and a PhD in Finance and Marketing, all from Rutgers. Professor Koku also holds the Juris Doctor degree from the University of Miami, School of Law, and practices law pro bono.

ACKNOWLEDGMENTS

I would like to thank all those who have contributed directly or indirectly to getting ideas for this book from being simply thoughts in my head to being words on paper. My former and current students have contributed in no small measure because I get to "practice my arguments" on them. My nephew Dan, an intellectual historian, contributed immensely to this book by indulging me in my never-ending discussions on many topics that became a part of this book whenever I visited him. "Absolute" my old classmate and Ali, a dear friend, who have had first-hand experiences, provided information for two cases in this book.

The staff of Routledge, particularly Levine Sophia and Emmie Shand, were extremely helpful. The former offered several thoughtful comments and coordinated the review process. I deeply thank "Dr. Ruth" for her unconditional love, support, and encouragement.

CAVEATS AND DISCLAIMERS

To minimize distractions, I used "they" instead of "they" in most parts of this book. The cases in this book are exercises intended to provide further opportunities for readers to interrogate themselves on the issues discussed in the chapters. Thus, they are for purely academic purposes and not intended to serve as a criticism of or commendation to any institution. While I benefited from the advice and the encouragement of many, I am solely responsible for all the errors in this book.

1

MARKETING IN UNIVERSITIES

Introduction

Have you ever thought about the nature of a university's business? What business did you think that is? This chapter introduces the book and argues that universities are involved in the business of *selling knowledge* which people acquire in the process of investing in themselves. The chapter therefore talks about human capital theory and value creation when universities sell knowledge, and relates all these to the marketing of universities.

The Essence of Marketing

A more fundamental objective of marketing is to develop a long-term mutually satisfying relationship between the customer and an entity. This entity could be a service provider such as a hotel, a bank, a university, or a product manufacturer such as an automobile or a computer manufacturer, and the customer could be a household, a consumer, a business organization, or a government agency. The purchaser need not necessarily be the consumer though. The relationship between the entity and the customer is created when the entity, regardless of what it is, be it for-profit business or a nonprofit entity (such as the United Way, the Red Cross, or Red Crescent), or government agency such as municipal transportation agency, delivers value to the customer.

  The entity makes the customer happy by delivering value, and this happy customer chooses the same entity (provider) from among many providers each time they need the same product (thing). Fundamentally, by delivering value which fulfils the customer's needs, both sides (the customer and the entity) end up achieving their respective objectives. The customer is happy getting their bundle of "satisfaction" through whatever it is that they purchased from the entity. An economist might say that the customer is happy maximizing their utility, while the provider is also happy from having accomplished what they set out to accomplish. This is the essence of marketing – meeting unmet needs in a time, place, and manner desired by the customer. This sounds simple, but behind this simple story are several activities and techniques.

DOI: 10.4324/9781003160267-1

We will discuss some of these activities and techniques in the following sections, and relate them to universities which are the focus of this book.

What Is a University Selling?

What business are we in? This is the basic question that every business executive, including university presidents, must first ask themselves and their executive teams because the answer provides a basic plank in their strategy formulation. Clearly, the answer to this question may not be exactly the same for different universities, for reasons we will discuss later, nonetheless the common strand that must be found in all the answers, because they all do about the same thing, is the fact that they are in the business of creating and disseminating knowledge. This is their *raison d'être,* and they do this through research and lectures which enhance the general welfare. By these, universities build intellectual capitals and/or expand the intellectual capacities of their students.

So, what are universities *selling?* The answer depends on who is asked and when the question is asked. This simple question should not elicit a complicated answer; however, a complicated answer is what one gets these days. Around 50–60 years ago, the answer would have been the same regardless of who is asked. Yet, the rules of the game have changed and so have the landscapes, and that is why individuals who are responsible for marketing universities have to be abreast with the changing landscape.

About 50–60 years ago, one could offer a simple answer by stating that universities *sell* knowledge, that is, knowledge is their core product (note that we use the term *product* to refer to tangible and intangible offerings), but this core product is embedded in several supplementary services. These supplementary services include but are not limited to the state-of-the-art lecture rooms, state-of-the-art computer labs, nice and well-equipped residential halls, recreational facilities, libraries, etc. which will be discussed in detail later. As a core product, universities provided a place for intellectual enlightenment and commitment to critical inquiry into humanist projects. However, things are shifting as far as the core offering is concerned; hence those who are responsible for marketing universities need to be abreast with the changing tides.

The Human Capital Theory

The human capital theory which began with Adam Smith in 1776 argued that labor is inextricably linked to the wealth of every nation (Smith, 1952). While this theory continued to play an important role in discussions on the wealth of nations, scholars such as Mincer (1958, 1974), Schultz (1961, 1963), and Becker (1964, 1993) extended the human capital theory to include the economics of education. Mincer in a series of empirical studies found that earnings given up to pursue education were compensated with higher earnings paid by occupations which required higher levels of education. Schultz (1961) further relates human capital to education in explaining the role of human capital in the significant increase in the national income between 1900 and 1956 when he observed that the estimated stock of education in the workforce had grown about twice the rate of reproducible capital.

Becker (1962) explained the relationship between human capital and education by describing investment in human capital as a wide range of activities including but not limited to "schooling, on-the-job training, medical care, vitamin consumption, and acquiring information about the economic system." Naturally, these investments differ in several respects. Take, for example, the relative effects on earning and consumptions. The important thing about the human capital theory and education is that even though the investment and the returns on investment are private, there is a spillover effect which is beneficial to society in general. That is so because in addition to an individual's acquisition of knowledge in a specific field, education also provides the means to an enlightened citizenry that is able to "participate in democratic and legal due process and to pursue values such as equality, fraternity, and liberty at both private and social levels" (Sweetland, 1966).

Let us take the case of Ms. Browne to illustrate these points. Ms. Jane Browne passed on the opportunity to work full-time as a cashier in the local grocery store, where she used to work part-time while attending high school, and instead went to college. After earning the bachelor's degree in history, Ms. Browne takes a job as a high school social science teacher. She also works as a volunteer in the local chapter of League of Women Voters. Besides using the specialized knowledge that she acquired from the university to do her job as a social science teacher, Ms. Browne uses the other experiences that she gained from the university to participate in civic activities. In this example, streams of income that Ms. Browne earns from her teaching job could be viewed as the private returns on her investment in her education. This according to Mincer (1958, 1974) would be more than what Ms. Browne would have made over the same amount of time (interests included) if she had taken her job as a full-time cashier with only a high school diploma. However, the social returns from Ms. Browne's higher education are not limited to the fact that she is making the society better off by teaching, but also from participating in civic activities. For these reasons, education is regarded largely as a public good in which many governments are prepared to invest, and have invested for hundreds of years as evidenced the founding of public universities.

Economic Rationale for Change

The economic shocks experienced around the globe in the twentieth century have led many governments to revisit their expenditure on education, particularly university education as the economic rationale for investment in human capital has been revisited. Instead of the liberal ideal of the university where knowledge is acquired for the sake of knowing something new that one did not know before, governments started calling for university education that is linked to employability. In other words, universities have to produce graduates with skills that were needed in the economy.

New models for universities (particularly public universities) have been developed, and in countries such as the United Kingdom and Australia, the university has "emerged as the single provider of higher education, displacing other institutions of tertiary provision" such as the polytechnic institutes, colleges of advanced education, and institutes of technology that emerged in the post–World War period (Symes, 1996). Furthermore, new efficiency standards and accountability metrics have been developed for universities under the rubric of "quality assurance" with funding tied to meeting these metrics (Cullen, 1992).

In some instances, some universities or colleges within a university have developed other means to supplement their budget. To increase their financial resources some schools of business offer executive programs for which the enrollees pay much more for the same degree courses offered to regular students. Furthermore, some schools have made arranges with corporations in which they offer customized courses only to the employees of those corporations (Dover et al., 2018). Similarly, the traditional view which regarded the commercial use of university research in terms of spillovers has dramatically shifted to a practice in which universities transfer their technology and innovations to companies through licensing arrangements in order to appropriate the returns from faculty research (Thursby & Thursby, 2002).

These shifts have caused seismic changes on how universities are administered around the world. Although their mission statements have remained essentially unchanged, universities now have to do things differently. These changes require that universities are run more or less as businesses. To run a successful business requires having an effective marketing department that operates under a Vice President of Marketing or Chief Marketing Officer, hence it is no surprise that these positions have sprung up in many universities. However, marketing a university is different from running a public relations department in a university. The marketing department of a university must perform a wide array of activities including but not limited to clearly defining the university's target markets, understanding the needs of the markets, creating the educational services that meet the needs of this target markets, creating a brand name for the university so that it can be easily recognized and differentiated from competition, evoke some desired sentiments or emotions as well as create a message that sells what the university is offering.

To Whom Is the University Selling?

One of the basic rules of marketing for every successful company is to know the customers. So, the first order for successfully marketing a university is to know the university's customers. So, who is the customer? Is the university's customer the potential employer, or parents, the students, or the government? These questions must be answered even before the university decides on how to sell its core product. The university cannot successfully market what it is selling if it does not know the market or the market's needs. However, to answer this question properly, a number of points must first be understood.

1. The customer and the user need not be the same. In other words, the customer may not necessarily be the user. Furthermore, the buyer may not necessarily be the user. However, it is also possible that the customer or the buyer is one and the same as the user.
2. The buyer may not necessarily be the major decision maker with regard to the university that a potential student enrolls in. In other words, the person or agency that pays the costs involved (tuition, books, room and board, etc.) may not be the entity that selects the university.
3. It is perfectly all right, in fact, it is a must to develop different messages for the different role players, but this means that university must identify the different roles that the different entities play. A message highlighting certain aspects of the university must be aimed at the potential students – for example, a message and classes and fun on campus might be aimed at potential students, while a message about campus safety and courses might be aimed at parents. These points will be discussed in detail in chapter 6.

Universities have to sell themselves and their products to several different target markets and in several different ways. For the ease of exposition we will settle on just one approach. First, a university must realize that it faces two distinct primary markets – the internal market and the external market. The internal market comprises all of its employees, both officers and nonofficers. All the rank and file of its employees must be sold on the universities' value proposition and they must believe in it. This of course requires a major ground work. Representatives of the faculty, staff and officers of the university must be involved in setting or creating this value proposition. Ideally, this value proposition must be periodically reexamined with input from all its stakeholders. Their involvement in creating the value proposition accomplishes two goals:

1. Makes it easy for them to buy in.
2. Allows them to without much effort (that is, naturally) reflect these beliefs in their interactions on behalf of the university.

A university can sell itself and its offerings to its target markets in the external market using a basic upstream and downstream model illustrated in Figure 1.1. We simplified things in the figure by assuming that the two-way communication is taking place only between the university and the entities depicted. However, in real life communication networks can be more complex. For example, there can be a communication channel between the alumni association (that may be acting on behalf of the university) and the government as well as parents, potential students, and other companies.

Upstream are entities that the university sells itself to for financial resources to pursue its mission. These include governments, funding agencies, and alumni associations, while downstream are entities that the university sells itself to in order to recruit students or develop opportunities for placement of students for permanent employment or internship opportunities.

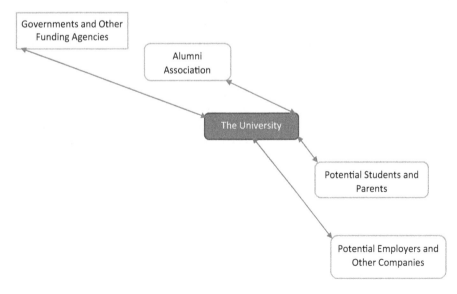

FIGURE 1.1 Upstream and Downstream Communication Pathways

Creating Value and Mutual Satisfaction

A university must know the needs of its target markets in order to be able to create value that can engender a mutually satisfying relationship. But how does a university do this? Many universities have an office for Institutional Research that has been grossly underutilized. In many schools these offices for years only kept track of alums. However, they have now become a major player in the "reimagined" role of universities. These offices are now responsible for conducting a wide array of research (studies) that include segmenting a university's market, determining the needs of a university's target markets, the financial impact of a university in its local markets, and the like. They are even responsible for creating the university's band in some schools.

Some universities supplement studies from the office of Institutional Research with studies from an external marketing research firm. Regardless of the approach, using the appropriate studies, a university must determine the unmet needs of its various market segments. However, it is obvious that a university does not have the resources to satisfactorily meet all the unmet needs in its various market segments, hence universities have to make hard choices. Which unmet needs is a university best equipped to meet, or can easily acquire the resources (faculty and equipment) to meet? This is where the difference between a **market segment** and a **market target** comes into play.

Take for instance a case where a university has determined that there is a great need for medical doctors in the area in which it operates. Furthermore, studies have shown that medical doctors tend to stay around the areas in which they attended medical school and did their residency (West et al., 1996). However, this university cannot afford the financial resources needed to establish a college of medicine. Here, what the university has the ability to do does not match the market's need; hence the university has to forgo meeting that specific need. The **market segment** needs physicians, but the university **does not have the expertise or the capacity** to train physicians

On the contrary, let us assume that the university also discovered that there is a need for trained personnel to fill entry and mid-level management positions in the local hospitality industry and the university has faculty with impeccable credentials and expertise in this area. In this case the university can offer degree programs in hospitality management or even consider creating a school or department in hospitality. Two things are happening here. First, the university "uncovers" a market segment and unmet need in the market, but unlike the case of medical doctors, the university has the means to meet this unmet need in the market. So, the second thing that has happened is the university now selects the market segment that it has a competency to serve well and proceeds to offer programs to train personnel for the hospitality industry. The **market segment** now becomes the university's **market target**. With further dialog with companies in the hospitality industry in the area, the university can create a *product* that they like (graduate well-trained personnel to fill the needs of the industry), hence the university creates value for companies in the industry. On the basis of this, a mutually satisfying relationship could develop.

Summary

This chapter tries to tie several concepts together and make a case for marketing universities. It begins with a definition of marketing which in itself shows the need for universities to market themselves. It then talks about value creation – a concept imbedded in marketing and how universities create value – for both the individual and the public. It then brings in the concept of human capital and education as an investment by discussing original economic arguments that one does not often see in marketing texts. The chapter concludes by discussing how market segmentation and market targeting are relevant to effectively market a university.

Questions

1. Who are a university's customers and why?
2. Who is a university's market segment?
3. Why is university a service?
4. Why is university education a public good?
5. How can university education be a personal investment if it is a public good?
6. How does marketing a university pose a unique challenge?
7. How does a university create value?

References

Becker, G.S. (1962). Investment in Human Capital: A Theoretical Analysis. *Journal of Political Economy* 70 (5, Part 2), 9–49.

Becker, G.S. (1964). *Human Capital: A Theoretical and Empirical Analysis, with Special Reference to Education*. New York: National Bureau of Economic Research.

Becker, G.S. (1993). *Human Capital: A Theoretical and Empirical Analysis, with Special Reference to Education*, 3rd ed. Chicago: University of Chicago Press.

Cullen, R.B. (1992). Running Academic Institutions: Is This Real Option. *Australian Journal of Public Administration* 51 (3), 297–303.

Dover, P.A., Manwani, S., & Munn, D. (2018). Creating Learning Solutions for Executive Education Programs. *The International Journal of Management Education* 16 (1), 80–91.

Mincer, J. (1958). Investment in Human Capital and Personal Income Distribution. *The Journal of Political Economy* 66 (4), 281–302.

Mincer, J. (1974). *Schooling, Experience, and Earnings*. New York: Columbia University Press.

Schultz, T.W. (1961). Investment in Human Capital [Presidential Address Delivered at the Annual Meeting of the American Economic Association, Saint Louis, MO, December, 1960]. *The American Economic Review* 51 (1), 1–17.

Schultz, T.W. (1963). *The Economic Value of Education*. New York: Columbia University Press.

Silk, A.J. (2006). *What Is Marketing?* Boston, MA: Harvard Business School Press.

Smith, A. (1952). An Inquiry into the Nature and Causes of the Wealth of Nations. In R.M. Hutchins & M.J. Adler (Eds.), *Great Books of the Western World: Vol. 39. Adam Smith*. Chicago: Encyclopedia Britannica. (Original work published 1776).

Symes, C. (1996). Selling Futures: A New Image for Australian Universities? *Studies in Higher Education* 21 (2), 133–147.

Sweetland, S.R. (1966). Human Capital Theory: Foundations of a Field Inquiry. *Review of Educational Research* 66 (3), 341–359.

Thursby, J.G., & Thursby, M.C. (2002). Who Is Selling the Ivory Tower? Sources of Growth in University Licensing. *Management Science* 48 (1), 109–124.

West, P.A., Norris, T.E., Gore, E.J., Baldwin, L-M., & Hart, L.G. (1996). The Geographic and Temporal Patterns of Residency-Trained Family Physicians: University of Washington Family Practice Residency Network. *Journal of American Board of Family Medicine* 9 (2), 100–108.

CASE #1 CREATING HUMAN CAPITAL: THE CASE OF UNDEREMPLOYMENT IN THE REPUBLIC OF NORTH MACEDONIA

This case discusses a university's role as not merely creating human capital, but creating human capital that is needed in building a society. It discusses the creation of "excess" human capital to the increasing rate of underemployment/unemployment of skilled labor (university graduates) that is currently being witnessed in transition economies and some developing countries.

"Tell me, Professor. Am I, stupid or what, for still living in this country? Am I doing the wrong thing? Perhaps, I should take my chances and try my luck elsewhere, Germany or wherever." That was Yusuf, pleading with those rhetorical questions and a comment. It was lunch time, but the small campus cafeteria was not busy, so the servers, two or three in total, could make small talks with patrons. By now, I have become a "regular" at the cafeteria where I ate my lunch, and about everyone knew me, the visiting professor from America (as they refer to the United States).

Yusuf works as a waiter in the only small cafeteria on campus and makes less than 300 Euros per month, and tipping in a restaurant is not a normal part of culture here, so he gets no tips. Yusuf graduated two years earlier from the same university with a bachelor's degree in Law, but as many of the underemployed, the only job he could find was to be a waiter in the cafeteria on campus. He talked to me almost every time I went to the cafeteria for lunch, and would ask about life in America. Sometimes his bitterness at his circumstance came through, but at other times he would simply make fun of himself. He confided in me that his situation was a little better than some of his friends who couldn't get any job at all, but explained that he was worse off than other friends who went to Germany to work as undocumented, because those guys could make at least €1,500 per month working in restaurants or doing other odd jobs. That was more than what a medical doctor (a general practitioner) or full professor could make in Macedonia, he offered. Anecdotal stories and online evidence seemed to confirm what Yusuf said. Almost everyone I spoke to knew someone who after graduating, and being unemployed, left the country out of frustration for Germany, France, or the United Kingdom, but Germany was by far the most popular destination.

What a waste of talent? Yusuf would sometimes ask rhetorically, smiling. He explained that it was not uncommon to find other university graduates unemployed, and blamed their sad circumstance on the fact that they did not know anyone in a political position or anyone who was "well-contacted," for that matter. As time went on I got to meet some of his former university classmates who would come to visit him in the restaurant and almost all of them were unemployed.

The Republic of North Macedonia formerly known as the Former Yugoslav Republic of Macedonia (FYROM) or simply Macedonia is a landlocked country of approximately 5,713 km² (9,928 sq. mi), and a population of approximately 2 million people. It is in Southeastern Europe and in the central part of the Balkan Peninsula. Its capital Skopje has a population of about 600,000. The country gained its independence in 1991 as one of the successor states of Yugoslavia. Its immediate neighbors are Kosovo to the northwest, Serbia to the north, Greece to the south, Bulgaria to the east, and Albania to the west. It used to be known as Macedonia, but it officially changed its name to the Republic of

North Macedonia in February 2019 to settle a dispute with Greece over its original name, Macedonia.

The country has six state universities – Ss. Cyril and Methodius University of Skopje, St. Clement of Ohrid University of Bitola, Goce Delčev University of Štip, State University of Tetova, University of Information Science and Technology "St. Paul the Apostle" in Ohrid, and Mother Theresa University in Skopje (the latest state university). There is also one public–private–not-for-profit university, and about 18 private universities. The question one can justifiably ask is whether all these universities are needed for a country whose population is just about 2 million?

The relevant economic statistics which are provided here were based on estimates made in 2003. They may be a little dated, yet still they do give clear pictures of the state of affairs: Labor force is about 860,000. GDP (purchasing power parity) is about $13.81 billion. Public debt is about 30.2% of GDP, and the unemployment rate is about 36.7%. Inflation rate is about 1.2%. The country's exports include food, beverages, tobacco, iron, and steel. Its export partners are Serbia and Montenegro 37.8%, Germany 27%, Italy 14.7%, Greece 9.7%, Croatia 6.9%, United States 6.1%, The Netherlands 4.8%.

With regard to the country's economic plans and reform measures, here is an excerpt from page 12 in the World Bank's report produced in 2020 titled *Republic of North Macedonia Action Plan for Recovery for Growth & Jobs:*

> The country's reforms have neither contributed substantially to improve the poor labor market outcomes observed since independence. Despite recent progress, North Macedonia continues to show high levels of unemployment and low labor force participation, as well as sub-par indicators of employment quality. In 2019, barely half of people of working-age in North Macedonia were employed, product of high unemployment rate (17.4 percent in 2019) and high inactivity rates (33.7 percent). Unemployment and inactivity cause workers to waste about 25 years of productive employment during their lifecycle (World Bank, 2018). Youth unemployment is considerably high, reflecting challenges to gain a foothold in the labor market for newcomers. The poor labor market situation of young people is also reflected in high rates of the youth population not in education, employment or training (NEET) (24.9 percent in 2017). These grim prospects for youth represent a challenge, as prolonged spells of unemployment and inactivity in these early years negatively affect subsequent labor market outcomes.

Yusuf's problem is not an isolated case; besides underemployment, there is also the problem of brain drain. Both issues need to be solved to build the country's economy in the long term.

Questions

1. How does Yusuf's problem implicate the case of education as a public good?
2. How does Yusuf's problem relate to education as an investment?
3. What are the public policy implications in this case?
4. How can you connect this case to university marketing?

CASE #2 WORK STUDY TAKES ON A NEW MEANING IN SOME COLLEGES IN THE UNITED STATES

The Case of Berea College, Kentucky

This case discusses how a university (Berea College in Kentucky in the United States) adapted to the changing market and rising cost of living which translated into school fees by creating opportunities for students to farm on campus and produce food items that are used in the university cafeteria.

"Work study," that is, working part-time on campus while going to school full-time is not new on university campuses in the United States. However, very often work-study assignments involved either working in an office or in the school's library helping to shelf books or assisting at the checkout desk. Seldom does it involve working on a farm until we heard of Berea College.

Berea College was founded in 1855 as a privately supported, nonsectarian institution. It is the first interracial and coeducational college in the South (the reader may want to read about the Black and White divide in the Southern States in the United States at that time to appreciate the bold statement that the founding of an interracial and coeducational college in the South made) and consistently ranks among the nation's leading liberal arts colleges, boasts the university's website. The college has a total of 1,652 undergraduate students representing 41 states, two US territories, and 76 other countries; however, over 71% of the students come from the Kentucky and the Appalachian. The family annual income of a typical first-year student at Berea is under $30,000, but tuition for a four-year degree at Berea is estimated to cost around $176,000 which averages around $44,000 per year excluding room and board. How do students from humble homes manage to pay this fairly hefty tuition?

No student pays tuition at Berea. All the admitted students to Berea receive Berea's "No-Tuition Promise," which covers 100% of tuition costs. At Berea, students are not simply admitted, but they are also "hired" because every student at Berea works anywhere between 10 and 15 hours per week while carrying a full academic load. Students can choose work options in more than 100 college positions, but prominent in all this is the Berea Farm which boasts on its own webpage, which declares:

> The Farm, located in the Knobs along the edge of the Bluegrass Region, borders Berea College's campus and the City of Berea. It consists of pastures, cropland, woodlots, and ponds. Much of the cropland is USDA certified organic and the Farm maintains animal-welfare certifications on several of the livestock enterprises.

The Berea Farm was established in 1871. It is now one of the oldest continuously run educational farms in North America. It operates on 500 acres that serves not only as a huge hands-on classroom for Agriculture and Natural Resources majors and labor students, but also as a laboratory for the latest techniques in sustainable farming. It offers students practical work and management experience through the Labor Program. The farm's website reads that it "maintains animal-welfare certifications on several of the livestock enterprises and its produce and grain are USDA certified organic, a value that is just one way Berea College lives out its commitment to mindful and sustainable living in Appalachia." The farm also has its own in-house butchery.

The farm store operates year-round. It sells lunch prepared by students who use fresh organic ingredients from the Berea College Farm. Seasonal organic ingredients, freshly prepared bread and pastries from the bakery made from scratch by Berea College students, grains, herbs, fruits, and vegetables, and frozen meats and other dry goods are sold daily from the farm store.

All the produce used in preparing meals at the Campus Cafeteria at Berea Campus comes from the Berea Farms and with the exception of a skeletal permanent staff, all the work in the store, farm, cafeteria, and kitchen are done by students. Berea is a living example of the kind of thinking outside the box that is required in the academia. They seem to be over a century and a half ahead of its time. But have you ever heard of Berea? If not, you would have to wonder why. Is this due to a marketing failure of some sort? Think about the number of students who may not have had college education, let alone at Berea, if they were required to pay tuition. With tuition fee increasing every year, it is a surprise that many more "Bereas" are not coming up to help students.

Questions

1. Can you think of another university that operates like Berea?
2. What is the objective of the Berea Farms?
3. Can you think of ways in which Berea can use its farm to market the university?
4. Would you want to be a student at Berea? Why or why not?

2

MARKET SEGMENTATION

Introduction

How are market segments formed and what are the major market segments? This chapter answers these questions. It discusses the techniques used in forming the major marketing segments and the segmentation variables, and relates them university marketing.

What Is Segmentation?

Segmentation is typically a process of aggregating *things* that have a high degree of commonality. It is used in several academic fields including marketing. Segmentation is used in typological studies in linguistics, for example, to cluster motion events in language into syntactic or intonational units (Ibarretxe-Antunano, 2004). In marketing, several scholars have argued that because "customers demonstrate heterogeneity in their product and service requirements," and in their buying behavior, segmenting them into homogenous units is necessary to give the producer a clearer picture (Dibb & Simkin, 1997; Wind, 1978). Indeed, segmentation is a fundamental component of marketing strategy formulation (Yankelovich & Meer, 2006).

Segmentation is achieved in marketing by aggregating customers that have a high degree of commonality in their purchase behavior or needs into distinct groups or segments. Kotler defined market segmentation as "the subdividing of a market into distinct subsets of customers, where any subset may conceivably be selected as a target market to be reached with a distinct marketing mix" (Kotler, 1980). In actuality, segmentation is based on two practical realizations: (1) There are many competitors in the marketplace who are fighting for the same consumers; hence to achieve a mutually satisfying relationship with consumers, a company must select only a group or groups of consumers that it can best serve; (2) Resources that are available to anyone company are not unlimited, hence a company has to deploy its resources efficiently by choosing products that it can make well, and consumer groups upon whom it can make the greatest impact. These rationales apply to universities as well.

DOI: 10.4324/9781003160267-2

A company can enjoy several advantages by segmenting its market. (1) It can more efficiently deploy its resources by focusing on a narrow group of consumers. (2) It can develop a better understanding of the needs of its customers and of their buying habits (Dibb & Simkin, 1997). (3) A company can use the better understanding that it gains from customers to develop more competitive offerings and marketing programs (Powers, 1991). (4) Segmenting can help a company to identify new opportunities and underserved customers (Hooley & Saunders, 1993). (5) It can assist a company in developing a competitive advantage (Dibb & Simkin, 1997).

Why a University Must Segment Its Markets

There are several compelling reasons for university administrators in the twenty-first century to segment their market. Here are a few of them:

1. The intensity of the competition that they are now facing is not only unprecedented, but it is also far reaching, and consequential. Unlike half a century ago, with the winds of "deregulation" of university ownership that is now sweeping through several countries, competition amongst universities can result in a complete failure and closure of some of them.
2. The relevant publics that a university has to deal with now are rather diverse and heterogeneous. It not only includes domestic traditional students who come to school directly from high school and live in residence halls, domestic nontraditional students, some of whom work have families and take courses on part-time basis in the evening or on weekends, but also includes traditional international students and nontraditional international students who wish to take courses online.
3. Besides competition from other universities in geographic proximity, universities now compete with virtual universities and MOOC courses to whom geographical barriers are nonexistent, satellite campuses of some other universities (domestic or international), and some courses even being offered by private companies.

It is important to note that these competitions are not limited to students alone, but extend to such other resources as faculty, staff, and funds. Thus, for a university to attain the full benefits of segmentation, it is important that the process be thorough. A comprehensive answer must be provided to the first question which is *who* is our market? The answer to this question may at first blush lead to the stakeholders, but the market is more than the stakeholders. A university with foresight will have to think about the future generations too. Similarly, a university with an international reach may have to think in terms of globalization too.

Factors and Methods for Segmentation

Academics and practitioners have developed several different methods and approaches for segmenting markets. Customer characteristics and needs-based approaches are the two common methods used (Greengrove, 2002). The common segmentation variables include, but are not limited to, demographic factors, socioeconomic factors, geographic factors, psychographic factors, behavioral factors, volume-based factors, and needs/benefits sought.

Demographic Segmentation

These are perhaps the most frequently used variables to divide a market. They include age, gender, race, education, family size, family cycle, income, occupation, nationality, and religion. In addition to their utility, the ease with which some of these variables can be collected might explain why they are most frequently used. Age can be very useful in segmenting age-related markets, for example, "consumables" such as clothes, television programs, music, plays, and toys. Furthermore, life cycle stage and family size which are a function of age can also be useful in segmenting markets such as housing and automobile. However, they may not be very useful by themselves in segmenting the market for universities.

Gender: As a segmenting variable, gender can useful, and has been widely used for markets such as cosmetics, clothing, and toiletries. It can also be used by supplements and physical fitness industries, perhaps used together with other variables by single sex universities.

Race: Among other things, race and ethnicity have been found to be useful variables for segmenting markets for television shows, foods, colors for clothes, and even education. Historical Black Colleges and Universities (HBCUs) which played an invaluable role in making university education accessible to many Blacks during the era of racial segregation in the United States are examples of how race was used, and to some extent, still being used as a segmenting variable in higher education.

Education: Education has been used as a segmentation variable in markets such as dietary supplements, life insurance, and investment where it is thought that persons with higher levels of education are more likely to understand the benefits.

Income: Because people's income generally determines their purchasing power, income as a part of demographic factors became a useful segmentation variable. Income would be a useful segmentation variable in the case of a healthcare center for low-income earners, while a private university, for example, could use income as a proxy for the ability or inability to pay tuition in conjunction with scholastic achievement to segment its potential student market.

Occupation: Dividing a market into groups of titles, seniority, or types of jobs or industry is useful for a firm to deploy its resources efficiently. For example, a book that is titled *A Handbook for Managers* is clearly signaling its target market, and another book that is titled *For Managers in the Hospitality Industry* is not only signaling the segment, but also its target market by its title. Similarly, it could be useful for a university that is offering customized courses for businesses to segment its market using occupation.

Nationality: Even though nationality and citizenship are technically different, the two are essentially the same as a segmentation variable. Nationality can be a useful segmentation variable in such industries as travel and tourism. Universities do keep track of the nationality of their students. In some cases, a university can use this record as a basis to propose a special relationship between a foreign government in which the university can offer a special program, for example, for the civil servants, or aviation authorities, etc.

Religion: Segmenting a market on the basis of religion is useful, but can be tricky. The insight gained from using this variable can help a company to design strategies that allow it to more effectively reach consumers whose purchases are driven by their religious beliefs. For example, make Halal products for observant Muslims and Kosher products for observant Jews, etc.

Geographic Segmentation

Data on geographic segmentation variables as in the case of demographic variables can be easily collected by marketers, and the ease with which these data con be collected might explain why their use is popular. Geographic segmentation variables provide information on the characteristics of consumers' place, and therefore consist of country, region, city, zip code, and climate.

Country: Segmentation variable is generally used to collect macro-level data such as Gross National Product (GNP), GNP per capita, level of education, average size of family, etc. Marketers generally combine these macro-level data with other micro-level data to generate better insight. For a university, using country-level data can help it design a special program for the more attractive international markets. Some universities have used country- level data to choose locations for their satellite campuses. For example, George Mason University in the United States has a campus in Seoul, South Korea, New York University (NYU) has a campus in Ghana, West Africa, and Lancaster University, United Kingdom, has a campus in Accra, Ghana.

Region: Region as a segmentation variable could either include a number of countries or simply consist of a part of country depending on the boundary being used. Language, culture, or climate is often the common thread found in regions.

City: A city is defined as an area where a large number of people live closely together. They are generally incorporated by a charter and have their own administrative agencies. As a segmentation variable, marketers use characteristics of cities such as density, the city government, types of major employers in the city, types of jobs available in the city, cost of living, urban transportation modality, tax rate, how utilities are provided, etc., to determine if a city is an appropriate target for what their company offers. A university can use a city's characteristics such as density, the major employers in the city, and how utilities are provided in a city to determine its location. Before the popularity of virtual classes, some universities have used these characteristics to determine the location of their satellite campus. For example, George Mason University which is located in Fairfax, Virginia, used such variables to locate its satellite campus and law school at Arlington, Virginia, which is about 20 minutes' drive (13.5 miles) from the university's main campus. Similarly, Florida Atlantic University, which is located in Boca Raton, used such characteristics to locate the business school's graduate programs in Fort Lauderdale. It is important to note that universities change the location of satellite campuses from time to time depending on the changing characteristics of the cities and the visions of the university's leadership.

Zip Code: Even though zip codes are used for mail delivery in the United States and other countries, they are often used as a segmentation variable because of their connection to other demographic factors. For example, they serve as a precise location of households, and in cases where the wealthy live together and apart from the rest, a zip code could be an efficient means to reach them as a single cluster of consumers.

Climate: The prevailing weather conditions in a region can be a useful segmentation variable for a company in the clothing or weather-related business. The fact that climatic conditions can be divided into zones ties the climatic variable to such other variables as region and zip codes. Useful as the climatic variable may be to companies for segmentation, its utility as a segmentation variable to universities may be limited.

Psychographic Segmentation

Psychographic segmentation is used to divide customers into separate and distinct clusters on the basis of the lifestyle, personality traits, social class, opinions, and values.

Lifestyles: Whether a consumer is a runner, swimmer, biker, or someone who practices yoga will determine the kind of clothes they wear while exercising, hence a marker of clothes for exercising would be interested in segmenting its market based on consumers' lifestyle. A university may use lifestyles as segmentation variable to select impactful extra curricula activities that it may want to offer using a limited means. It can also be used to help design menu items for the cafeteria on campus.

Personality Traits: Companies attempt to deliver a product that adds value to their customers by clustering customers based on their personality traits. This may include individuals labeled as creative, emotional, friendly, opinionated, introvert, and extrovert. Again, useful as these traits are, they may be of limited utility to a university. However, some universities may use such classifications for fundraising purpose to design the appropriate message for the different personality types.

Social Class: Social class is useful in segmenting markets for brand name items, luxury goods, and automobiles because the consumer's social status generally determines the products they buy or use. However, because universities seem to be particularly sensitive to being labelled as elitist, they are likely to use social class as a segmenting variable only to ensure diversity of all classes on their campuses.

Opinions: A consumer's opinions reflect the person's viewpoint or judgment on things/ issues. Opinions may not be based on facts, but they are nonetheless deeply held. Because opinions influence a person's interest and activities, the three are combined into activities, interests, and opinions (AIO) to segment consumers. AIO can be useful in segmenting consumers who may be amenable to certain political messages. A university can use AIO in communicating its brands or mission statement.

Values: Values are important segmentation variables amongst psychographic factors. They are the basic or fundamental beliefs behind an individual's actions or attitude. A consumer's values play a role in what they prioritize or how they prioritize. The value of data on consumers' values lies in the fact that they motive consumers' actions and attitude. Because consumers' values are closely connected to their religious beliefs, some religious and parochial universities may find it useful to segment their market on the basis of values. Some church-affiliated universities such as Liberty University in Lynchburg, Virginia, have successfully segmented their market on religious values; however, other nonreligious universities have to be careful in doing so.

Behavioral Segmentation

Behavioral segmentation approach allows marketers to gain deeper insight into consumers by using what consumers do or how they behave as a basis to divide them into groups. Behavioral segmentation approach uses such variables as occasions, benefits, user status, loyalty status, attitude toward product, and user rates to segment consumers.

Occasions: Occasion generally refers to the time or an event at which the consumer uses a product. Occasions can be observed by many people at a particular time, for example, Christmas, Valentine's day, Halloween, and the like. They can also be observed regularly by individuals, for example, birthdays, or observed rarely, for example, celebrating an anniversary or promotion, etc. Although occasions are useful marketing segmentation variables to marketers, they may not be useful variables for universities.

Benefits Sought: Because consumers generally purchase for specific benefits, it is not surprising that benefit sought becomes one of the most used bases for segmentation. Because universities try to differentiate themselves in the consumer's mind by projecting an array of benefits that its potential students seek, segmenting its market using benefits sought is a particularly useful segmentation variable. Some potential students or donors may be interested in a university that has small class sizes, that offers excellent liberal arts education, or is located in a small town, while others might be interested in a large state university with a good football team and good basketball team with a good placement record. Private universities such as Swarthmore College and Bryn Mawr College have successfully used some of these attributes. Duke University also successfully uses good education and good basketball team as some of the major benefits it confers on its "consumers."

Loyalty Status: Loyalty status measures the level of an ongoing relationship or emotional engagement between a product, brand, or company and a consumer. Loyalty is exhibited in how often a consumer chooses a company's product over that of a competitor. Companies tend to treat their loyal customers differently in order to maintain their loyalty. Using loyalty to segment the market for a university is not obvious; however, it is not uncommon to find a successive generation of a family going to a particular university. There was a case where a student's grandfather, father, and mother attended the same university, of course at different times. The question is why? One can say that is a university's version loyalty, but universities need to know what keeps these families coming back. Knowing that can be used to fashion a message and a marketing program that can encourage such behavior.

Attitude toward Product: How individuals think or feel about a company or its policy may spillover into their attitude toward the company's product which in turn determines whether they purchase the product. This connection is often explained by the Theory of Reason Action (TRA) which was developed by Ajzen and Fishbein (1980) which posits that behavior is solely driven by personal agency (i.e., the formation of an intention) (see also Armitage & Christian, 2004). The theory has been the basis of several empirical studies in consumer behavior, and has been validated by several studies including a meta-analytical study by Sheppard et al. (1988). Thus, companies that are able to cultivate consumers' favorable attitude will more likely experience patronage by those consumers. For this reason, universities can do well by segmenting their market on the bases of attitude toward the university. Different messages can therefore be crafted for the different segments. Those who have a negative attitude will be targeted with messages designed to persuade them to change their attitude while those who already have positive attitude will be targeted by messages designed to reinforce those attitudes.

User Rates: How often a consumer uses a product is of interest to marketers because there could be a connection between use rate and loyalty. For example, a consumer who regularly chooses a particular product from a collection of other products available, may likely be a loyal consumer, hence a message designed for this consumer may not be intended to make them regular, but rather to make them increase their volume of purchase. Depending on the objective, user rate as in the case of loyalty might be useful to a university in terms of segmenting the market for its potential students, but it can be very useful in segmenting the market for its donors.

Volume-Based Segmentation

Segmenting a market on the basis of the quantity of products demanded could give a useful insight to a marketer; however, universities have to be creative with the use of this variable. Its use could reveal countries, states, or regions where most of their students come from. Similarly, its use can also reveal where the least number of their students come from. Delving into the reasons for those numbers could be revealing and informative, and could impact their communication/marketing strategy. Volume segmentation need not be limited only to student market, but could be applied to the donor market also. Volume-based segmentation includes such variables as need segmentation, specific motivations, and barriers.

Need Segmentation: It is not unusual for a company to try to solve a nonexistent problem, in other words a problem that its customer or potential customer does not have. It is also not uncommon for people to confuse benefits-sought segmentation with needs segmentation. The two may look alike, but are not the same. With benefits sought, both the customer and the provider will be dealing with perceptions. The customers deal with perceived benefits of the product while the company deals with consumers' perceptions; however, with needs, the customer is dealing with actual lack, deprivation, or unmet needs that must be satisfied. For example, patients' need for a drug may spur on a pharmaceutical company to produce it. The variables for need segmentation can be specific motives, requirements, and barriers.

Greenberg and McDonald (1989) have argued that there are two varieties of need segmentation – person-based segmentation whose objective is to group persons on the basis of common product motivations or barriers to purchase, and occasion-based segmentation which attempts to segment not persons but purchase or consumption occasions on the basis of "the patterns of needs operating when consumers decide to buy or consume a product." In either case the driver of the purchase is the underlying factor, hence specific motivations are also an important segmentation variable.

Specific Motivations: There are many instances such as in tourism where situational approach to segmentation provides useful insight. However, this approach to segmentation focuses on types or classes of travels, and fails to take motivations of travelers, for instance, into consideration. The use of specific motivation as a segmentation variable cures this deficiency as it goes to the heart of why the consumer is using the product. For universities, the use of specific motivation for segmentation could yield valuable information in a number of ways. First, it can provide information on why persons (potential students or donors) in the university's space (market) are interested in universities in general (i.e., the market for higher education). Second, it could give information on why the group of individuals (students or philanthropists) is interested in a particular university. It may be the university's liberal credits for work experience, as used in the United States by many private for-profit universities that focus on adult learners, or it may be the university's flexible schedules. In either case, specific messages could be developed for each segment.

Barriers: Underlying the use of many of the segmentation variables is the assumption that consumers have "perfect information," "behave rationally," and can "move freely" in the market. However, as every market participant can testify to, these assumptions are practically nonexistent in the "real world." So, factors that impose impediments on consumers' choice in the market, in themselves, also constitute segmentation variable. While contract terms with early termination penalties could prevent some customers from switching phone companies, fewer hassles and sign-up bonuses could encourage some consumers to break their contracts nonetheless. Thus, segmenting consumers using choice barriers can be useful for a company to defeat the exit barrier that a competitor may have for its customers.

Similar to companies, a university could segment its market using choice barriers as a variable. By doing so, it can understand how to defeat some of the barriers that its competitors may have set up. Take, for instance, one of the commonly cited fears: what prevents students from transferring from one university to another is the loss of credit hours when they do transfer to another university. If a university discovers through segmentation that this fear is grounded on facts, then it can devise a strategy to defeat this barrier, if it is worth its while.

Multiple Segmentation Variables

Using multiple segmentation variables allows the marketer to divide a market into segments using more than one characteristic. This approach provides more information about the individuals in each segment than does single-variable segmentation approach, and can allow a marketer to better satisfy its customers. A university can use multiple variables by applying overlapping clustering technique, for example, to segment its market. Instead of using income, or geography, for example, one variable at time to segment its market, a university can use both variables at the same time.

Segmentation Techniques

As there are many segmentation variables, it should not come as a surprise that there are also several different segmentation techniques and programs for market segmentation. These are of varying degrees of complexity and sophistication that range from a simple cross-tabulation to a more sophisticated algorithm. Depending on the objective, some programs and techniques work very well while others work less well. The singular objective of the segmentation process is to minimize within group differences although it maximizes between group differences, which leads to achieving a high level of homogeneity within segments, while segments are clearly different from each other.

However, the advent of advanced segmentation techniques such as Artificial Neural Networks, Latent Class Models (Mixture Models), Fuzzy and Overlapping Clustering has shifted the focus to understanding different market structures depending on different occasions to use a product.

University Markets

It is noteworthy to quote Kotler's definition of market segmentation, which was cited earlier, as a process that involves dividing "the market" into what we can call mini-markets of homogeneous consumers. However, one can argue upon looking closely at universities that despite their unifying statement of being in the knowledge-providing business, they in fact do not operate in a single market. A university operates in several markets; it may operate in a market that involves traditional students, that is students who go directly to the university from high schools, and students who enroll on full-time basis after being out of high school (and working) for several years. Amongst students who enrolled directly from high schools are commuting students and students who live in residence halls. This group alone presents at least two subgroups. Focusing on this segment (those who enroll in the university directly after high school) for a moment, because the needs of the two subgroups could be completely different, we can discern that aggregating them could lead to loss of information and therefore a loss of insight.

Other markets include nontraditional students (students who are older than the average high school graduates who might be returning to school, either full-time or part-time, after having been in the workforce), international students who may come from all over the world, faculty, staff, corporate employers, the government (from different levels – local government, state and governmental agencies), and philanthropist. The diversity of the markets faced by a university is apparent from these examples, hence a more comprehensive segmentation approach on each of the markets faced by the university would yield a deeper insight. Some studies have suggested that because students' needs are quite diverse, universities should use the benefits-/needs-based approach to segment (Blasko & Saura, 2006; Dailey et al., 2006; Ghosh et al., 2008).

Haley (1968) proposed the need/benefit segmentation approach that is based on causal rather than descriptive factors (such as demography, geography, and volume-based) that are used as the traditional segmenting variables in an attempt to provide a better understanding of consumers and to better predict their buying behavior. Using the tooth paste market for illustration, the Haley divided buyers of the product into four different segments (sensory, sociable, worrier, and independent). The sensory segment is attracted by attributes such as flavor and product appearance. The sociable segment seeks to brighten their teeth, the worrier segment seeks to prevent tooth decay, while the independent is attracted by price. Contrasting these segments of users with segments that could be obtained using the traditional approaches, Haley (1968) demonstrated the advantages that are inherent in using the needs/benefit approach (We must note that Haley sated in his 1968 *Journal of Marketing* article, the need/benefit segmentation approach was available since 1961 but not disclosed because of proprietary reasons). The method has been widely applied since Haley (1968), in such areas as transportation, travel and tourism, higher education, television news audiences, fund raising, the pharmaceutical industry, etc. (Haley, 1971; Frochot & Morrison, 2000)

Even though market segmentation has been heavily promoted, it is not a panacea to marketing problems. It is a process that is helpful in strategy formulation, so the question is when must marketing segmentation be done, in other words when do the costs justify the benefits? In answering this question, Kotler (1991) and other marketing scholars such as Saunders (1980) suggested that market segmentation provides value when some basic conditions exist. For example, the segments must be measurable in the first place. Because segmentation is done to assist in developing actionable marketing strategy, a market segment must be such that the company should be able to evaluate its current size vis-à-vis its future potential. It is also important that the segment be substantial and that is large and potentially profitable in order to justify pursuing it. Furthermore, it is also important that the market segment be accessible to the company. It offers no advantage to the company if the company cannot reach it or serve it with its programs.

Summary

Like other business organizations, a university "cannot be everything to everyone." This is dictated because resources are not without limits, and a university does not have the expertise to excel in everything, therefore choices have to be made. To deliver the best value means that universities must choose the group(s) (segments) that they can best serve, and thus the market has to be divided into mini-markets of similar consumers (segments). Several variables as well as techniques are available for segmentation. The variable as well as techniques used depend on the objectives. Hence, the key question that must be asked at the outset is, "What are we looking for?" Though it shows one's ignorance, it is the right question to ask.

Questions

1. How does segmentation help in marketing a university?
2. Which variables do you think can be most useful for a university in segmenting its market?
3. How can governments, for example, be used as a variable for segmentation?
4. How can psychographic variables be used by a university in segmentation?
5. Does loyalty matter in university marketing?
6. What role does the assumption of perfect information play in segmentation?
7. What is the rationale for segmentation, to begin with?

References

Ajzen, I., & Fishbein, M. (1980). *Understanding Attitudes and Predicting Social Behaviors*. New Jersey: Prentice Hall.

Armitage, C.J., & Christian, J. (Eds.) (2004). *Planned Behavior*. New Brunswick: Transaction.

Blasko, M.F., & Saura, I.G. (2006). Segmenting University Students on the Basis of Their Expectations. *Journal of Marketing for Higher Education* 16 (1), 25–45.

Dailey, L., Anderson, M., Ingentio, C., Duffy, D., Krim, P., & Thompson, S. (2006). Understanding MBA Consumer Needs and the Development of Marketing Strategy. *Journal of Marketing for Higher Education* 16 (1), 143–158.

Dibb, S., & Simkin, L. (1997). A Program for Implementing Market Segmentation. *Journal of Business & Industrial Marketing* 12 (1), 51–65.

Frochot, I., & Morrison, M.A. (2000). Benefit Segmentation: A Review of Its Applications to Travel and Tourism Research. *Journal of Travel & Tourism Marketing* 9 (4), 21–45.

Ghosh, A.K., Javalgi, R., & Whipple, T.W. (2008). Service Strategies for Higher Educational Institutions Based on Student Segmentation. *Journal of Marketing for Higher Education* 17 (2), 238–255.

Greenberg, M., & McDonald, S.S. (1989). Successful Needs/Benefits Segmentation: A User's Guide. *Journal of Consumer Marketing* 6 (3), 29–36.

Greengrove, K. (2002). Needs-Based Segmentation: Principles and Practice. *International Journal of Market Research* 44 (4), 405–421.

Haley, R. (1968). Benefit Segmentation: A Decision-Orientated Research Tool. *Journal of Marketing* 32 (July), 30–35.

Haley, R. (1971). Beyond Benefit Segmentation. *Journal of Advertising Research* 11 (4), 3–8.

Hooley, G.J., & Saunders, J. (1993). *Competitive Positioning: The Key to Marketing Strategy*. New York: Prentice-Hall.

Ibarretxe-Antunano, I. (2004). Language Typologies in Our Language Use: The Case of Basque Motion Events in Adult Oral Narratives. *Cognitive Linguistics* 15 (3), 317–349.

Kotler, P. (1980 and 1991). *Marketing Management: Analysis, Planning, Implementation and Control*. New York: Prentice-Hall.

Powers, T.L. (1991). *Modern Business Marketing: A Strategic Planning Approach to Business and Industrial Markets*. St Paul, MN: West.

Saunders, J.A. (1980). Cluster Analysis for Market Segmentation. *European Journal of Marketing* 14 (7), 422–435.

Sheppard, B.H., Hartwick, J., & Warshaw, P.R. (1988). The Theory of Reasoned Action: A Meta-Analysis of Past Research with Recommendations for Modifications and Future Research. *Journal of Consumer Research* 15 (3), 325–343.

Wind, Y. (1978). Issues and Advances in Segmentation Research. *Journal of Marketing Research* 15 (3), 317–337.

Yankelovich, D., & Meer, D. (2006). Rediscovering Market Segmentation. *Harvard Business Review* (February) 84 (2), 122–131.

CASE #3 WORKERS COLLEGE

This case discusses the evolution of Workers College for educating adult learners in a developing country.

As the name suggests, one thing that all the students have in common at Workers College is that they all work on full-time basis (generally during the day). The name could be misleading, but the word "college" is used in the former British colonies for what some may call a secondary school or a high school, but when used together with "university" as in "university college," then it refers to a university that is not yet autonomous.

So, Real Workers College (a fictitious name) was founded around 1963 in the capital of one of the former British colonies to provide the equivalent of high school education to workers. High school education at that time was relatively expensive and actually could be accessed generally only by children of families that had some wealth. So, one can even say that going to high school of any kind, whether public or private (which were mostly church-affiliated, better-equipped and therefore a little expensive), was considered elitist. Against, this background, Real Workers College emerged, clearly as a nonresidential institution. A bare-bone instructional facility. The building was funded by the government, but the instructors who were all part-timers were paid from the fees paid by the students. Classes were coordinated by the local university through its extramural program.

As one would expect, those who enrolled in Real Workers College were therefore people from very humble means. They had graduated from elementary school and were sent to the city to look for work to help their parents and siblings back in the village, hence they were mostly males. Some of them worked as "messengers," paper delivery boys, or simply as factory hands in the capital city; a few lucky ones even got jobs as clerks in offices (government's or a private company's). What they did not have in means they made it up with ambition and drive.

They would attend classes five nights each week after work between 6 and 10pm. It was a hassle making it to school on time and home after classes as some of them lived or worked outside the city limits. Classes were not conducted on strictly cohort basis, so each student can pick and choose a course and progress at his or her own pace. Those who kept a strict schedule could be ready to take the General Certificate of Education – Ordinary level ("O" level) exams in five or six courses (which is the same examination students in the regular high schools take), after four, five, or six years depending on the student's pace and ability.

A successful student at the "O" levels, that is, someone who passed all the five or six courses with a certain passing grade could continue with night courses for two or three years to take the General Certificate of Education – Advanced level ("A" level) examinations. Passing three courses at the Advanced level at the same time generally qualifies a student to enroll in a university.

The local public university's control over Workers College strengthened over the years, and by the mid-1970s university degree courses were being offered at Workers College. The students were considered external candidates of the local public university, but the courses were being taught by the lecturers from the local university. By 2000s Workers College has been transformed into what is now referred to as "City Campus" of the local university. It still carters to workers, continues to be nonresidential, but the high school component of the College has been eliminated.

Questions

1. What is the arching commonality that students at Workers College have?
2. What are the advantages in the takeover by the local university?
3. What other options did Workers College have and why?
4. What else could have made Workers College better as Workers College and why?

CASE #4 OPEN UNIVERSITY, UNITED KINGDOM

The potential university student market can be divided into two main segments – the traditional students and nontraditional students. The traditional students are full-time and younger, and on the other, the nontraditional students are relatively older part-timers who need a lot of flexibility. This case discusses how developing a pathway to university education for people who because of their circumstances need flexibility gave birth to United Kingdom's largest university – the Open University. (This case is based on available public records.)

The Open University (OU) is the largest public research university in the United Kingdom with a total of 175,000 students of whom around 7,700 are overseas students. The majority of the students are based in the United Kingdom, but study off campus as many of the university's courses can be studied anywhere in the world.

The idea for an OU could be attributed to the Labor Prime Minister Harold Wilson who was committed to modernizing the British Society. Wilson believed that OU would help transform the British economy to be more competitive while also promoting greater equality of opportunity and social mobility. The planned use of television and radio to broadcast the university's courses was supposed to link the OU to the technological revolution underway, which the Prime Minister saw as a major plank in his modernization plans.

The university was founded in 1969 and was initially housed in a facility vacated by the British Broadcasting Corporation (BBC) at Alexandria Palace, north London. Its first students enrolled in January 1971. Currently about 34% of the newly enrolled undergraduate students are below 25 years. The university awards both undergraduate and graduate (postgraduate) degrees and there are also a number of full-time graduate (postgraduate) research students based at the university's campus in Milton Keynes. This campus works as the university's hub with over 2,500 administrative staff and 1,000 academic and research faculty (staff). The university also offers nondegree qualifications such as certificates, diplomas, and continuing education units.

Over 2 million students have taken courses at OU since it was founded, and the university produces more CEOs than any other university in the United Kingdom. The school's economic impact on United Kingdom is over £2.77 billion in 2018–2019 fiscal year. A variety of teaching modalities including written and audio materials, the Internet, disc-based software, and television programs on DVD are used. Course-based television broadcasts which were started in 1971 by the BBC were discontinued in December 2006. Materials which comprise originally authored work by in-house and external academic contributors, and from third-party materials licensed for use by OU students are used. For most modules, students are supported by tutors ("Associate Lecturers") who provide feedback on their work and are generally available to them at face-to-face tutorials, by telephone, and/or on the Internet.

A number of short courses worth ten credits are now available that do not have an assigned tutor but offer an online conferencing service (Internet forum) where help and advice is offered through conferencing "Moderators." For some modules, day schools are mandatory, however, permission to be absent could be obtained for health-related reasons (or other extenuating circumstances), but many courses have no mandatory face-to-face component. The Quality Assurance Agency for Higher Education review which was published in December 2015 found five areas of good practice at OU and made three recommendations for improvement. The university won the first place twice on the English national survey of student satisfaction.

As a mostly distance learning–based school, fair assessment of students' mastery of the course materials is important and this is what is reported about the university's assessment method:

> The University modules are generally assessed using an equal weighting of examinations and coursework. The coursework component normally takes the form of between two and seven Tutor-Marked Assignments (TMAs) and, occasionally, may also include up to six multiple-choice or "missing word" ten-question Interactive Computer Marked Assignments (ICMAs). The examinable component is usually an invigilated three-hour paper regardless of the size of the module (although on some modules it can be up to three three-hour papers), but an increasing number of modules instead have an End of Module Assessment (EMA) which is similar to a TMA, in that it is completed at home, but is regarded as an exam for grading purposes.

As far as the grades go, there are five grading categories including a fail. Grade 1 is distinction with score over 85%, grade 2 is 70–84%, grade 3 is 55–69%, grade 4 is 40–54%, and fail is below 40%. This grade is calculated based on the Overall Continuous Assessment Score (OCAS) and Overall Examination Score (OES). Grades can be weighted according to their level and combined to calculate the classification of a degree. An undergraduate degree will weight level 3 modules twice as much as level 2, and in post-graduate (graduate) program modules are equally weighted.

Questions

1. Should OU have age restriction on enrollment? Why or why not?
2. Who are the market targets for OU?
3. In which segment is OU competing?
4. Do you personally know anyone who has been to OU or is going to OU? If you do not know anyone, then explain why that is the case, and if you know someone, explain the circumstances under which you met this individual.

3
HIGHER EDUCATION AS A *PRODUCT*

An economic activity offered by one party to another, most commonly employing time-based performances to bring about desired results in recipients or in objects or others assets for which purchasers have responsibility. In exchange for their money, time, and effort, service customers expect to obtain value from access to goods, labor, professional skills, facilities, networks, and systems; but they do not normally take ownership of any of the physical elements involved.

(Lovelock & Wirtz, 2011, p. 601)

On the basis of these definitions, the chapter will discuss how the salient features of services marketing apply to universities.

Introduction

In this chapter, we discuss and relate the concept of a product to university education and argue that a university is a producer of service. The relevant concepts of value, value co-creation, and service attributes are discussed as they relate to universities and how they could be used in marketing universities.

What Is a Product?

Just like how the definition for *marketing* has been offered by different scholars (see Grewal & Levy, 2020), the word *product* has also been defined in several different ways by different scholars. Here are a few definitions which not only reflect the stability of marketing thought on what a product is over time, but also the very essence of a product – the *thing* being traded. Miracle (1965) defined a product as "the sum of the physical and psychological satisfactions the buyer receives when he makes a purchase." Grewal and Levy (2020) defined a product as "anything that is of value to a consumer and can be offered through a voluntary marketing

DOI: 10.4324/9781003160267-3

exchange." Kotler and Armstrong (2008) defined it as "anything that can be offered to a market for attention, acquisition, use or consumption that might satisfy a want or need" (p. 218), while Perreault et al. (2021) suggest that *a product is* "the need-satisfying offering of a firm." Kerin et al. (2020) also defined a product as "a good, service or idea consisting of a bundle or tangible and intangible attributes that satisfies consumers' needs and is received and exchanged for money or something else of value."

Two questions are important here. (1) Why is the definition of a product necessary, and (2) What do all these different definitions have in common. As Lewis Carrol reminds in *Alice's Adventures in Wonderland*, if one does not have any particular destination, then it does not matter much which direction one goes! The moral of that lesson is that unless the marketers know which product(s) the consumer wants, they would offer *anything*. But, of course, that *anything* may not be what the consumer wants, and that brings us to question #2. The common themes that all these seemingly different definitions carry are as follows: (1) a product can be tangible or intangible, which means a product can be a good such as an automobile or computer or a service such as insurance; (2) a product must have value to the consumer; and (3) a product must be offered through a voluntary exchange. Understanding these three elements of a product are important to not only doing things right by the consumer, but also being successful in the marketplace. A good marketer scrupulously applies these three elements.

In applying these elements, we can emphatically say yes, higher education is a product. It is an intangible product, an offering according to Perreault et al.'s (2021) definition of a product. However, we know from these definitions that a product must create value, hence the next logical question is, how does higher education create value?

Value and Value Creation

The consensus amongst marketing scholars is that marketing creates value for the consumer, therefore to be successful a company must create value. But to create value, the company or marketer must first understand what value is. So, what is value? Neap and Celik (1999) suggested that the value of a product to a consumer reflects the consumer's desire to obtain and retain the product. However, let us take two hypothetical customers – A & B who have different levels of desire for the same product. Because customer A's desire for the product, let's say university education, is different from customer B's desire for the same product (university education), the value of a university education would be different for these two consumers. Why do you think this might the case and what might it suggest?

This suggests that the term value is subjective and differs from one individual to the next. However, value can also be viewed as conferring "bundle of utilities" on the consumer. These "utilities" come from the product itself as a composite of several attributes. Thus, it is in the interest of the company to try a find out which attributes the potential consumers "desire" in a product and how high that "desire" level is. Obviously, except in the case of customization, it is impossible to design a product that meets every consumer's "desire," hence the need for segmentation which we discussed in Chapter 2.

Several scholars have suggested several ways in which a company can operationalize consumers' value, bearing in mind that it is subjectively determined by the consumer. Some scholars suggest that value takes a ratio form and is a relation between consumer's perceived benefits that can be derived from a product and the price at which the product is being sold. Using this argument, value could be written as:

$$Value = \frac{perceived\ benefits}{price}$$

On the contrary, other scholars have argued that in addition to out-of-pocket cost (the price of a product) there are other costs associated with a product which reflect such other attributes as place and time that the product is obtained, as such consumers focus on **net value** instead of **value** (Wirtz & Lovelock, 2018). Net value is operationalized as the sum of all the perceived benefits (gross value) minus the sum of all the perceived costs. Thus, instead of a ratio, value can be operationalized as a simple additive and subtractive function. For example, where and when the product has been purchased is considered part of the benefits enjoyed by the consumer, therefore the costs associated with place and time are also relevant in determining the value of a product. Hence,

Net Value = Total Perceived Benefits − Total Perceived Costs

To illustrate this point further, consider this scenario. Your car breaks down at point X on a highway at 10am. Point X is 20 miles from the closest garage, Yuletide garage. You called Ziggie's towing company which offered to tow you to the garage for $50.00. However, you declined the service because you considered it to be too expensive. Your reservation price was $40.00. Now, let us pretend that instead of 10am your car broke down at the same point X at 10pm and you called the same towing company. Instead of $50.00, the towing company offered to tow you to the same garage for $100.00 and you agreed. What has changed here? Certainly, your valuation of the service has changed, but what is it that must have influenced your valuation differently at this time around? After all, it is the same distance? For one thing, the time of the day is different. You may think it is dangerous being out there at 10pm compared to 10am. From this illustration, it would seem that the cost of a product can be broken down into monetary and nonmonetary costs. The nonmonetary costs include such other costs as time cost, physical cost, psychological costs, and sensory costs (Wirtz & Lovelock, 2018). You may therefore have reasoned that the towing cost at 10 pm is equal to or less than the $50.00 that the company wanted to charge at 10 am when the nonmonetary costs are subtracted from $100.00. Thus, the towing cost at night is actually equal to or less than your reservation price.

In summary, for the consumer, value is a relation between the sum total of the perceived benefits and the costs, therefore companies seek to satisfy consumers by incorporating in a product, as much as possible, all the attributes that give value to the customer at a given price. Similarly, universities can create value for their consumers by first knowing what their customers desire and want to have at a given price. It would be simplistic to say that universities offer knowledge as their product because a product is an embodiment of component parts or sum total of attributes. Therefore, in designing their product, universities would benefit greatly, we can say, by using a combination of the arguments made by Miracle (1965) and by Theodore Levitt in (1980).

Gordon Miracle (1965) in one of the earliest papers on product characteristics argued that a total product includes all the features and conveniences for which the buyer pays when a purchase is made. Levitt (1980), building on the idea of a product having several attributes, conceptualized a product as having three levels: the *core product*, which is the fundamental benefit or problem-solution that consumers seek; the *expected (or actual) product*, which is the basic physical product which delivers those benefits; and the *augmented product*, which is the addition of extra or unsolicited services or benefits that the customer did not require nor expect, but needed to nudge them to make the purchase (Crane, 2001). A university as a product therefore includes several features and conveniences, but educating students (selling knowledge) could be considered its core product. This core is delivered by lecturers with different array of expertise who teach in lecture halls, laboratories, and gyms (for physical education) on campuses, or virtually through cyberspace (as we have seen during the recent COVID-19 pandemic). The issue then is how universities include these other attributes in their value proposition and in their marketing statements?

Value Co-creation

Since value is subjective, the customers' perception could be influenced if they are co-opted into the production process. Co-opting the customer into the production process ensures that the product meets their expectations. Furthermore, it is also a practical acknowledgment of the evolution in the marketplace in which consumers have been transformed from "passive audiences" to "active players" as observed by Prahalad and Ramaswamy (2000). However, there is no well-defined structure for involving customers in co-creating value. Vargo and Lusch (2004) in proposing the Service Dominant Logic (SDL) developed a comprehensive foundation which emphasizes the development of customer–supplier relationships through interaction and dialog (Payne et al., 2008). One of the ten foundational propositions that Vargo and Lusch (2004) developed that succinctly captures customer involvement in the value creation as pointed out by Payne and his colleagues (2008) is Foundational Proposition 6 (FP6). FP6 states that "The customer is always a co-creator of value: There is no value until an offering is used – experience and perception are essential to value determination."

Even though the SDL appears convincing and clear, it is not without criticism. Grönroos (2011), for example, argues that some of the foundational premises "do not fully support an understanding of value creation and co-creation in a way that is meaningful for theoretical development and decision making in business and marketing practice." Grönroos further makes the point that "customers always are co-creators of value, but rather that under certain circumstances the service provider gets opportunities to co-create value together with its customers."

Applicable Features to a University

The primary features of services which set them apart from goods with regard to marketing strategy development apply to universities also, as such understanding of these features and how they relate to universities is important. Services have long been distinguished from goods along some primary features such as intangibility, inseparability, heterogeneity, and perishability (Edgett & Parkinson, 1993; Zeithaml et al., 1985). However, it is important to know also that these are not the only means of distinguishing services from goods and that distinguishing services from goods on the bases of intangibility, inseparability, heterogeneity, and perishability has been challenged by some authors (see, e.g., Wyckham et al., 1975;

Moeller, 2010). Some scholars (see Lovelock, 1983, for example) have distinguished services from goods on the basis of the difference in how these two categories of products are processed (a process perspective).

Intangibility

Because services cannot be touched or held, they are not subjected to same kind of prepurchase inspection that goods are subjected to. For example, a potential car buyer may test drive the car to feel how it handles on the road before deciding to purchase it. Certainly, a wide range of other considerations, such as reputation of the maker (in terms of reliability, durability, safety, value retention, maintenance cost, the dealer, etc.) goes into the decision-making process. However, a university as a *product*, similar to a bank or a hotel, cannot be tried before purchase. How can a product that has experience instead of search attributes be marketed?

There is an ad with a tag line that says "image" is everything. Well, that is not exactly the case, however, in the absence of the potential customer being able "to test drive" a university as car, creative ways could be found to assure the potential buyer of the service quality, or at least give them a sample of how it feels like. It is therefore not an accident that some universities give potential students, that is, students who are considering the school as one of their choices the opportunity to come and sit in class for a day. Even though it is not a perfect substitute for "test driving," it at least gives a feel of what the potential student can expect. Furthermore, in place of tangibility, the entire servicescape – the appearance of the university's campus, lecture halls, lawns, roads, and in fact the entire ambience can be used as a package. Note though that just as the reputation of the car marker features in the consideration set when deciding which car to buy, so does the reputation of the university.

What is the university known for? Who are some of its famous alums, what is its overall ranking? What about the ranking of its individual programs of schools? What is its placement record? What is the average salary of its graduates? The list is by no means exhaustive; however, it gives you a sense of a long list of points that a university could consider using in place of tangibility to persuade a potential student, employee, or donor.

Inseparability

Most services, especially personal services, are consumed simultaneously as they are being produced. So, the audience at a live concert "consume" the concert as it is being produced. A close substitute is to have the concert on tape. Every concert attendee would attest to the fact that there is something electric or magical about live performances that cannot be duplicated on tape. Similarly, a student receives "knowledge" or "wisdom" embodied in a lecturer's expertise and experience as a lecture is being given. The "burden" here on a service provider is huge. Unlike goods, there is no room for "recalling" defective products. However, universities can reduce this burden through internal marketing.

Heterogeneity

Because services, even in the same establishment, a bank for example, are often performed by different people, standardization of quality and pricing to reflect quality become problematic. It can be seen from the earlier discussions on *value* that this lack of standardization of quality can pose difficulties for the potential consumer in assessing value before purchase. However, universities can allay consumers' concerns by giving detailed descriptions of courses and different aspects of the university, for example, research, internships, practicum, co-opts, and university life in general in the catalog/prospectus and on websites. These must be substantive information as opposed to glitz that some universities are unfortunately settling for these days.

Perishability

Services unlike goods cannot be inventoried to be sold at a future date. For example, the unsold seats for a concert cannot be stored and sold after the performance, unlike cars at a dealership that can be sold at any time. The problem of perishability makes demand forecasting particularly important in services industries. At a time when universities are expected to do more with less, capacity utilization (classrooms, lab spaces, residence halls, etc.) becomes increasingly important. Hence, accurate forecasting of enrollment figures and meeting the anticipated targets are important.

Other Conceptualizations of Services

Using the *process* perspective, Lovelock (1983) distinguished between services and goods on the basis of what is being processed. He argued that there are primarily two ways of processing things in services, which are either tangible or intangible, and that there are three main groups of things that can be processed – people, physical objects, and data. "Intangible actions are performed on people's minds or to their non-physical assets," while "tangible actions are performed on people's bodies or to their physical possessions." Four broad categories of services result from the viewpoint of processing. These are people processing, possession processing, mental stimulus processing, and information processing. Table 3.1 shows the resulting typology.

The process viewpoint on what distinguishes services from goods could give universities another framework through which they could sell themselves to their consumers. As illustrated in Table 3.1, universities can market themselves to different constituencies,

TABLE 3.1 Types of Processing – People and Possessions★

Processing	People	Possessions
Tangible Actions	• Knowledge transforming the individual as a person (People Processing)	• An owner taking their pet to the university's veterinary clinic (Possession Processing)
Intangible Actions	• A student getting new information (knowledge) • A student receiving psychological counseling at the university's counseling center (Mental Stimulus Processing)	• Individuals getting legal free assistance from the university's law school's clinic • Individuals getting free assistance from the accounting club to file their taxes. (Information Processing)

★ On the basis of Lovelock's 1980 Process Perspective.

not only to potential students, but also to businesses, pet owners, those who need clinical services (legal, psychological, dental, etc.), in fact, to the entire community in which they exist, if the university has the different schools such as veterinary school, dentistry school, medical school, law school, and business school. With regard to Table 3.1, we must add that we are aware that some people consider their pets as part of the household and not as a possession. However, the laws in the United States (at least) regard pets as possessions, hence our classification.

Service Quality

The quality of services is harder to evaluate compared to goods partly because of their intangibility. However, having a sense of the q*uality* of a service is important to both service providers and service consumers. But what is service quality? Wirtz and Lovelock (2018) defined service quality as "a high standard of performance that consistently meets or exceeds customer expectations."

Borrowing from the expectancy-disconfirmation model in organizational management (Oliver, 1977; Oliver et al., 1994), service quality has been conceptualized as the difference between perceived service expectation and the perceived service performance. Thus,

$$SQ = PSE - PSP$$

Where,

Service quality = SQ
Perceived Service Expectation = PSE
Perceived Service Performance = PSP

But how do consumers get to form their expectations? Zeithaml et al. (1993) in a conceptual paper on service quality argued that consumers form their service expectations based on such sources as word of mouth, news stories, information search, and a firm's own marketing efforts and website. Previous experiences also inform consumers' service expectation, for those who have previously encountered the service. With expectations formed, consumers are now in a position to evaluate service quality by comparing their expectations with the performance received. The quality of service received can meet expectation, exceed expectation, or fall below expectation.

Studies such as Parasuraman et al. (1985) have shown that consumers evaluate service quality using five broad dimensions: tangibles (the appearance of the physical elements); reliability (dependable and accurate performance); responsiveness (promptness and helpfulness); assurance (credibility, security, competence and courtesy); and empathy (easy access, good communication, and customer understanding).

The question is how can universities use these dimensions to their advantage? We will discuss some of these issues in detail in later chapters. Suffice it to say that universities have to use both internal and external marketing to achieve their objectives. Servicescape will be used to address issues such as appearance and physical elements and internal marketing will be used to address reliability, responsiveness, assurance, and empathy because these must be conveyed by staff and faculty through their interactions with the relevant publics.

Service providers want to make sure that they deliver the quality level expected by the consumer not only because they provide value to the consumer by doing so, but also because it is profitable in doing so. Several studies have shown that service providers who deliver high quality not only earn customers' loyalty but also enjoy profitability (Reichheld & Teal, 1996). Universities like any other service business must aim at meeting or exceeding the expectations of its market (stakeholders). They can do this by carefully managing expectation. They must not overpromise (e.g., inflate placement rates or exaggerate rankings, etc.). Some universities like to tout the percentage of their premed students who make it into medical schools, and some universities like to tout the percentage of their medical school graduates who get residency spots, or the percentage of law school students (graduates) who pass the bar exam. All these help in setting expectations, and definitely help in attracting new students.

Service Quality Gap

A service quality gap is the difference between what customers expected and what they perceived to have received. According to Parasuraman et al. (1985), a service quality gap occurs as a result of four other antecedent gaps: (1) The knowledge gap which occurs when there is a difference between what senior management personnel believes the customer expects and what the customer actually needs and expects. (2) The policy gap which is the difference between management personnel's understanding of the customer's expectations and the service standards that management has set for service delivery. Because management has "misread" the customer's service expectations, the incorrect policies have been set, hence the gap. (3) The delivery gap which is the difference in the specified service delivery standards and the service delivery team's actual performance using the specified standards. This can be caused by several factors including improper training of employees which leads to their lack of knowledge or lack of team efforts. (4) The communication gap which is the difference between what the company communicates and what the customer understands as well as the customer's subsequent experiences. This can occur when advertising messages are not clear or raise the customer's expectations beyond and above what the company actually delivers.

Creating a university experience that maximizes customers' satisfaction improves most likely improves customers' value as well as loyalty. However, because services cannot be standardized to negatively deviate from the consumer's expectation, and if they do deviate, the provider/university must quickly make sincere efforts to make the customer whole.

Service Recovery

Service recovery is a concerted effort taken by a company to address a consumer's dissatisfaction after receiving a service. Because a service provider's objective is to make the customer's experience an enjoyable one, an incident leading to a dissatisfied customer is referred to as a service failure. Because no matter how competent a provider is, service failures will occur, and a good service provider will have procedures in place to address service failures; otherwise they risk alienating customers. A good service provider will have processes in place that manage and resolve complaints. A *service recovery paradox* is a phenomenon in which customers who experienced service failures feel happier after the recovery than those who did not experience any problems in the first place.

Universities can have service recovery processes in place not only to address constituents who may complain after an encounter, but also to address dropout rates. Frequent surveys of stakeholders can be used to help design a recovery strategy.

Loyalty

A loyal customer is not simply a consumer who repeatedly buys from the same company, but who really patronizes the same company, even when other options are available. It is important to understand the point that some customers will repeatedly buy from one company not out of loyalty, but simply because they do not have another option. This means that those customers will stop patronizing that company immediately when another option is available to them. A loyal customer not only patronizes a company over a long term, but also encourages others to buy from that company.

The key to loyalty is goodwill. Because there is goodwill between a customer and a company, for example, company "A," a loyal customer is prepared to convince others to patronize that company "A." That is exactly what universities need. Certainly, the number of repeat purchases is limited for one individual in the case of universities, however, a loyal customer of a university, let's say university Z, will convince other people to attend university Z. Therein comes the invaluable role of alums who can attest to the value of the experiences that they had at university Z, a particular university more than anything else.

The question now is how can a university cultivate this loyalty? There are no easy answers, but we can start from the premise that consumers are intrinsically honest, and that someone who failed in classes or failed to get a job despite the good attempts of the university to offer "help programs" for failing students and to find jobs for its graduates would admit to their own failings. That being the case, as part of their marketing programs, universities could periodically make available to all students and potential students, faculty, and staff what we may refer to as a "Success Compact" – a list of all the programs and steps available in the university to ensure students' success. This compact must be designed with input from all the relevant stakeholders to ensure a maximum buy-in. The compact should not be merely words on paper, but must also be things in action. If all these are done, all else being equal, it would be obvious to even students who have not been successful that the university has done its possible best, and those who have been successful will continue to share stories of their positive experiences with others and encourage them to attend their alma mater.

Summary

Drawing on the definitions of marketing, product, and service, this chapter makes an argument for why higher education is a special product – a service and ought to be marketed as such. It uses such relevant concepts in marketing in general such as exchange, value and value creation, and loyalty, and services marketing in particular such as service attributes, service quality, service quality gap, and service to recovery to show how universities could be effectively marketed.

Questions

1. What is the difference between goods and services?
2. What is the difference between a product and a good? Is there really one?
3. How can a university use loyalty in its recruiting programs?
4. Answer a cynic who asks why a university should be advertising at all?
5. Is the concept of service gap applicable to universities? How?
6. How do universities "process" people?
7. Give an example of how universities can process possessions.

References

Crane, A. (2001). Unpacking Ethical Products. *Journal of Business Ethics* 30 (4), 361–373.

Edgett, S., & Parkinson, S. (1993). Marketing for Service Industries. *The Services Industries Journal* 13 (3), 19–39.

Grewal, D., & Levy, M. (2020). *Marketing*, 7th ed. New York: McGraw Hill/Irwin.

Grönroos, C. (2011). Value Co-creation in Service Logic: A Critical Analysis. *Marketing Theory* 11 (3), 279–301.

Kerin, R., Hartley, S., & Rudelius., W. (2020). *Marketing*, 15th ed. New York: McGraw Hill/Irwin.

Kotler, P., & Armstrong, G. (2008). *Principles of Marketing*, 12th ed. Upper Saddle River, NJ: Pearson Prentice Hall.

Levitt, T. (1980). Marketing Success through Differentiation – Of Anything. *Harvard Business Review* 58 (1), 83–91

Lovelock, C.H. (1980). Towards a Classification of Services. In C. Lamb and P. Dunne (Eds.), *Theoretical Developments in Marketing*, pp. 72–76. Chicago: American Marketing.

Lovelock, C.H. (1983). Classifying Services to Gain Strategic Marketing Insights. *Journal of Marketing* 47 (3), 9–20.

Lovelock, C. and Wirtz, J. (2011). *Services Marketing-People, Technology, and Strategy*. 7th Edition. Pearson Prentice Hall.

Miracle, G. (1965). Product Characteristics and Marketing Strategy. *Journal of Marketing* 29 (1), 18–24.

Moeller, S. (2010). Characteristics of Services – A New Approach Uncovers Their Value. *Journal of Services Marketing* 24 (5), 359–368.

Neap, H.S., & Celik, T. (1999). Value of a Product: A Definition. *International Journal of Value-Based Management* 12 (2), 181–191.

Oliver, R.L. (1977). The Effect of Expectation and Disconfirmation on Postexposure Product Evaluations: An Alternative Interpretation. *Journal of Applied Psychology* 62 (4), 480–486.

Oliver, R.L., Balakrishnan, P.V.S., & Barry, B. (1994). Outcome Satisfaction in Negotiation: A Test of Expectancy Disconfirmation. *Organizational Behavior and Human Decision Processes* 60 (2), 252–275.

Parasuraman, A., Zeithaml, V.A., & Berry, L. (1985). A Conceptual Model of Service Quality and Its Implication for Future Research. *Journal of Marketing* 49 (4), 41–50.

Payne, A.F., Storbacka, K., & Frow, P. (2008). Managing the Co-creation of Value. *Journal of the Academy of Marketing Sciences* 36 (1), 83–96.

Perreault, W., Cannon, J., & McCarthy, E.J. (2021). *Essentials of Marketing*, 17th ed. Irwin, New York: McGraw Hill.

Prahalad, C.K., & Ramaswamy, V. (2000). Co-opting Customer Competence. *Harvard Business Review* 78 (January), 79–90.

Reichheld, F.F., & Teal, T. (1996). *The Loyalty Effect*. Boston, MA: Harvard Business School Press.

Silk, A.J. (2006). *What Is Marketing?* Boston, MA: Harvard Business School Press.

Vargo, S.L., & Lusch, R.F. (2004). Evolving to a New Dominant Logic for Marketing. *Journal of Marketing* 68 (1), 1–17.

Wirtz J., & Lovelock, C. (2018). *Essentials of Services Marketing*, 3rd ed. Upper Saddle River, NJ: Pearson Prentice Hall.

Wyckham, R.G., Fitzroy, P.T., & Mandry, G.D. (1975). Marketing of Services: An Evaluation of the Theory. *European Journal of Marketing* 9 (1), 59–67.

Zeithaml, V.A., Berry, L.L., & Parasuraman, A. (1983). The Nature and Determinants of Customer Expectations of Service. *Journal of Academy of Marketing Science* 21 (1), 1–12.

Zeithaml, V.A., Parasuraman, A., & Berry, L.L. (1985). Problems and Strategies in Service Marketing. *Journal of Marketing* 49 (2), 33–46.

CASE #5 THE UNIVERSITY AS A UNIQUE SERVICE FACTORY

This case discusses universities as the provider of a unique service.

The picture that a factory generally evokes is a complex of several buildings filled with machines constantly humming, and workers attending to them to produce things. Factories are a critical part of modern economic production, with the majority of the world's goods being created or processed within them.

Such is the mental picture of a factory, so perhaps it is a stretch for some people when we compare a university to a factory. But going beyond the machines, people will agree that both universities and manufacturing plants are equally important to modern economic production and both "factories" produce "products" that are a necessary part for modern-day economic engines.

Modern factories generally have, at least, five main components: laboratory, the manufacturing plant, consultation, showroom, and dispatch. The laboratory is where the research and developments take place. In some cases, the laboratory is located at a remote location, separate from the manufacturing plant. Nonetheless, it is the feeder to the manufacturing plant. The manufacturing plant is where the production or processing takes place. It is where the machines hum. Consultation occurs when and where quality control occurs. It can also be, to some extent, where order taking occurs and specifications, etc. are discussed. The showroom is of course where some of the finished products are kept on display. It is generally where visitors go, or rather where they are often shown or taken so that the company can show off its shining new products with pride. "Dispatch" is where the finished products are kept, to be shipped to buyers.

Universities around the world serve primarily as a vehicle through which nations invest in their human capital. A university, therefore, is a complex service factory that produces human capital stock and knowledge. Like an industrial factory, it does these things using people (faculty, administrators, and staff), technology (computers and research equipment), lecture rooms, laboratories, studios and theatres (buildings), students (materials), faculty offices (for consultation), and placement offices (show rooms).

Let us take the case of Ziggie University (a fictitious name), that has over 30,000 students (undergraduate and graduate students combined), and faculty and staff of over 3,000. The university awards degrees at all the three levels (bachelor's, master's, and doctorates) and therefore has active research programs and attracts millions of dollars in research grants each year. The university's research faculty have developed several patented innovations.

Similar to an industrial factory, Ziggie University has employees – faculty, staff, and administrators. The lecture halls/classrooms, laboratories, and studios, like the manufacturing plants, are where production takes place. The equivalent of the production in the case of Ziggie University or any other university for that matter is that knowledge is impacted to students in those spaces. Laboratories in universities also double up as places for invention. What about faculty offices? These are where consultations take place, however, some inventions and quality assurance activities also take place there. The university's equivalent of a showroom is the placement office and campus job fairs. Graduation day is the university's dispatch.

So, even though the equivalences are not clear cut, it is evident from this example that equating a university to a factory, a service factory, is not a hyperbole. Both factories and universities produce outputs. The outputs of a university are the human stock and the new knowledge created through research.

Questions

1. What is human stock?
2. Can you draw other parallels between a university and a factory?
3. What are the five critical characteristics of a factory?
4. If a university can be equated to a factory, then what is the business equivalent role and title of a university president?

CASE #6 STANDING BEHIND THE QUALITY OF THEIR SERVICE – STATE UNIVERSITY OF NEW YORK AT BUFFALO IN THE UNITED STATES

Offering a warranty is a way for some manufacturers to signal the quality of their product. Can the same concept be applied by universities? This case discusses the use of the concept of warranty by universities.

The University of Buffalo was founded in 1846, originally as a private medical college, and merged with the State University of New York system in 1962. It is known variously as the State University of New York at Buffalo, the University at Buffalo (UB), or SUNY Buffalo. It is a public research university with campuses in Buffalo and Amherst, New York, United States.

The University of Buffalo is one of the four university centers in the system, in addition to Albany, Binghamton, and Stony Brook. As of fall 2020, the university enrolled about 32,347 students in 13 colleges, making it the largest public university in the state of New York. In addition to the College of Arts and Sciences, the university houses the largest state-operated medical school, dental school, education school, business school, engineering school, and pharmacy school, and is also home to SUNY's only law school. The university has the largest enrollment, largest endowment, and most research funding among the universities in the SUNY system, and offers the bachelor's degrees in over 100 areas of study, as well as 205 master's degrees, 84 doctoral degrees, and 10 professional degrees. It is the fourth largest state university along the east coast behind Temple University, Pennsylvania State University, and Rutgers University.

In-state tuition fees for an undergraduate degree is around $20,000.00 per year and around $30,000 per year for out-of-state students. Studies showed that students are taking long time, anywhere between five and six years, to complete the bachelor's degree, which in the United States should under normal circumstance take just four years. The cause of this common delay in graduation is not clear, but to encourage students to complete their degree on time, University of Buffalo came up with an innovative program called "Finish in 4 pledge" which is similar to warranties used in industry.

In the industry of experience products where there is information asymmetry and buyers cannot tell the quality of products prior to purchase, producers of high quality distinguish themselves by signaling their quality through expensive warranties. Similarly, in "Finish in 4 pledge," both parties make the pledge. The student pledges to do what it takes to earn the four-year degree in four years, and the university pledges to provide the student with the resources needed to keep the pledge, that is, to graduate in four years. If a student takes the pledge and fulfills all of the requirements, but still cannot graduate in four years, the university will provide the opportunity to complete the needed courses free of tuition and comprehensive fee charges.

While this program can be viewed as a service quality guarantee and a signal, it can also serve as a service recovery strategy.

Questions

1. Can you think of another purpose that the "Finish in 4 pledge" serves?
2. What are *experience* products?
3. Does University of Buffalo's "Finish in 4 pledge" advance the argument for viewing universities as a service factory?
4. In which way can "Finish in 4 pledge" impact University of Buffalo's reputation?

4

PRICING ISSUES

Introduction

What is a price of a product and how is it determined? These are two questions that consumers often consider. They often ask the first question, and the second is less often asked, but nonetheless thought of. Answers to these questions often help to determine the value of what they are buying. So, for the consumer price is connected to value through perceived benefits. To the producer, price plays a more fundamental role – it allows them to remain in business and realize a profit. Price therefore plays a very important role in business to both parties – the buyer and seller. We discuss those notions and the common pricing methods in this chapter. We also discuss the concept of price as a signal of high quality in the market of information asymmetry.

Price and Factors that Influence Price

Price seems simple enough, but is it? What is a fare, a tariff, a commission, an interest, fees, tolls, rent, premiums, and tuition? They are all prices of one form or the other, but with different names depending on the industry. For goods in commercial exchange, price is called "price," but for services, prices are referred to by several different names depending on the industry. The fact that price can come under several different names may be an indication of its complexity. Price, according to Kotler and Armstrong (2008), is "the amount of money charged for a product or service, or the sum of the values that consumers exchange for the benefits of having or using the product or service." This definition is simple but comprehensive.

The importance of price to the continuing operation of a business cannot be overstated. A business will simply cease to exist if the price charged is not high enough to cover the cost of its operations. The same is true for universities also, however, universities have a more complex problem since their students, in most cases, are not directly charged or asked to pay the full cost of the product (education) that they receive. We will discuss the complexities a little later, however, to charge the appropriate prices to cover the cost of a product means that the cost of the product must first be identified. This may not be an easy process

DOI: 10.4324/9781003160267-4

particularly because most companies produce many different kinds of products whose costs vary. Within the same automobile company, the cost of producing a 1600cc (cubic capacity) sedan may be vastly different from the cost of producing a 2400cc SUV (Sport Utility Vehicle). The same is true for universities. Have you ever wondered why tuition (the monetary price charged for education) for business majors is different from the tuition of engineering majors within the same university? Or the tuition of students in the medical school is different from the tuition of students in the law school within the same university? This is because the cost of education (or better yet "producing education") in those different disciplines or schools is different.

There are three main categories of costs – sunk cost, fixed cost, and variable costs. We will refer to the fixed cost and the variable costs as the **relevant costs** to pricing, because they are recoverable and taken into consideration when a product is being priced. In other words a product is priced in such a way that the **selling price** covers the relevant costs. **The sunk** cost is not a relevant cost because it is not recoverable or taken into consideration when a product is being priced. An example of sunk cost for a university could be the cost incurred to conduct a feasibility study for possibly introducing a new school or program in the university. To attempt to recover sunk cost may make the price of product uncompetitive. What about the fixed and variable costs? Because they can be traced to the outputs, generally they must out of necessity be recovered, if the company wants to remain in business.

Fixed costs are costs that do not vary with respect to the volume of units produced. In other words, these costs remain the same, at least in the short term, regardless of the volume produced. In the context of universities, these costs will not change in the short term regardless of the number of students admitted. Examples include the cost of keeping certain infrastructures functional even when school is not in session, the salaries of administrators, and the salaries of some faculty and staff depending on the terms of their contracts and the spheres of their operations.

Variable costs include those costs that are incurred because a university is in session. In other words, they are costs that can be traced directly to the university's production (i.e., doing what it is supposed to be doing – educating students, conducting research, etc.,). Because these costs can be traced directly to outputs, they are also referred to as direct costs. Variable costs can in turn be divided into two – direct labor and direct material (see Figure 4.1). Within the context of universities, this may include books and computers which are supplied fee-free to students because they have already included the tuition (for some programs such as executive

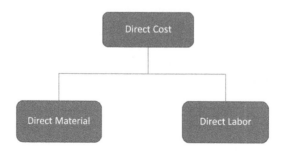

FIGURE 4.1 Variable Costs

education programs in many schools) and, of course, the salaries of some such as adjunct lecturers and term professors.

How Price Is Determined

Price of the product which is sometimes technically referred to as monetary price (to distinguish it from nonmonetary price (see, e.g., Obst, 1989; Vistnes & Hamilton, 1995; Yu et al., 2011) is what the buyer pays out of pocket for their product. It is influenced by several factors; however, the three main factors are the fixed costs, the variable costs, and desired profit (see Figure 4.2). Note that we have assumed away the semivariable category and have fitted everything into fixed and variable categories.

Other relevant factors are competition, supply and demand, reputation, and the supporting strategy. These same factors are important in determining tuition in universities also, but perhaps in a slightly different way. Take the case of private not-for profit and private for-profit universities. Can you see how these factors apply?

A university will adjust tuition accordingly depending on market conditions. For example, a private university decided to not increase its tuition despite the rising cost of living (labor, electricity, etc.) because according to the president, "we do not want to price ourselves out of the market." Look closely at Figure 4.2 to see what the university will have to vary in order to keep tuition at the same level without sacrificing quality? You can see from Figure 4.2 that the university will have to settle for less desired profit now. This means that the university will have to reduce its profit margin in order to keep tuition at the same level.

The interplay between cost profit can be represented simply in a linear form as follows:

Profit = Total revenue − Total cost
For goods, total revenue = (price) × quantity
Total cost = (cost/unit) × quantity
Hence, profit = (price) × quantity − (cost/unit) × quantity
Profit = quantity (price − cost/unit)

We do know that before a company realizes profits, it must first cover all its relevant costs, which is known as to breakeven. At the breakeven point the company realizes no profit, and it does not lose any money as well, hence estimating the breakeven point is important to

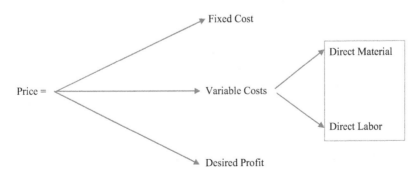

FIGURE 4.2 The Relationship Between Price and Relevant Costs

every company including universities. The formula for calculating the breakeven volume is as follows:

$$Unit\ breakeven\ volume = \frac{Total\ Fixed\ Cost}{Unit\ Selling\ price - Unit\ variable\ cost}$$

Unit breakeven volume generally refers to the number of units that the provider not only has to produce but also has to sell in order to breakeven. The unit breakeven in the context of universities could be the enrollment necessary to breakeven. Again, even though the unit selling price in the equation is not necessarily the price charged to individual students (we will discuss this point shortly under the section on pricing) it underscores why enrollment management is so important to the smooth functioning of universities. This is more so for private for-profit universities than for not-for-profit or public universities.

It must be noted that even though we are discussing breaking-even for a university as a whole entity, the breakeven analysis can and should be calculated for the individual schools, colleges, and departments within the university in order to get a sense of how many students a program needs in order to be viable. In fact, this analysis is now more important and needed than ever as universities, even public universities, are being asked to generate funding on their own for some of their programs. The breakeven analysis gives university administrators a deeper insight when they have to make tough decisions such as eliminating programs or closing a school or college within the university in order to keep the university running. Can you see this happening? Can you think of a university that eliminated a school or program in order to eliminate or reduce an unsustainable cost?

Consider the case of Fairleigh Dickinson University's four-year Doctor of Dental Medicine Program. Fairleigh Dickinson University is the largest private university in the state of New Jersey. It has several other schools and programs such as the Maxwell Becton College of Arts and Sciences, Peter Sammartino School of Education, Silberman College of Business, and several others. Fairleigh Dickinson University's four-year Doctor of Dental Medicine Program used to admit about 150 students each year into the four-year program. However, on March 28, 1989, the university's president announced that the university would close its 33-year Doctor of Dental Medicine Program after the 1989–1990 academic year. The gut-wrenching decision was made because of cuts in state aid to the university's dentistry program. The university's other colleges and programs continued unaffected. How would you have felt, if you were a first-year dentistry student in the four-year program, and only started dentistry school the previous August? How do you think the president felt making this announcement?

Similarly, in the wake of COVID-19 which "rocked" the financial standing of many academic institutions, some universities wisely decided to eliminate some programs or schools in order to save the university as a whole from a financial disaster. Examples include the University of Akron, Ohio, which announced plans to eliminate 6 of the university's 11 colleges (Cleveland.com), Ohio Wesleyan University eliminated 18 majors. the University of South Florida, Tampa, has eliminated its undergraduate program in education, the University of California, Berkeley, has paused admissions to its PhD programs in anthropology, sociology, and art history (Hubler, 2020), and several four-year colleges have eliminated their athletics program (*Los Angeles Times*, 2020).

Other Factors

While price determines a company's customers or a university's student pool, it also determines a company's or a university's competitors. Why is this the case? It is easy to see why price can determine the customers or the market segment that a company will attract simply because of affordability. If the price of a product or the tuition of a university is high, it is logical that only consumers with high income could afford it, all else being equal. However, let us look at price a little more closely.

Price signaling theory (Gabor & Granger, 1966) suggests that in the absence of complete information, consumers are likely to take a high price of a product as a signal of high quality. But how does a high price determine a company's competitors? The answer to this question is rather subtle. If you were my competitor and you do not know how much it costs me to produce a product, but what you can see, or know objectively, is only the high price that I charge for the product, then besides thinking that it costs me a lot of money to make the product, you are also more likely to think that I must be making a lot of profit for making the product, right? What are you likely to do then? Most people would say that they too will more likely make the same product so that they too can "enjoy" some of the perceived high profit. This line of thinking explains why charging a high price can determine a company's competitors. This is true of universities also, particularly for-profit private universities that depend on tuition as the major part of their revenue.

There are two important lessons here: (1) Because prices can be easily mimicked by competition as illustrated by the example above, price should not constitute the thrust of a company's or a university's marketing strategy. However, as part of the marketing mix, price can play an important part in the company's or university's strategy. (2) Following a competitor's price "blindly" without knowing the product's true cost may not be a good strategy. Many private universities in some developing countries (Ghana, Kenya, Nigeria), where private ownership of universities is a recent development, have learned this lesson the hard way through bankruptcy.

Besides the obvious cost and profit motives, the price of a product is influenced by several other factors including the market conditions and value to customers

Market Conditions

By market conditions we mean (1) the market segment or segments that a university is catering to and (2) the intensity of competition for those segments. With regard to (1) the market segments that a university is catering to, let us take the case of a small private university. This university may choose to cater to a **small and exclusive** market that may be interested in a certain type of education (e.g., liberal arts, fine arts, or physical sciences and engineering). This exclusive market segment may not be price sensitive, therefore the university can afford to charge high tuition, and still be able to attract enough students to make the institution financially stable. Of course, several other attributes such as size, servicescape, instructional quality, reputation, and qualifications and experience of faculty and staff will have to be "curated" to support the university's exclusive image.

With regard to (2) the level of competition in the segments chosen, we mean the number of other universities that are also operating in the same segment(s). Tuition (i.e., price) could be affected if there are many universities that are competing for the same resources (students, faculty and staff, etc.), but price changes would largely depend on how elastic or inelastic these resources are to price changes.

Price Elasticity

Price elasticity is the degree of responsiveness of quantity demanded to price changes. It is mathematically written as

$$E = \frac{\Delta Q}{\Delta P}$$

Where E = elasticity, and ΔQ is the degree of responsiveness of quantity demanded to price changes, and ΔP is a unit change in price. If the market demand is price elastic and the university lowers tuition by a percentage, it will experience a disproportionately higher increase in enrollment. On the contrary, if the demand is price inelastic, the university can increase tuition to a point without experiencing any decrease in enrollment.

In for-profit private universities, the market conditions will influence their profit objectives, hence they can seek to maximize profit by increasing tuition, if demand is price inelastic; however, we should note that the appropriate marketing strategies must be used to support the increase in tuition. Some of these universities support their high tuition with other marketing attributes such as flexibility with courses, liberal acceptance of work experience for college credits, installment payment of tuition, and the like.

Value to Customers

We have already discussed the "value" of a product to consumers, and how consumers assess "value" using price and perceived benefits in the previous chapter, hence it should not come as a surprise that we are again discussing value here in a chapter on pricing. The truth of the matter is price matters in whatever the customer perceives "value," hence universities can influence the consumers' perception of the value of the education they receive from a particular university not only by "playing" around with tuition, but also by adjusting the supporting marketing attributes which make university experience more holistic.

Other Factors

There are other factors besides the monetary costs and market conditions which even though do not influence price directly are nonetheless taken into consideration. For example, the pricing of a company's product may be influenced by the availability of a close substitute in the market. Furthermore, ethical and fairness considerations as well as government regulations and policies also influence pricing decisions in companies as well as in universities.

Generally, companies use different pricing approaches to arrive at the selling price. When the price of a product reflects all the costs (the variable cost and the allocated part of the fixed cost) and profit as depicted in Figure 4.2, it is said that a **full-cost pricing** approach is being used. On the one hand, when a company because of market conditions and strategic considerations decides to sell a product at only the variable cost, then it is said that a **variable-cost pricing** approach is being used.

While the full-cost and the variable-cost approach to pricing is simple and appealing they may not capture all the relevant costs in service firms such as universities, retail banking, and hospitals. Hence, a more complex Activity-Based Costing (ABC) approach has been proposed, and evidence suggests that applying this method in real life is more complex than initially thought. However, running a university involves more than organizing lectures; it often involves running a complex web of operations such as residence halls, cafeterias, transportation, gyms, clinics, counseling centers, and in some cases entertainment centers or movie theaters. The major decision that must be made is which of the services to include in tuition and which are made available on pay-as-you-use basis? Some universities charge facilities user fees separately. For example, students taking science courses are charged extra for lab fees, and others technology fees and athletics fees. Whether this is a better costing approach or another means to improve a university's revenue is yet to be decided.

Because of the rising cost of living in many countries, including the United States, prices of certain products including tuition keep increasing to the point where school fees in some private schools have become so high that they have become practically unaffordable to students from certain segments of the population, for example, students from lower-income households who also tend to be students of minority backgrounds. Take, for instance, tuition for 2021–2022 academic year for an undergraduate program at Grinnell College (a liberal arts college in Iowa) is $58,156, with room and board plus activity fees, the school fees for the academic year is $72,998 (at www.grinnell.edu/admission/financial-aid/affording-grinnell/cost). Similarly, the school fees for 2021–2022 academic year for an undergraduate program at Swarthmore College in Pennsylvania is $73,206 (at www.swarthmore.edu/student-accounts-office/tuition-room-and-board-fees) while the median annual income for a Black family in the United States in 2019 is approximately $42,000 (see Berube, 2019).

This shows that without any intervention, access to education in such universities is outside the reach of the average Black family in the United States. Thus, the population at some of those universities would not be reflective of the population of the United States, if the market forces were allowed to operate unchecked in setting school fees. Diversity of viewpoints that reflects that of the population would be absent on some campuses and in classrooms which might lead to one-sided education. To forestall this, the administrators of such exclusive universities have raised funds to assist qualified minority students to attend such universities fee-free. To assist qualified minority students and prevent lack of finance to get in their way of attending good but expensive private universities, financial aid programs have been instituted in some exclusive universities to grant free tuition to qualified students. Take for example the program in the Ivy League universities to allow admission to every qualified and admitted student from a household where the annual income is between $65,000 and $150,000 (see Wyland, 2013) free tuition.

Innovative thinking of the kind reflected here is not only good for society in general, but it also makes for good public policy, public relations, and an excellent marketing opportunity for the universities involved.

Pay What You Want

Pay What You Want (PWYW) is a new pricing strategy that emerged in the 1980s in the services industry. The name of the strategy pretty much says what it is. In its purest form, the price of the service is completely delegated to the buyer or the consumer, hence the buyer can pay nothing if they so choose. However, variations of the pure form have appeared where there is either a suggested price or coupons to be used.

While pinning down the origin of the strategy is at best elusive, two things are clear: one, it originated in the services industry; two, it has certainly made its way into the academia, specifically in the field of behavioral economics. Kim et al. (2009) in one of the earliest academic studies on PWYW suggested that sellers using PWYW face the risk that consumers will exploit their control or take advantage of the condition and pay nothing at all or pay a price below the seller's costs. However, in three field studies conducted involving movie tickets, restaurant buffet lunch, and hot beverages, the authors found that the prices paid by consumers were significantly greater than zero. Kim and his colleagues suggested that such factors as fairness, altruism, loyalty, price consciousness, and satisfaction may have positively impacted consumers' price decisions, while other factors such as income and reference price played no significant role.

In another study, Regner and Barria (2009) investigated customers' behavior regarding their choice of price paid for music using a real-world music label and online store Magnatune. In the study, customers could pay what they want for albums, as long as the payment was within a given price range ($5–$18). Magnatune's comprehensive prepurchase access facilitated discovery of the music and allowed informed buying decision. This arrangement set Magnatune apart from conventional online music stores.

The study found that on average customers paid $8.20, far more than the minimum of $5 and even higher than the recommended price of $8. The authors suggested that the relationship between artists/labels with regard to social preferences, particularly reciprocity, guided the customers to behave in a particular manner, and that Magnatune's open contracts design can encourage people to make voluntary payments. The authors also noted Magnatune's approach might be a viable business option.

These are by no means the end of the application of PWYW pricing strategy in real life nor does it signify the end of academic examinations of the strategy. However, we cannot see its immediate application to tuition in general, nonetheless an opportunity exists where some universities may try payment for a course or two on PWYW basis. The results of such an experiment would certainly be interesting.

Dynamic Pricing

Have you ever wondered why the toll on the high way changes several times during the day, or the price for an airline between the same two cities changes several times during the week? This is because the Department of Highway, or the airline, is using dynamic pricing also known variously as surge pricing, time-based pricing, or demand pricing strategy. Dynamic pricing is fairly common these days and is used by several industries particularly by the services industry – car rental companies, airlines, hostels, and even entertainment venues. Dynamic pricing is based on sophisticated algorithms that take into consideration demand and supply at any given time, competitors' position, and environmental conditions to arrive at an optimal price for that time. As indicated earlier, even though it is commonly used in the services industry, its use in pricing (setting tuition) in universities seems infeasible.

Summary

This chapter examines the different pricing methods, particularly the full-cost pricing approach since it is the most commonly used approach. It talks about the dual objective of pricing as a means to make profit and also as a signaling device. The chapter also covers the activity-based costing approach since it is the most amenable to services industry though not popularly used. Finally, the chapter discusses the PWYW approach which is still somewhat a novelty in real life.

Questions

1. Do you think universities can easily use activity-based pricing method?
2. Do you think universities will ever use the PWYW approach? Why not?
3. Do you think the PWYW approach is culture or context specific?
4. Do you think universities can use pricing as signal? (Tip – you will have to distinguish public universities from private universities to answer this question satisfactorily)
5. Why do you think the tip given in question 4 in necessary?
6. What is a separating equilibrium and why is it necessary for signaling to work?
7. What is elasticity of demand?

References

Berube, A. (2019). Black Household Income Is Rising across the United States. www.brookings. edu/blog/the-avenue/2019/10/03/black-household-income-is-rising-across-the-united-states/. Retrieved on September 10, 2021.

Gabor, A., & Granger, C.W.J. (1966). Price as an Indicator of Quality: Report on an Inquiry. *Economica* 33 (129), 43–70.

Hubler, S. (2020). Colleges Slash Budgets in the Pandemic, with "Nothing Off-Limits." *The New York Times.* www.nytimes.com/2020/10/26/us/colleges-coronavirus-budget-cuts.html. Retrieved on August 17, 2021.

Kim, J.Y., Natter, M., & Spann, M. (2009). Pay What You Want: A New Participative Pricing Mechanism. *Journal of Marketing* 73 (1), 44–58.

Kotler, P., & Armstrong, G. (2008). *Principles of Marketing.* Upper Saddle River, NJ: Pearson Prentice Hall.

Los Angeles Times (2020). Nearly 100 College Sports Programs Have Been Cut during Pandemic. www. latimes.com/sports/story/2020-05-30/nearly-100-college-sports-programs-have-been-cut-during-pandemic. Retrieved on August 17, 2021.

Obst, N.P. (1989). Monetary Price Rules for Alternative Steady-State Regimes. *Metroeconomica* 40 (3), 179–277.

Regner, T., & Barria, J. (2009). Do Consumers Pay Voluntarily? The Case of Online Music. *Journal of Economic Behavior & Organization* 71 (2), 395–406.

Vistnes, J.P., & Hamilton, V. (1995). The Time and Monetary Costs of Outpatient Care for Children Source. *The American Economic Review* 85 (2), 117–121.

Wyland, M. (2013). Harvard Initiative to Attract Low-Income Students Includes Free Tuition NPQ Non-Profit Quarterly Report, https://nonprofitquarterly.org/harvard-initiative-to-attract-low-income-students-includes-free-tuition/. Retrieved on September 10, 2021.

Yu, U-J, Niehm, L.S., & Russell, D.W. (2011). Exploring Perceived Channel Price, Quality, and Value as Antecedents of Channel Choice and Usage in Multichannel Shopping. *Journal of Marketing Channels* 18 (2), 79–102.

CASE #7 IS FREE TUITION (TUITION FEE) IN PUBLIC UNIVERSITIES SUSTAINABLE? THE CASE OF UNIVERSITIES IN GERMANY

State or government universities in some countries do not charge any tuition (tuition fees). The government covers these expenses as a way to build intellectual capital. This case discusses this practice and asks whether it is sustainable.

A commonly cited quotation whose source is unknown is "an *educated citizenry* is a vital requisite for our survival as a free people." However, a steady stream of research in economics and education has demonstrated both by empirical evidence and theoretical proofs the wisdom of investing in education. Recognizing this, education, in many countries around the world, is considered a public good, and must as such be provided by the government without cost to the recipients, at least up to a point. The question is up to which level? Should it be up to elementary school or high school level? Or better still should university education also be free?

Because of resource constraints, many governments limit free and compulsory education up to the high school level. University education in many advanced countries, even in public universities, does not come with free tuition. The situation is, however, different in Germany where university education is tuition free not only to citizens, but to foreign nationals as well. In fact, Germany is one of the few countries in the world where one can study for free, independent of where one comes from. The German public seems to believe that education should not be treated as a commercial product and that free access to higher education ensures economic growth and welfare for the greater population. The interesting thing about Germany is that this argument extends to even foreign nationals who happen to be in Germany. This belief is not, however, without counterarguments.

Those who opposed free education in public universities were able to get a legislation passed allowing a modest tuition (tuition fees) in public universities. However, with mounting public protests, this legislation was reversed in 2014, once again allowing everyone, including international students, free tuition. The question is how long can this practice go given the rising cost of education?

The debate on free education in public universities continue. Some constituent German states have reintroduced tuition fees for international students studying in Germany. These fees are, however, much lower than tuition fees in public universities in many other countries. Some argue that having no tuition fees or setting tuition fees relatively low in public universities in Germany is a well-thought strategy to attract best brains to come and study, live and work in Germany whose population growth rate was only 0.2% in 2020. It is worth noting that even this marginal growth rate was primarily due to migration.

Questions

1. Do you think the cost of free university education outweighs the benefits?
2. Should the German government consider paying for students' tuition fees in private universities in Germany, if it really considers education to improve welfare?
3. What do you think is the future of tuition-free public university education in Germany?
4. Would you consider going to Germany to pursue your university education? Why or why not?

CASE #8 ARRIVING AT TUITION IN STATE UNIVERSITIES

There are several suggestions in services marketing on how to determine the price of a service. However, we are not aware of any of such suggestions for university education. This case discusses an approach to determining the price of university education

The price of services goes by many different names: tolls on the freeway, fare for the airline, premium for insurance, and tuition or tuition fees for university education. Most businesses use defined accounting methods to determine how much it costs them to produce an item. To that cost, they add a predetermined desired profit to arrive at the selling price per unit. But with the rising cost of tuition, have you ever wondered how tuition at many state universities is determined, and how schools play around with it?

Tuition, the price, students pay for instructions at many state universities is actually set by one of the three different bodies depending on the state. In some states, they are set by the Legislature (e.g., Florida and Louisiana), or by the State System of Board of Higher Education (Arizona, California, and Connecticut). There is also another entity, the State Board of Higher Education, which sets tuition in Idaho. Because in some states such as Arkansas the local governing boards such as the boards of trustees have the authority to set tuition, any increases in tuition can be offset by decreases in state appropriations, hence universities have resorted to resourceful ways of disguising tuition raises.

According to *US News & World Report* (February, 2020) several state universities disguised tuition increases at the university level by charging several different fees that they did not charge in the past. For example, some universities such as the University of North Carolina at Asheville charge between $50 and $300 as orientation fee which is one-time fee charged to freshmen. Some schools such as the University of Arizona charge freshmen $10.00 per semester for freshmen fee which is different from orientation fee. This is charged to cover the support services supposedly given to freshmen. Other schools including Rutgers University, New Brunswick, charge undergraduates as much as $1,347 per year for what they call "campus fee" which covers such things as student services, health services, and facilities use.

Other fees include lab fees which are charged when a student is taking a science course that requires use of the labs, and surprisingly of all is an environment fee of $14.40 per year that is charged by the University of California at Los Angeles (UCLA) for green initiatives. Texas at Austin charges $5.00 per semester for what it calls "green fee." What about "campus spirit fee"? The University of California, Irvine, charges every undergraduate student $99.00 per year for "campus spirit" fee which is used to support athletic and campus spirit programs. Tech fees are common these days – used to support computer labs and Wi-Fi.

Another innovative fee that has made its way to campuses is transportation fee. The University of Central Florida, for example, charges a $9.10 transportation fee that is tacked on for every credit hour a student takes. A student taking a 15-hour course load would therefore pay $136.50 in transportation access charges. Paying for athletics has also become common these days. For example, at the University of Virginia, students paid $678 during the 2020–2021 academic year for athletics on top of a $428 mandatory fee for recreational facilities. Mandatory health and wellness fees are also common these days. Fairleigh Dickinson University in New Jersey, for example, charges full-time undergraduate students $70 per semester for health and wellness, while the University of Colorado charges wellness fees on per credit basis and up to $90 for students taking 15 credits or more hours. Finally, there is no school without graduation ceremonies, right? So, commencement fees are also being charged. The University of Massachusetts, Amherst, for example, charges $110 to students in the first semester of their senior year while Chicago State University and Ohio University charge "graduation application" fees of $50. At this time, we believe the list of innovative fees or what we call disguised tuition raises is endless and can be limited only by our imagination.

Questions

1. Can you come up with three other ways in which universities can disguise tuition raises?
2. What do you think about these tuition raises? Are they appropriate, ethical, or deceptive?
3. Can you name three other schools that charge these "innovative fees"?
4. Can you suggest other viable ways in which universities can generate funds without raising tuition?

5

LOCATION AND A UNIVERSITY

Introduction

Even though the mantra in real estate is "location, location, location," and location is one of the four elements of the marketing mix, "location" does not seem to be relevant in decisions on where a university must be sited. In this chapter, we review the relevant literature and concepts in economics and marketing on the location of industries and relate them to universities and how they can be used in the marketing of universities. We also discuss other topical issues including infrastructure and quality of life issues that can be implicated in discussions on location and relate them also to university marketing.

The Concept of Location of Industries

The factors of production as discussed in classical economics are land, labor, capital, and entrepreneurship (see O'Sullivan & Sheffrin, 2003; Friedman, 2007). Land as a factor of production was broadly defined to include land in all forms, for example, agricultural land, commercial real estate, etc., and natural resources such as oil, gold, and minerals that can be extracted from land and refined for human consumption (see Krzyzanowski, 1927).

Place, however, assumed a larger role in discussions of location of industries around the turn of the twentieth century when Alfred Weber propounded a theory on the location of industries (1909). Industry in this context refers to an economic activity in which raw materials are transformed into goods and services and business activities which surround the use of these goods and services. The term industry is used to refer to a wide array of business activities which may include only manufacturing – the making of goods in the narrowest sense or in the broadest sense to "all stages and types of economic activity including extraction, construction and services."

Location of an industry is an idea referring to the practice of establishing an industry in a given area for economic, geographical, social, or political reasons. Industrial location can also be defined as the strategic placement of various economic activities in relation to some specific factors.

DOI: 10.4324/9781003160267-5

Under Weber's theory, an industry would be located where the transportation costs of raw materials and final product are at its minimum. This would occur when the weight of the final product is less than the weight of the raw material that goes into making the product. Under this theory we can see why industries that process products such as gold and bauxite, for example, locate close to where the mines are located. Weber's theory lost favor to August Losch's theory of "Profit Maximization" in which Losch argued that "profit maximization" is the only objective of the entrepreneur, whether the entrepreneur is a state or an individual (Losch, 1954). Because maximizing profit is the objective of the entrepreneur and not the minimization of transportation costs, an entrepreneur would only locate an industry at any location that furthers the profit maximization objective.

The discussions of place in the services marketing literature is largely restricted to discussions on place in the marketing mix which focuses primarily on distribution (Constantinides, 2006; Warnaby & Medway, 2013). However, we argue that "place" in the marketing of services (including universities) goes beyond matters involving distribution per se or the marketing mix for that matter. It may involve fusion of theories on the location of industries, the theory of retail gravitation, and the marketing mix. Place in the marketing mix is more closely aligned to land or geographical location, particularly in the pre-Internet era. Decisions regarding where to locate a brick-and-mortar store at that time amongst other things reflected discussions of the retail gravitational theory which argues that a retailer's physical location defines the "target geographical market" where the firm competes for its customers (see Converse, 1949; Reilly, 1953; Ingene & Lusch, 1981).

Even though the presence of international students on university campuses may belie the fact that the retail gravitational theory plays a role in decisions to locate university campuses, particularly in the age of the Internet and the holding of virtual classes, a closer look at where university campuses, particularly where some satellite campuses, are located may suggest otherwise. However, several other factors such as the market, government policies (especially with public universities), availability of land, etc., may play a role in the decision. We summarize the factors that traditionally play a role in deciding the location of industries in Figure 5.1.

Raw Materials

The availability of raw materials in the location of industries stems from the fact generally that raw materials in some industries such as gold are heavy and bulky compared to the output as discussed by Weber (1909). Hence, industries that process such materials are located close to the source of the raw materials. Raw materials are, however, not relevant in the location of universities. Even if the argument were made that students are the "inputs" (as in the "input-output model" of production), they (students) are still mobile.

Energy

Industries such as fertilizer and copper smelting plants that consume a lot of power are generally located near power sources. However, because power can now be inexpensively transmitted over long distances, energy no longer wields much influence over the location of industries. In any case, energy by itself does not appear to wield any influence in the location of a university.

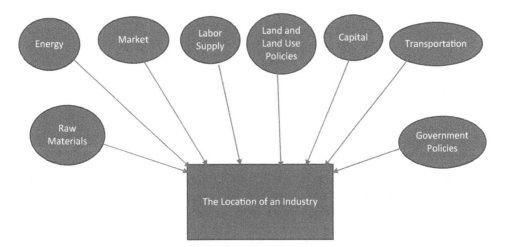

FIGURE 5.1 Factors Affecting Location of Industries

Note: We use the term industries here broadly as defined in the beginning of the chapter, e.g., a factory, and universities in this context can be regarded as a service factory.

Market

Access to easily available market is essential to some industries, for example, those whose finished products are fragile or perishable, however, with the advancement in modes of transportation, nearness to markets is no longer as important as it used to be in locating factories and certainly not in the case of universities.

Labor Supply

Even though labor is fairly mobile (Sassen, 1990) the availability of skilled labor in a particular area can influence the location of certain industries (Rodrik, 1998; Cardi & Restout, 2015). For example, high technology companies tend to locate in states where there are many high-quality universities. For example, Silicon Valley in California attracts a disproportionately high number of high technology companies; however, availability of labor per se does not appear to influence the location of universities.

Land and land Use Policies

Land as a factor of production naturally plays an important part in the decision to locate an industry, primarily because of prices and regulations (Randall & Castle, 1985; Palmquist, 1989). Hence, a decision to locate a university would have to be made taking into considerations land prices and regulations concerning their use (Metzemakers, 2005; Brandao & Feder, 1996). Some properties (parcels of land) maybe readily available or even available for free, or at a heavily discounted price because a municipal or county government may want to encourage certain economic activities in those areas. In this regard, a university may also take availability of housing stock for faculty, staff, and nonresidential students in an area into consideration.

Capital

The argument in favor of the influence of capital is that many industries require investment of capital and because capital is more readily available in urban centers these industries would locate close to where it is easy to raise capital. Again, this argument is not very persuasive anymore knowing how mobile capital is in the twenty-first century (see Sassen, 1990). In any case, the role of capital in attracting a university to a particular location is minimal.

Transportation

Transportation is important for getting raw materials to factories for processing and also in getting the finished products to the market, hence it plays an important role in the location of factories; however, its role in the location of a university might be limited. It is foreseeable that nearness to an airport or transportation hub could be considered in siting location though students and faculty will need to move to and from conferences as well as their homes for holidays.

Government Policies

A government's economic and social policies can greatly influence the location of industries. A government can give tax and other incentives to influence industries to locate at a place preferred by the government. Similarly, a government can influence the location of universities by its policies (see Brandao & Feder, 1996). This is particularly true in the case of private universities (for-profit or otherwise), while the legislatures in some states in the United States or the governments in some developing countries simply dictate where the next state university should be located or tie the location to the funding of the university (see Marginson & Considine, 2000; Boucher et al., 2003; Wright & Ørberg, 2008; King, 2009).

Infrastructure

While we discussed above a set of factors that in classical economics are necessary for the location of industries in general, it seems one word that would describe a constellation of factors that is necessary for the location of a university is infrastructure. By infrastructure we mean a set of fundamental facilities and systems that are necessary to support the functionality of households or companies and therefore a university. It includes public and private physical amenities such as parks and recreational facilities, and structures such as roads, bridges, electrical grids, telecommunications, and Internet and broadbands. These items are important for the maintenance of a level of quality of life that the university can use to position itself.

Quality of Life

There is no consensus on the definition of Quality of Life (QOL). However, the World Health Organization defines QOL as "an individual's perception of their position in life in the context of the culture and value systems in which they live and in relation to their goals, expectations, standards and concerns" (THE WHOQOL GROUP, 1998). Even though QOL is subjective, most people agree that it is something they seek. They consider easy access to the arts, afford-able housing, entertainment, good restaurants and food, good hospitals, good shopping malls, and good infrastructure as factors that would contribute to their QOL. This being the case universities can use their location, that is, their nearness to these facilities and perhaps the low crime rate (which is enjoyed in many university towns) to promote themselves to their poten-tial customers (students, faculty, and staff).

A university that is conducting cutting-edge research (in technology or pharmacology) could create a research park and business incubator offices which can be used to attract businesses to locate close to them. A symbiotic relationship in which internships and employ-ment opportunities are created could be forged between the university and the businesses that have responded.

Summary

We discussed in this chapter factors that can affect the location of industries in general and uni-versities in particular. We discussed the eight factors discussed in economics which influence the location of industries – land, labor, capital, raw materials, government policies, markets, transportation, and energy. However, not all the eight factors are relevant to decisions to locate a university. We discussed those that are important to locating a university such as infrastruc-ture and quality of life issues. We have to remember though that the same factors that are rele-vant to locating a university could also be useful in marketing a university.

Questions

1.   What are the eight factors that can affect the location of an industry?
2.   Which of the eight are relevant to locating a university?
3.   How can the factors used in answering question 2 be used in marketing a university?
4.   How vital is infrastructure in the decision to locate a university?
5.   What role can quality of life issues play in locating a university? Why?
6.   What role can government policies play in locating a university?
7.   Are political considerations equally important in locating public and private universities?

References

Boucher, G., Conway, C., & Van Der Meer, E. (2003). Tiers of Engagement by Universities in their Region's Development. *Regional Studies* 37 (9), 887–897.

Brandao, A.A.P., & Feder, G. (1996). *Regulatory Policies and Reform: The Case of Land Markets, Private Sector Development Department.* Washington, DC: World Bank.

Cant, M.C., & van Heerde, C.V. (2004). *Personal Selling.* Cape Town, South Africa: Juta.

Cardi, O., & Restout, R. (2015). Imperfect Mobility of Labor across Sectors: A Reappraisal of the Balassa–Samuelson Effect. *Journal of International Economics* 97 (2), 249–265.

Constantinides, E. (2006). The Marketing Mix Revisited: Towards the 21st Century Marketing. *Journal of Marketing Management* 22 (3–4), 407–438.

Converse, P.D. (1949). New Laws of Retail Gravitation. *Journal of Marketing,* 14 (January), 379–384.

Friedman, M. (2007). *Price Theory,* 4th ed. New Brunswick, NJ: Transaction.

Ingene, C.A., & Lusch, R.F. (1981). The Declining Rate of Return on Capital in US Retailing. *International Journal of Physical Distribution & Materials Management* 11 (1), 25–39.

King, R. (2009). *Governing Universities Globally, Organizations, Regulations and Ranking*. Northampton, MA: Edward Elgar.

Kotler, P., & Keller, K.L. (2008). *Marketing Management*. Upper Saddle River, NJ: Pearson Prentice Hall.

Krzyzanowski, W. (1927). Review of the Literature of the Location of Industries. *Journal of Political Economy* 35 (2), 278–291.

Losch, A. (1954). *The Economics of Location*. New Haven: Yale University Press

Marginson, S., & Considine, M. (2000). *The Enterprise University, Power, Governance and Reinvention in Australia*. Cambridge: Cambridge University Press.

Metzemakers, P. (2005). Land as Production Factor. Paper presented at 45th Congress of the European Regional Science Association: "Land Use and Water Management in a Sustainable Network Society," August 23–27, 2005, Amsterdam, The Netherlands. http://hdl.handle.net/10419/117520

O'Sullivan, A., & Sheffrin, S.M. (2003). *Economics: Principles in Action*. Upper Saddle River, NJ: Pearson Prentice Hall.

Palmquist, R.B. (1989). Land as a Differentiated Factor of Production: A Hedonic Model and Its Implications for Welfare Measurement. *Land Economics* 65 (1), 23–28.

Randall, A., & Castle, E.N. (1985). *Land Resources and Land Markets in Handbook of Natural Resource and Energy Economics*, Vol. 2, A.V. Kneese & J.L. Sweeney (Eds.), pp. 571–620. Amsterdam, The Netherlands: Elsevier Science.

Reilly, W.J. (1953). *The Law of Retail Gravitation*, 2nd ed. New York: Pillsbury.

Rodrik, D. (1998). Capital Mobility and Labor. Manuscript. http://ksghome.harvard.edu/~drodrik/capitalm.pdf

Sassen, S. (1990). *The Mobility of Labor and Capital*. Cambridge: Cambridge University Press.

Warnaby, G., & Medway, D. (2013). What about the "Place" in Place Marketing? *Marketing Theory* 13 (3), 345–363.

Weber, A (1909) Theory of the Location of Industries ([Translated by Carl J. Friedrich from Weber's 1909 book in 1929). Chicago, IL: University of Chicago Press.

WHOQOL GROUP. (1998). Development of the World Health Organization WHOQOL –BREF Quality of Life Assessment. *Psychological Medicine* 28 (3), 551–558.

World Health Organization Quality of Life (WHOQOL). www.who.int/publications/i/item/WHO-HIS-HSI-Rev.2012.03

Wright, S., & Ørberg, J.W. (2008). Autonomy and Control: Danish University Reform in the Context of Modern Governance. *Learning & Teaching: The International Journal of Higher Education in the Social Sciences* 1 (2), 27–57.

CASE #9 LOCATION, LOCATION, LOCATION

This case illustrates how one private university made its location decision and the factors it considered.

"Location, location, and location" are the three most important factors that one should consider when looking for a residential home, but how are these factors important in deciding the location for a university? This study deals with the factors considered while deciding on the location of a small private university, Lloyd University (fictitious name).

Political considerations play a major role in deciding the location of public universities all over the world. The situation is, however, different for private universities where political consideration play a little or no role at all. For private universities several factors play a role, but underlying all the factors is how to parlay them into a successful marketing statement for the university.

Lloyd University is a small private university founded in 2010 in Accra, the capital of Ghana, by two friends. Lloyd was a born entrepreneur who initially conceived plans for the university. Having spent most of his time outside Ghana, he needed a reliable person who knew the ropes, as it were, in terms of whom to contact, etc., to get the paperwork approved expeditiously. Contacts still matter here. So, Lloyd shared his plans with his friend Martin, and asked if he was interested in pattering with him as the cofounder and a minority shareholder of the university. Martin agreed, so the Lloyd University was founded. The two men initially made all decisions regarding the university. They formed a board of trustees as required by the National Accreditation Board (NAB) to get the school registered, but the board of trustees was simply a "rubber stamp" that approved everything Lloyd wanted.

The initial decision was where to house the university. After a brief search, Martin found a building whose owner was known to a friend of his. The rent was a little high, but they considered the location ideal for visibility and marketing purposes, so they took a five-year lease on the house with an option to purchase at the end of the lease. Lloyd and Martin operated on shoe-string budget and assumed several roles to save money. After a six-month intensive advertising and going to high schools to recruit, Lloyd University opened its doors to freshmen students in August 2010. The university enrolled 60 students.

After four years, the student population increased to 1000 students. The lease on the three-story house would be due the next year and Lloyd and Martin need to decide on whether they should buy the house and try to acquire some adjoining properties also, or try and relocate to the suburb where rent could be a lot lower. Factors that they need to consider are students' access to cultural activities, students' internship opportunities with large companies located downtown, job opportunities for students with large companies, network opportunities for students and the university, easy access to public transportation, and tax break from the city. These advantages would have to be compared with the advantages of locating in suburb such as lower rent, higher tax break to relocate in the suburb, lower visibility, less access to public transportation, and access to much more space and inexpensive land available for acquisition for long-term expansion.

Lloyd and Martin have to decide in about three months.

Questions

1. With current advancements in technology, how much importance do universities have to attach to location?
2. Do universities have to consider faculty viewpoints in deciding on a site to locate its main, or satellite campuses?
3. What roles do the boards of trustees play in the decision to locate or relocate a university's campus?
4. What role can marketing play in a university's decision to locate a campus?

CASE #10 DOWNTOWN OR NOWHERE – THE MBA PROGRAM AT FLORIDA ATLANTIC UNIVERSITY, BOCA RATON, FLORIDA, UNITED STATES

This case discusses a decision-making scenario in a College of Business on whether to locate the executive master's degree in Business Administration (MBA) in a facility in the downtown of a city which is far away from the university's main campus or to run the program out of the university's main campus. Why is the location of a program still a debatable issue?

Florida Atlantic University (FAU) was founded in October 1964 as the fifth of the state's university system. In attendance at the dedication ceremony was Lyndon Baines Johnson, the 36th president of the United States. It certainly was unusual for a sitting US chief executive to officiate the dedication of a new regional university, but such was the beginning of FAU.

The university's main and only campus at its inception was located at a former Boca Raton Army Air Field base. This facility which opened in October 1942 was one of the few radar training schools, operated by the US Army Air Corps during World War II. The base which covered more than 5,800 acres played an active part in helping to win the war as it was the site where thousands of airmen were then taught a relatively new art of radar operation. Amongst its trainees were those who were aboard the Enola Gay on its fateful run to Hiroshima in 1945.

The base had outlived its usefulness by the 1950s when the war was over. The radar training school had moved to Biloxi, Mississippi. After complex negotiations in Washington, the Civil Aeronautics Administration permitted the state to build the university on 1,000 acres of the former airbase, reserving another 200 acres for airport use. Boca Raton Municipal Airport was built on a 200-acre site adjoining the campus and remains in active use to this day.

FAU was one of the first universities in the country to offer only upper-division and graduate-level work. The school operated on the theory that freshmen and sophomores could be served by the growing community college system. Even with these enrollment restrictions, the initial student body was expected to be about 2,000, but by September 8, 1964, the scheduled opening day, fewer than half that number had registered for classes. This shortfall was attributed to the campus' lack of dormitories and dining facilities, South Florida's inadequate system of highways, the absence of public transportation, and the administration's failure to actively recruit students. Because a feasibility study had indicated that the new university stood in the middle of a region that was home to 30,000 potential students, little or no marketing effort had been made.

The university had five colleges in the beginning – the College of Business, the College of Education, the College of Humanities, the College of Science, and the College of Social Science. The College of Education also offered master's degrees in elementary, secondary, and higher education, administration, guidance, special education, and human behavior. Under FAU's third president, Dr. Popovich, the Reuben O'D. Askew, a nine-story University Tower was built in downtown Fort Lauderdale in 1987 to serve students from Broward

County. The University Tower served as classrooms and offices for programs in business and public administration. Downtown Fort Lauderdale is a hub of businesses and government offices. The Federal and County Courts which employ hundreds of employees were located with a one-mile radius from the University Tower. Similarly, the county mayor's office and the county's court house were within a few hundred yards from the Tower.

Because of the University Tower's proximity to businesses, it was thought that an opportunity to attract students from the local businesses exists. The most attractive segment of these businesses is their middle- and lower-level managers. Hence, a decision was made to locate the Graduate School of Business at downtown Fort Lauderdale. This program was charged with the responsibility of offering classes towards the MBA degree. The nagging question, however, is whether the location of the program matters? About 12–15 years later, the program was moved to FAU's main campus in Boca.

Questions

1. Does the MBA program need to be located downtown or near businesses?
2. Do know any other university that started as a senior and graduate-level institution? What is their rationale for doing so and how was it marketed?
3. Given FAU's nearness to an active airport, what explains why it has never offered a program in aviation management?
4. Do you think FAU's history can be leveraged as a marketing asset to offer a program in military leadership or the US military history? Why not?

6

PROMOTING AND ADVERTISING UNIVERSITIES

Introduction

This chapter has combined two common means through which organizations communicate with their target audiences and relates them to university marketing. It discusses the need to have communication objectives, and how universities can use the communication mix to reach their various targets. The chapter also defines advertising and discusses some seminal papers in advertising to set the basis for why and how universities must advertise. It concludes by discussing the communication channel and how it can be used by universities to effectively market themselves.

Promotion

Promotion is an element of the 4Ps – the marketing mixes. Because part of its objectives is to educate the target markets, many marketing textbooks often refer to promotion and education in the same context. Promotion consists of several marketing activities that are designed to inform, educate, and build preference for a brand, a product, or a producer. Its targeted audiences are employees (the internal market), prospective users, and current users of the product or brand.

Most organizations including universities use promotion mix, a subset of the marketing mix, that is a specific mixture of advertising, sales promotion, personal selling, publicity and public relations, instructional materials, direct marketing, product placements, and corporate design to communicate with their target markets within the framework of an Integrated Marketing Communication Model (IMC). As a tactical framework, the IMC should guide universities on how to be judicious in their communications by addressing the 5Ws –

> *Who* is our target audience?
> *What* do we need to communicate to achieve our goal?
> *How* should we communicate this?
> *Where* should we communicate this?
> *When* do the communications need to take place?

DOI: 10.4324/9781003160267-6

How Should Universities Use the 5Ws?

For universities, the _Who_ in the 5Ws could be very broad (current employees – faculty and staff, current students, potential and current donors, and governments). For universities, reaching _who_ may call for a concurrent use of several different elements of the promotion mix.

Internal Market: As indicated earlier, this includes current employees and current students. Because these targets are internal, they could be reached through internal marketing communication channels which typically include the use of email messages, on-campus banners, newsletters, seminars, meetings, and occasional university get-togethers.

External Market: These are broad and diverse and include audiences such as potential students and parents, potential faculty and staff, potential donors, legislators and business organizations. Because of their diversity, to be effective, a variety of different communication channels have to be used.

What addresses the content of the message which varies according to the target as well as what the university hopes to accomplish by the communication. Certainly, sharing the university's achievements is a relevant message to all the target audiences. The achievements that are emphasized will depend on the target market. For example, to potential students the university's achievements with regard to job placement and performance in national athletics can be effective in recruiting. For example, application pool to Florida Gulf Coast University increased by 40% when the school's basketball team made the "Sweet Sixteen" (the National Collegiate Athletic Association [NCAA] Men's Division 1 Basketball Tournament in 2013 (Collier et al., 2020)). Similarly, Butler University also experienced a 40% bump in its applicant pool after it reached the national championship game in 2010 (Collier at al., 2020). To donors, scholastic and other achievements would serve as a reason to donate or acquiesce to the university's request as people generally want to be associated with success or something creative (Xu et al., 2021).

How addresses what should be communicated. Because education or what universities offer are services, they are intangible. Unlike goods, the nature of services (nonsearchability, abstractness, and mental impalpability) poses a challenge when it comes to how it should be communicated. Here, advertising the university's achievements such as its ranking on the various metrics by the various reputable ranking organizations such as _US News & World Report_'s "Best College Rankings," Princeton Review, etc. would be useful. Advertising using testimonials from successful former students, having campus tours and "open house" which allow potential students and parents to visit campus and even sit in some of the lectures can be employed.

The use of tangible cues that can help potential students and their parents visualize the benefits that can be obtained from attending a particular university can be used here. Similarly, metaphors, the university's logo, school slogans, and even school mascots can be used here not only to help the target with their visualization, but also to position as well as distinguish one university from the other. For example, a relatively "young" private university in Ghana captured its targets attention by the extensive use of two catch phrases "Dare to Dream" and "A Place of Possibilities." Those two slogans have repeated over and over that potential students began to internalize it. They wanted to dream, and dreamt big, besides they too wanted to see what they could achieve.

Where addresses the communication channels that will be used to reach the target market, hence one can see how the _how_ ties closely to the _who_? Different channels will be more effective for the different targets; are they parents, donors, legislators, or potential business partners? That is the question that will set the ball rolling.

Students and their parents, for example, could be reached using catalogues (in print or electronic form using disk, jump drive, etc.) which can contain information on courses, programs, and degrees being offered, university life (intramurals, etc.), faculty (including information on their education and research), pictures of buildings – classrooms and residence halls (which give a sense of the servicescape), staff with information on their dedication, etc. Potential donors and legislators (particularly public universities) can be more effectively reached through university representatives (periodic visit by the university president or lobbies, for example). These targets can also be updated on the achievements of the university through periodic magazines, personalized mail, etc. Alumni associations that can also serve as official and unofficial recruiters can also be reached through similar means.

When addresses the timing of the communication. There are three stages in the service consumption process; these are the prepurchase stage, the encounter stage, and the postpurchase stage. Universities can use advertisements which invite students to enroll during the prepurchase. Because university education is an expensive monetary purchase, it is not likely to be purchased upon impulse, therefore a university needs to give rational and factual explanations during the prepurchase stage as to why an individual must make the purchase. The encounter stage is when a student has actually enrolled in the institution. Every communication at this stage must be made to reinforce the positive attributes or reasons which motivated the student to enroll in the first place. It is important to note that communication during this phase goes beyond words and symbols and must include orchestration of the whole educational experience.

University's Communication Objectives

The Awareness, Interest, Desire, and Action (AIDA) and the *hierarchy-of-effects* models have been used to describe the phases that consumers go through in the prepurchase stage. Because they capture the phases that consumers go through (in the prepurchase stage), both models (the hierarchy-of-effects model which is essentially an extension of the AIDA model) provide a useful framework that guides the tactical plan for the marketing communication of service companies. A university as a service company can also greatly benefit from using this framework to accomplish its communication objectives.

Awareness is the first step in the AIDA model when consumers first become aware of the service. Generally, from a state of unawareness, the consumer becomes aware of the product. Within the context of a university marketing, the goal must be to not only make the market aware of the university's existence, but to also sufficiently retain the target's attention. To make a large number of people become aware of its existence/presence at the least possible cost, a university must advertise.

Interest is generated from being aware of the university and being susceptible to its message. Hence, a university must very carefully choose the contents of its advertisements to generate and capture the target's interest.

Desire comes after the target's interest has been sufficiently aroused in the university. The desire may be a result of both cognitive analysis and/or emotional appeals, hence universities must be careful in selecting the content of their messages.

Action is of course the ultimate goal of the communication, that is, to get the target of the communication to act in a way and manner that the communicator has planned, in this case the university.

In summary the AIDA model lays down a framework that guides the communicator (a university marketer) with regard to what to say and how to say it to be effective. It is important to note, however, that studies have shown that no true *hierarchy-of-effects* actually governs consumers' product adoption process. For example, Vakratsas and Ambler (1999) reviewed more than 250 journal articles and books "to establish what is and should be known about how advertising affects the consumer and how it works." After a thorough analysis, the authors concluded that there is "little support for any hierarchy, in the sense of temporal sequence, of effects." On the basis of their findings, Vakratsas and Ambler (1999) proposed "that advertising effects should be studied in a space, with affect, cognition, and experience as the three dimensions," and that "advertising's positioning in this space should be determined by context, which reflects advertising's goal diversity, product category, competition, other aspects of mix, stage of product life cycle, and target market" (p. 26).

How Universities Can Use the Communication Mix

As alluded to earlier, the communication mix includes several communication elements that universities can effectively use to achieve their communication objectives. As shown in Figure 6.1, these elements are advertising, corporate design, instructional materials, personal communication, publicity and public relations, and sales promotion. Instead of *instructional materials*, some authors (Wirtz and Lovelock, for example) use different words such as *service delivery points* to capture the communication channels available under *instructional materials*.

As we have explained earlier, the choice of an element or elements and channels will depend on the university's objectives, some of which for illustrative purposes are summarized here. However, it must be understood that the use of some elements or channels for that matter does not preclude the use of another. In fact, several different channels could be used simultaneously to achieve the same or different objectives.

Summary of a university's communication objectives

- To build awareness
- To create lasting impression
- To build preference through communicating achievements
- To position or reposition
- To encourage action
- To educate/inform
- To compare with other or similar institutions
- To provide reassurance by using placement records or average salary of graduates
- To express appreciation to the community and supporters
- To ask for support (financial or otherwise)
- To communicate financial aid/scholarship opportunities available

It is clear in the era of the Internet and the social media that not all the communication that the target market receives will originate from the university, its officials, or even from

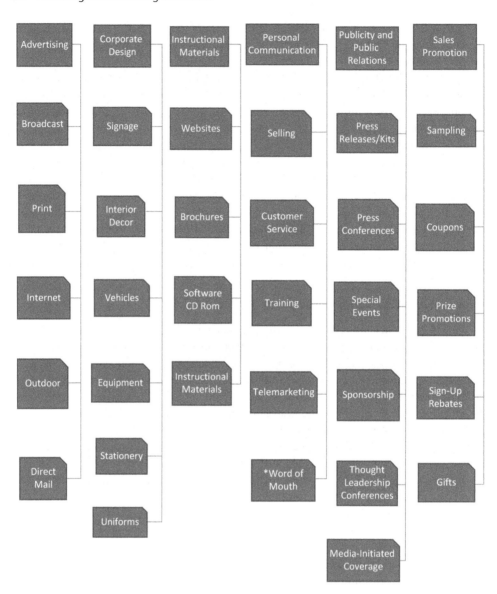

FIGURE 6.1 The Marketing Communication Mix
Note: ★Communication originates outside the organization/university.

authorized personnel. Thus, universities have to take into consideration the "controlled" and "uncontrolled" sources of information to the public as they plan their communication strategy.

Figure 6.2 illustrates the two main sources of information to the target audience and the different channels through which messages are sent to get to the target audience.

What Is Advertising and Why Universities Must Advertise?

The marketplace can be characterized as information asymmetric world in which sellers know more about their products (what they are selling) than do consumers, as such it makes sense

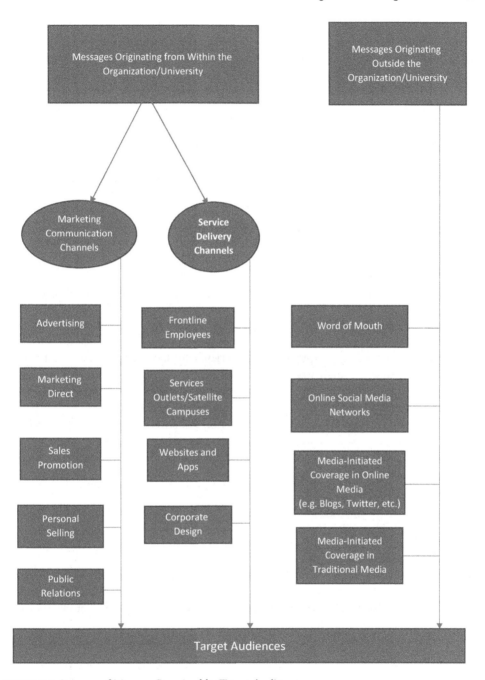

FIGURE 6.2 Sources of Message Received by Target Audiences

for the seller to convey this superior information to the consumer. This superior information is valuable to the consumer because it helps the consumer in assessing the *value* of the product. The preceding statement establishes one of the reasons for an organization to communicate with its target audiences and advertising is one of the means to do so.

There is hardly any organization – including universities, political parties, and churches (i.e., for-profit and not-for-profit organizations) – that does not advertise in one form or the other. As a communication device that is within the control of the organization, advertising is used to accomplish several objectives. It can be used to inform, educate, persuade, build a brand, and elicit action. Advertising is defined as "any paid form of nonpersonal presentation and promotion of ideas, goods, or services by an identified sponsor" (Kotler & Armstrong, 2017). Advertising may be the most cost-effective means of communicating with target audiences when the audiences are spread over a wide geographic location, and when the message is simple enough. However, before we proceed with discussions on advertising as a useful communication channel, we must first discuss the issue of credibility in advertising messages.

Despite regulations in many advanced countries to ensure that claims made in advertising are true or based on facts, particularly with advertisements for prescription drugs, in the United States, for example (see Koku, 2021), there is a continuing tension between regulating advertising and corporate free speech in the United States (Tucker, 2010). Knowing this, the marketplace is sometimes skeptical of advertising claims. This has led to a series of studies in economics and marketing.

Nelson (1974) in his seminal paper argues the major features of advertising can be explained by "advertising's information function." He makes a distinction between search and experience "qualities" and argues that for search "qualities," advertising provides direct information, for example, the braking distance of a sports car or the woolen content of a jacket. However, the information that advertising provides for experience "qualities" such as services or universities, for that matter, is "simply that the brand advertises." Consumers know that advertising is not cheap, and therefore advertising in itself says something about the organization that is spending money to advertise.

Kihlstrom and Riordan (1984) revisited the notion that advertising conveys credible information on product qualities to consumers. The authors argued that advertising could indirectly signal product quality if there "exist market mechanisms that produce a positive relationship between product quality and advertising expenditures" and presented two models to make this point.

In the first, all high-quality firms ultimately establish reputations for high quality whether they advertise or not.

> This is shown to imply that advertising can signal quality if and only if high-quality production requires investments in specialized assets that increase fixed costs but not marginal costs. In the second model, where non-advertising firms never acquire a reputation for high quality, advertising might signal quality even if marginal production costs are somewhat lower for low quality.
>
> *(Kihlstrom & Riordan 1984, p. 427)*

These conclusions are consistent with Nelson's 1974 arguments.

The marketplace for higher education (worldwide) has undergone several changes (including regulatory and funding models) during the past five decades (this is discussed in detail in Chapter 12). These changes have led, amongst other things, to increasing competition for talents (students, faculty, and staff) as well as funding. As such, universities worldwide (unlike half a century or so ago) have been actively advertising. The ubiquity of university advertising in the United States is evident during televised conference football and basketball games when almost unending ads are shown to highlight the history and the accomplishments of the universities that are playing. It is no wonder that universities that have done well during each year's conference games (football and basketball) realize a significant increment in the number of students who apply for admission in the following year (see Collier et al., 2020; Chung, 2013).

According to Cellini and Chaudhary (2020) university advertising grew throughout the early 2000s and seemed to peak in 2013 when $1.2 billion was spent on university advertising in United States alone. However, Brock (2017) reports that paid advertising by US colleges and universities continued to increase after 2013 and reached an all-time high of a $1.65 billion in 2016. The 2016 expenditure represents an increase of 18.5% after 2015 and an increase of 22% since 2013, despite declines in advertising by the "troubled for-profit educational sector."

Direct Marketing

As indicated in Figure 6.2 direct marketing is another communication channel under the direct control of universities. Direct marketing is the practice of connecting directly with a carefully targeted audience to obtain an immediate response and/or cultivate a lasting customer relationship. Universities like organizations can use the telephone, use direct mail, email, the Internet, and other tools to communicate directly with the target audiences. To give the feeling of authenticity, some universities solicit faculty and student volunteers to call potential students and encourage them to enroll. Similarly, faculty and student volunteers are asked to invite students to attend open house and informational sessions on campus. The advantages in using direct marketing besides giving the feeling of authenticity and welcoming ambience is that the callers can answer questions and provide additional information that the targets may have. They can also convince people that are "uncommitted" by handling possible objections.

Sales Promotion

Sales promotions can be communications with special short-term incentives that are intended to elicit immediate purchase or response. Can you see how a university can use sales promotion? Some universities use sales promotion-like tactics by waiving such fees as application fees if a student were to apply for admission during a designated period. Other universities even provide partial expenses-reimbursement programs to targeted students, for example, minority students to certain graduate programs if they were to visit campus during certain periods during their application process.

Personal Selling

Personal selling refers to interpersonal encounters in which efforts are made to provide personalized information to a potential customer. Universities use personal selling by sending recruiting officers to different high schools to meet and provide information to graduating seniors. Recruiting staff is sent to college fairs where different universities and colleges meet graduating high school students from different high schools at a common forum to provide information on their universities/colleges. Some universities enlist the assistance of the appropriate personnel at US embassies overseas to facilitate meeting high school students as part of their recruiting efforts. Because the costs involved in personal selling are high many universities use the alternative lower-cost telemarketing even though it is not a perfect substitute. In spite of all the destructions that COVID-19 has brought, one thing it has facilitated is the high acceptance of video meetings as a substitute for in-person meetings, hence we expect meeting high school recruits via video meetings to be more common in the future.

Public Relations

Public relations for universities involves efforts to stimulate positive interest in the university by sending out news releases on research projects and discoveries that are taking place in the university, holding free and paid seminars on topics of interest, organizing special events, and sponsoring news-worthy events. Sometimes this can be achieved through events such as cancer awareness programs, health and fitness programs, and beach cleaning programs that student organizations/groups organize.

Communications that Take Place in the Delivery Channels

Service Delivery

Clear signs and campus maps that direct people to the appropriate departments, colleges, and buildings on campus are an important part of the university's service delivery and hence must be done with that in mind. They not only facilitate the consumption of what the university is selling (education), but also communicate unspoken messages about the university. In addition to physical directions and maps, some universities have apps that can be downloaded on mobile phones, but conspicuous signs and instructions need to be provided to ensure that people are aware that such apps are available for downloads.

Frontline Employees

There are several categories of frontline employees in universities through whom planned and unplanned or unintended messages are communicated. They include telephone exchange operators, campus security personnel, department secretaries, and the faculty. The messages these individuals convey cover the core and supplementary services that the university offers. Because it is important to communicate a unified theme, training frontline employees on "what to say" is necessary.

Service Outlets/Satellite Campus

Planned and unintended messages are transmitted to customers through the service delivery environment. Universities transmit impersonal messages to target audiences through signage, posters, banners, video screens (with monitors placed at strategic locations on campus), audios, and brochures. The entire servicescape (the university campus architecture, buildings, and flora and fauna) and interior and exterior designs are a part of the impersonal means of communicating with the audience. The use of satellite campuses has become common and important to some universities, in addition to structure, and the location of such satellite campuses is important because it (location) also says something about the university.

Websites

Practically every university now has a website which is used to accomplish a variety of communication tasks including but not limited to promoting awareness, providing information, facilitating two-way communications through email and chat rooms, and enabling enrolment. Some universities also use their websites to measure the effectiveness of promotional campaigns and the like.

As a means through which a university interfaces and communicates with the public, it is important that certain steps be taken to create a memorable impression. Here are a few but necessary steps:

1. The website must be easy to navigate.
2. Information provided at the website must be accurate and up-to-date.
3. The appropriate university colors must be used.
4. The fonts must be legible.
5. Downloads must be quick.
6. All associated links must be functional.

Websites that are difficult to navigate or whose fonts are inelegible cause visitors to abort their search or leave without finding what they came for. Such visitors are not likely to return and may result in the loss of a potential student or donor.

Corporate Design

While corporate design that ensures consistency in the style and message that is communicated is important to companies operating in competitive environment to stand out apart from others, the same could be said about universities as well. A university like other service organizations operating in a competitive space must "employ a unified and distinctive visual appearance for all tangible elements to facilitate recognition and reinforced a desired brand image." The use of a university logo and colors on stationary, vehicles, t-shirts, exercise clothes, and other promotional literature are part and parcel of presenting a university as a unifying and recognizable brand to the public.

Communications that Take Place Outside the Organization/University

Word of Mouth

Word of Mouth (WOM) is a personal communication between targeted buyers outside an organization. Generally, it is between a friend or family member who has already had an encounter with the service or a provider. Recommendations, outside an organization, between individuals are often perceived to be more credible than firm-initiated promotional activities.

Several studies have been conducted on the role and effect of WOM in services marketing and have shown that the greater the perceived risk with the purchase, the more actively customers seek and rely on WOM (Bansal & Voyer, 2000). Furthermore, customers who are less knowledgeable about the service rely more on WOM than do expert consumers

(Mattila & Wirtz, 2002). With regard to satisfaction and dissatisfaction, studies have shown that customers who hold strong views are likely to tell more people than customers who hold mild views, and extremely dissatisfied customers will tell more people about their negative experience than do customers who are highly satisfied (Anderson, 1998; Söderland, 1998; Augusto de Matos & Vargas Rossi, 2008). Furthermore, even those who were initially dissatisfied with a service can end up spreading positive WOM if they are delighted with the way the organization handled service recovery.

What are the implications of these studies for marketing a university? These studies suggest that not only should universities have strong ties with their alums, but they should also keep track of those who dropped out. It is important to find out why a student dropped out and try to find the reason for their dropping out and seek a solution. A student who dropped for financial reasons would be more than delighted to find out from the university that there is "pool of money" within the university that needy students who are in good academic standing could access to complete their studies. Such a student is more likely to spread positive WOM about the university. Incidentally this suggests the need for an office that deals with or reaches out to students who dropped out or fail to complete their degree without finding a solution for their problems.

There is no group of students more loyal to their alma mater than a satisfied alum; this group of former students are more likely to spread positive WOM, actively recruit students, and even participate in fundraising activities for their alma mater, hence the need for an alumni office on campus that communicates regularly with alums and forges a strong bond with them through a variety of regular activities.

Online Social Media Networks

Online networks or communities such as Facebook or LinkedIn and Internet-based virtual worlds such as Second Life offer universities new communication opportunities that did not exist three decades ago. The growing popularity of these networks provide universities an additional opportunity to spread positive electronic word of mouth (eWOM) by identifying and using individuals who are influential on these social networks. A university can create its own Facebook account through which it can highlight the accomplishments of its faculty, staff, and students or simply spread news and other positive developments about the university.

Media-Initiated Coverage in Online Media (Blogs, Twitter, etc.)

Web logs usually referred to as blogs are not only ubiquitous, but have also become powerful and influential means through which consumers get the information they need. Blog writers are referred to as bloggers, who for lack of better word, are self-appointed opinion leaders who often specialize in a narrow topic. Blogs are web pages that are frequently updated and the entries are listed in reverse chronological order. They are best described as online journals, diaries, or news listings where people can post anything and on whatever they like. Blogs have become a new form of interaction on the Internet, as messages posted on the blog are of interest to marketers. Some companies follow blogs very carefully as a way to monitor their image. Universities could do likewise. They can use positive postings to burnish their image while negative postings could be used as feedback to act on and address a perceived or real problem before it becomes uncontrollable.

Twitter is a social network and microblogging service that allows its users to post messages or updates or read messages of updates of other users. Messages on Twitter are limited to 280 characters in length, and can be sent and received through Twitter website, SMS, or external applications. Twitter can be useful to universities in sending out messages about fairs, meetings, and other events. Similar to bogs, universities can use Twitter to advance their brand and create a following.

Media-Initiated Coverage in Traditional Media

Even though the online world has become very popular and active, it would be a mistake for a university to overlook and discard the traditional media as a means of spreading its message. Media coverage of a university and its activities are often initiated by the university's public relations or media relations department. However, the media also initiate their own coverages. Journalists and other media personalities often contact faculty for their expertise when they are writing or speaking on technical topics. The use of faculty by the media gives the university a good exposure and builds on its credibility, hence it is useful for a university to maintain or post a list of experts and their areas of expertise on its website.

Podcasting

Nowadays it has become common to use the Internet to make digital recordings of broadcasts that are available for downloading to a computer or mobile device. Podcasting refers to a series of digitized audio files of episodic nature that can be downloaded and played at one's convenience, hence university officials can use podcasting to share good news about the university. They can also use it to periodically remind people of the university's mission.

Push and Pull Strategies

There are two other points to make before we end this chapter. First, the push and pull strategies and, second, the metric for choosing a means through which a university advertises. The push and pull strategies are the two basic forms of the promotion mix strategies that a university can use just like other organizations. In push strategy, the producing organization uses intermediaries through whom it *pushes* the offerings to the final consumer. Hence, the producer's marketing activities are directed at the intermediaries. On the contrary, the producing organization directs its marketing activities at the final consumer in pull strategy. The major question here is who are the intermediaries to a university? The answer is less obvious and counterintuitive than it is for a producer of goods where the distribution channel is clear and often distinct.

Universities sell education (or knowledge) to students. So, in the pull strategy a university will focus its marketing activities directly at attracting potential students. On the contrary, in the push strategy, a university could form an alliance with two-year universities (through 2 plus 2 arrangements in which students finish their first two years in the community college and the remaining two years in the four-year university to get their degree) and/or companies from which it can draw students. However, because students drawn from both arrangements are generally not sufficient, universities must use both push and pull strategies simultaneously to recruit students.

Which Means to Use to Advertise?

We are sure that you have more than once reached out into the backseat pocket for one of those glossy airplane magazines on your flight back home from school or vacation only to see advertisements for a number of MBA programs in some of the top universities and wondered why they were advertising in those magazines. Similarly, you would have been driving on the highway (freeway) the other day and would have seen a big billboard advertising the local university's master's program in sports management and wondered why the university was advertising there. Well, it should be apparent from the discussions in this chapter that a university can use several different media to communicate with its target audience.

Which media a university uses will be determined by a combination of factors including the media's reach, frequency, and impact. *Reach* is the number of buyers potentially exposed to an ad in a particular vehicle. It can also be expressed as the percentage of people in the target audience who are exposed to the ad. For instance, if 80% of a university's target audience was exposed to the ad during the first quarter of an ad campaign, then the reach is 80%. *Frequency* is the number of times that buyers are exposed to the ad during a given period. For example, a university might want an average exposure frequency for an ad to be 5. And the desired *impact* is the qualitative value of a message exposure through a given medium. With these metrics a university might decide that the most cost-effective means to reach its target audience is through the use of a billboard by the local highway, the local daily newspaper, or during a Super Bowl (the annual championship game of the American Football Season).

To standardize the cost for using different vehicles, advertisers generally use Cost per Thousand (CPM) which is the cost for reaching 1,000 readers or viewers per period. There are several ad timing strategies that companies and universities use. They can use a *blitz* strategy and/or a *pulse* strategy. A university might adopt a blitz strategy when a new program is introduced or a new school/college is established within the university. In this strategy the advertising dollars is concentrated in a relatively short period. This strategy is intended to give the message sufficient power to break through the chatter within a very short period. On the contrary, the pulse strategy in which advertising is periodically concentrated, some semblance of continuity is maintained and might be employed when the university wants to periodically highlight an achievement, but maintains a continuous presence throughout the period.

Summary

Judging from the increasing expenditure on university advertising, it is safe to say that the practice is here to stay. Also, universities take advertising seriously, hence this chapter discusses the relevant communication framework that universities can use to get their messages across to their target audience. The chapter discusses all the elements in the integrated communication model and how universities can effectively use them. It also analyzes in detail the AIDA model and the communication channel.

Question

1. Why must universities advertise?
2   What is the communication mix?
3. How can universities use the communication mix?
4. How can universities use personal selling? When?
5. Is the choice of means that a university uses to advertise an important decision? Why and why not?
6. Can you think of how WOM would work in advertising a university?
7. What is a media-initiated coverage?

References

Anderson, E.W. (1998). Customer Satisfaction and Word of Mouth. *Journal of Service Research* 1 (1), 5–17.

Augusto de Matos, C., & Vargas Rossi, C.A. (2008). Word-of-Mouth Communications in Marketing: A Meta-Analytic Review of the Antecedents and Moderators. *Journal of Academy of Marketing Science* 36 (4), 578–596.

Bansal H.S., & Voyer, P.A. (2000). Word-of-Mouth Processes within a Services Purchase Decision Context. *Journal of Service Research* 2 (3), 166–177.

Brock, B. (2017). College Advertising at All-Time High. https://emgonline.com/2017/10/college-adve rtising-at-all-time-high/. Retrieved on October 2, 2021.

Cellini, S.R., & Chaudhary, L. (2020). *Commercials for College? Advertising in Higher Education.* Washington, DC: Report on Higher Education, Bookings Institution.

Chung, D.J. (2013). The Dynamic Advertising Effect of Collegiate Athletics. *Marketing Science* 32 (5), 679–698.

Collier, T., Haskell, N., Rotthoff, K.W., & Baker, A. (2020). The "Cinderella Effect": The Value of Unexpected March Madness Runs as Advertising for the Schools. *Journal of Sports Economics* 21 (8), 1–25

Kihlstrom, R.E., & Riordan, M.H. (1984). Advertising as a Signal. *Journal of Political Economy* 92 (3), 427–450.

Koku, P.S. (2021). The Legal and Ethical Dimensions of Direct-to-Consumer Advertising of Prescription Drugs: The Case of Pfizer and Lipitor in the United States. *Health Marketing Quarterly* 38 (1), 23–34.

Kotler, P., & Armstrong, G. (2017). *Principles of Marketing.* Upper Saddle River, NJ: Pearson Prentice Hall.

Mattila, A.S., & Wirtz, J. (2002). The Impact of Knowledge Types on Consumer Search Process – An Investigation in the Context of Credence Services. *International Journal of Research in Service Industry Management* 13 (3), 214–230.

Nelson, P. (1974). Advertising as Information. *Journal of Political Economy* 82 (4), 729–754.

Tucker, A. (2010). Flawed Assumptions: A Corporate Law Analysis of Free Speech and Corporate Personhood in Citizens United. *Case Western Reserve Law Review* 61 (2), 496–511.

Vakratsas, D., & Ambler, T. (1999). How Advertising Works: What Do We Really Know? *Journal of Advertising* 63 (1), 26–43.

Söderland, M. (1998). Customer Satisfaction and Its Consequences on Customer Behavior Revisited: The Impact of Different Levels of Satisfaction on Word of Mouth, Feedback to the Supplier, and Loyalty. *International Journal of Service Industry Management* 9 (2), 169–188.

Xu, L., Mehta, R., & Dahl, D.W. (2021). Leveraging Creativity in Charity Marketing: The Impact of Engaging in Creative Activities on Subsequent Donation Behavior. *Journal of Marketing.* https://doi. org/10.1177/00222429211037587.

CASE #11 THE BRAGGING RIGHTS

This case discusses how a university uses its bragging rights (e.g., an ad or a statement in its admission brochure claiming that the university's MBA program is ranked #1 for Business Executives in US Today *or in the* Financial Times*) to attract certain segment of students.*

What better way to convince people that you are good than citing a third party's assessment of how good you are? In the crowded market of business schools many business programs are learning to differentiate themselves by using third-party evidence, and here comes rankings.

Because business programs have become very popular with students, in an effort to attract students in a tight and competitive market, many universities are offering business programs. Even some liberal arts schools have decided to offer some limited business. About 15 years ago educational consultants remarked that thought many schools were using the MBA as a cash cow. However, we think the Executive MBA (which is the MBA designed for middle managers) is now the cash cow.

To catch the attention of potential students, many business schools are advertising aggressively on billboards, social media, magazines, and newspapers. However, to distinguish themselves in terms of the quality of their programs, they need a credible independent party's evaluations, hence they are using accreditations received from prestigious accreditation agencies such as the Association to Advance Collegiate Schools of Business (AACSB), Association of MBAs (AMBA), and European Quality Improvement System (EQUIS).

The AACSB is the longest standing and the most recognized professional accreditation that a business school can earn. The AACSB has now granted accreditation to about 567 institutions on 6 continents. The AMBA was founded in 1967 and offers accreditation to specific MBA, DBA, and MSc programs – not entire schools like AACSB and EQUIS. AMBA currently accredits about programs in about 180 business schools in 72 different countries. The EQUIS limits its scope to Europe. It grants accreditation to institutions as a whole, not on a program-by-program basis. Currently, EQUIS accredits approximately 127 business schools in 35 countries. In addition to these accreditation agencies are also independent ranking bodies such as the *US News & World Report* and the *Financial Times*.

To distinguish itself from its competitors, the business school at Florida Atlantic University (FAU) used to advertise that it was the only AACSB-accredited MBA program in its market. With other business schools in its market gaining the prestigious AACSB accreditation, FAU has switched over to advertising its rankings. For example, the business school's website banner advertises the following:

*Best Undergraduate in Business
US News & World Report (2022)
*#3 in Florida, #14 in North America, #19 in the World
SportBusiness Ranking 2021
*Best Graduate School – Part-Time MBA
US News & World Report (2022)

*Best Online Bachelor's in Business Program
US News & World Report (2021)
*The Princeton Review
Top 50 Undergraduate Program
Top 50 Graduate Programs
Entrepreneurship Programs 2021
#22
*Best International Business
US News & World Report (2021)

Some of these accomplishments are also advertised on billboards by the freeway and in the local newspapers.

Questions

1. Would you be persuaded by rankings in your school choice? Why and why not?
2. Do you think it is acceptable for universities to advertise? Why and why not?
3. What type of claims would you make if you were in charge of advertising your university? Why?
4. Do you think advertising a university's ranking is deceptive? Why and why not?

CASE #12 MS. UVI (UNIVERSITY OF THE VIRGIN ISLANDS) PAGEANTRY

While "Ms. Anything" is offensive to some people because of the implied sexism, for many universities, especially Historically Black Colleges and Universities (HBCUs), it is a highly anticipated annual event. This case discusses annual activities leading to the crowning of Ms. UVI at the University of the Virgin Islands, St. Thomas.

The title "Ms. Anything" is offensive to some people who see the use of such titles as an extension of commodification of women, particularly if the title relates to anything "beautiful" associated with it, yet the crowning of Ms. UVI at the University of the Virgin Islands, St. Thomas & St. Croix, is a highly anticipated annual event. However, it is not only UVI that celebrates the pageantry, rather it is common among HBCUs.

The UVI was chartered on March 16, 1962, as the College of the Virgin Islands – a publicly funded, coeducational, liberal arts institution. The US Virgin Islands are the US territory in the Caribbean. It consists of three Islands – St. Thomas, St. Johns, and St. Croix.

The first campus of UVI was opened on St. Thomas in July 1963, on 175 acres donated by the federal government. The first board of trustees took office in August 1963. In 1964, the college founded a second campus on St. Croix, on 130 acres also donated by the federal government. University of the Virgin Islands started operating first as College of the Virgin Island (CVI). CVI began by offering only associate of arts degrees. In 1967 it added bachelor's degree programs in liberal arts and education. The first baccalaureate degrees were awarded in 1970, and in 1976 the college awarded its first master's degrees in education. Two years later, master's degree programs in business administration and public administration were instituted on both campuses.

In 1986, the College of the Virgin Islands was renamed the University of the Virgin Islands to reflect the growth and diversification of its academic curricula, community and regional services, and research programs. That same year, the US Congress named UVI one of America's HBCU; therefore, it holds the distinction of being the only HBCU outside of the continental United States.

The Ms. UVI pageantry is a part of the university's annual carnival celebration in which the Calypso King is also crowned, generally after a fierce competition amongst the school's calypsonians. The contest takes place around March each year, a little ahead of the Island's carnival which is held around April–May. The calypso king from the university goes on to compete in the Island's calypso championship contest. As part of the evolution of tradition, Ms. UVI now goes to compete for MS. HBCU title in which the "Queens" of the individual HBCUs compete.

Ms. UVI reigns for a year during which she serves as the university's goodwill and cultural ambassador. She takes part in charity activities to raise funds for philanthropic purposes and to raise the school's image. Contestants vying for the title are judged on their performance in personal interview, oratory, poise, and projection, which includes the evening gown segment, and talent and performance in public question and answer sessions. Ms. UVI's participation in Ms. HBCU contest brings a lot of attention to the university and through these contests many people on the mainland United States became aware of the university.

Question:

1. Is the pageantry a relic of the past and must be abandoned?
2. Which other roles can you foresee for Ms. UVI?
3. Is the pageantry compatible with the academic mission of HBCUs?
4. Can you connect Ms. UVI's role with recruiting?

7
PERSONAL SELLING OF A UNIVERSITY

Introduction

When is personal selling best used, how can universities use personal selling, and which attributes must a salesperson have? The answers to these questions are fundamental to designing a good personal selling program. This chapter covers these issues together with the relevant research that discussed the use of technology in personal selling, the role of ethics in personal and other constructs such as authenticity in personal selling. In relating personal selling to university marketing, the chapter discusses the use of third-party recruiting agencies, admission fairs, and using US embassies abroad to assist in organizing college fairs.

What Is Personal Selling?

Personal selling according to Kotler and Armstrong is one of the oldest professions in the world (Kotler & Armstrong, 2017). Personal selling can be defined as

> the process of person-to-person communication between a salesperson and a prospective customer, in which the former learns about the customer's needs and seeks to satisfy those needs by offering the customer the opportunity to buy something of value, such as a good or service.
>
> *(Cant & van Heerde, 2004)*

It is used by many companies, especially those engaged in Business-to-Business (B2B) sales, and manufacturers of industrial goods typically maintain a team of dedicated personal sales people.

Personal selling is often used when the product being sold is complex and cannot be easily explained in advertisements. It is also ideal for products that are expensive and not often sought. Because face-to-face contact between the seller and prospective buyer is involved, personal selling is an expensive selling method. In the era of high technology, a less expensive alternative such as telemarketing or video marketing can be used instead of in-person contact.

DOI: 10.4324/9781003160267-7

Despite its high cost, personal marketing is often a preferred method of communication, because a seller can immediately handle the protective buyer's questions, read their body language, and can quickly put their fears to rest.

Although it is not obvious, universities, like other service organizations, rely or must rely, to a large extent, on the dedicated personal selling teams (known as the recruiting staff and foundation officers or fundraising officers) to sell the university to potential students (to recruit) and to persuade prospective donors to donate money to the university (fundraise). However, universities must realize that recruiting student recruiters and fundraisers not only calls for individuals with special attributes, but also managing them well requires a different approach. To complicate matters, methods of recruiting and managing these teams also change over time.

Several marketing scholars have chronicled significant changes that have taken place over the years in personal selling. Powers et al. (1987) described the historical origins as well as the early practices of selling prior to 1900, especially the changes that have occurred from 1900 to 1949. These perspectives showed distinct differences in the practice of selling in different time periods, particularly when they corresponded with changes in economic conditions and associated competitive and market variations as well as an environment in which technology is not only rapidly changing, but is also being integrated in how personal selling is done. Several studies have been conducted in marketing and in personal selling and management that provide guidance on the kinds of attributes to look for in personal salespersons as well as on how to manage them. We review a few of them here to give a sense of what is involved.

The Characteristics of Good Salesperson

Wotruba (1991) argued that the job category titled "personal selling" really encompasses a wide variety of positions and responsibilities. However, the general public as well as marketing students may not have appreciated these changes because their view, which is generally a misunderstanding of selling, may have been conditioned by the very narrow stereotype portrayed in movies, television shows, and cartoons (Thompson, 1972; Swan & Adkins, 1980–1981). Using inductive analysis based on the available literature, Wotruba (1991) presented a longitudinal view of how selling jobs changed or evolved, its history, and characteristics of competitive and market environments. The author identified five stages in this evolution of selling and salesmanship as (1) the provider; (2) persuader; (3) the prospector; (4) the problem-solver; and (5) the procreator. Wotruba (1991) discussed these stages and their implications in the management of selling practices.

However, besides identification of selling stages, other factors play important roles in the performance and evaluation of salespersons. Singhapakdi and Vitell (1991) examined the relative influences of corporate ethics codes, Machiavellianism, and gender on the various components of sales professionals' decision making in ethical situations. The authors collected data through a mail survey of 98 sales professionals who were members of the AMA. The results of the study suggest that the ethical climate of an organization influences a salesperson's perceptions of an ethical problem and their perceptions of alternative courses of action. The most ethically sensitive salespeople were found to be more agreeable to both punitive and nonpunitive types of remedial actions and less agreeable to a no-action alternative. The results also revealed a negative relationship between Machiavellianism and deontological norms. By the way, what is Machiavellianism and what are deontological norms? And how are these two related to personal selling?

Machiavellianism is defined slightly differently by different authorities to refer to the personality traits described by Machiavelli in *The Prince*. These characteristics generally describe an individual who is cunning, manipulative, and inclined to use whichever means they can to gain power (see Spielberger & Butcher, 2013). In sales, individuals with those tendencies tend to lie or use less than honest or coercive persuasion to achieve their ends, and have little regard for moral or ethical standards. Machiavellian focus on money, power, and competition can be destructive to an organization's long-term sales goals or long-term relationship with their clients. Deontological ethics, on the contrary, in simple terms, is a moral philosophy that emphasizes the relationship between duty and the morality in human actions. Unlike Machiavellianism, deontological norms value the means not just the ends (see Koku, 2022).

Given the caricatured and the stereotypical view of salespersons (Thompson, 1972), it is not surprising that the study of ethics has attracted a significant research effort in personal selling and sales management. The increasing research efforts in the area has resulted in a diversity of opinions and findings with no apparent coherence in the literature. To provide an assessment of the status of the existing knowledge and clarity, McClaren (2000) conducted a review of the literature which he arbitrarily divides into two main groups – "organization" and "personal" ethics.

From the review the literature, McClaren (2000) found that such factors as age, gender, cross-cultural aspects, Machiavellianism, personal values, and ethical perspective have been investigated as personal factors, and organizational factors that have been examined include selling role and organizational offerings, job tenure and professional background, income and competition, supervision, discipline, rewards and punishment, codes of ethics, climate, and culture. Although the factors examined appear comprehensive, because conceptual bases from which sales ethics research is developing appears to have shifted, the existing models do not appear to accurately reflect the multiple ways in which sales outcomes may be evaluated, hence the author concludes that further work is still needed "in the sales area to establish if the individual moral decision structures of salespeople and their organizational conditions in the sales area are different from other groups, such as marketers" (McClaren, 2000, p. 299).

Verbeke et al. (2000) posited that pride as an internal resource from which sales personnel draw their motivation (Brown et al., 1997; Frederickson, 2002) plays an important adaptive effect in the interaction between individuals engaged in personal selling and their colleagues as well as their customers. In two empirical studies, the first which consisted of 93 sales persons in the Netherlands, the authors found that pride increases sales person's performance-related motivations, "specifically it promotes the use of adaptive selling strategies, greater effort, and self-efficacy." Furthermore, a salesperson's pride has a positive effect on their organizational citizenship. The results of a structural equation analyses of the second study based on data obtained from 250 salespersons in the Netherlands suggest that salespersons are capable of self-regulating the expression of excessive pride and positive pride differently towards their colleagues and customers through anticipated feelings of fear, shame, and regret, and are also capable of controlling those fears to their advantage. What do you think about these findings? Are they consistent with previous readings such as McClaren (2000)?

Technology and Personal Selling

Technology has proliferated sales management and selling activities during the past three decades as evidenced in automation, customer relationship management, and communications. In a study conducted by *C&C Marketing Communications for Sales and Marketing Management* magazine, 78% of the respondents felt that technology was currently making their jobs easier, while 92% felt that technology would make their jobs easier in the future (see Colon, 1998). Other studies such as that of Taylor (1993) found that the benefits of technology include decreasing costs, while studies of Thetgyi (2000) focus on enhancing communications and reducing cycle time, Lejfer's (1999) showed improving organization and access to information. Other studies have shown that people perceive sales force automation, for example, as an absolute necessity for an organization to stay competitive (Peppers & Rogers, 1998; Rosen, 1999). However, how and where technology is actually being used in the field is neither well-known nor well-understood.

To shed further light on these issues, Widmier et al. (2002) undertook an empirical study in which 1,500 questionnaires were mailed to the randomly chosen subscribers of *Sales Marketing and Management*. The subscription list of *Sales Marketing and Management* was used to ensure the cross-sectional nature of the sample and to minimize the chances that multiple people from the same organization would be surveyed. The questionnaire was divided into three parts. The first part explored the salesforce's use of technology in organizing, presenting, reporting, informing, and supporting and processing transactions. The second part was used to obtain information on the salesforce's application of communication technology such as email, pagers, fax machines, and cell phones, and the use of location in the job and who initiated the use. The third part was used to obtain general demographic information and some additional information of the company and industry in which the respondents worked.

The results of the study showed that technology is being used for (1) organizing, presenting, reporting, informing, supporting and processing transactions, and communicating by sales person; (2) enhancing productivity of each function; (3) communicating in the field by salespeople; and (4) initiating transactions with both salespersons and companies. However, ethical issues continue to dominate discussions on the performance and conduct of salespersons particularly during economic downturns. For universities, especially the private for-profit universities, the issue of the use of deceptive tactics to get students to enroll became a common news item (Wong, 2010; also discussed in the case study #26 in this book).

Bombarded daily by heavy advertising messages, American consumers as well as consumers worldwide are demanding authenticity from products they consume (Lewis & Bridger, 2000), from the marketing messages they receive (Dolliver, 2001), and from their customer contact personnel (Winsted, 1999). But what is authenticity? Existential-humanistic scholars have conceptualized "authenticity as an autonomous behavioral construct" and Kahn (1992), on the contrary, conceptualized authenticity as "the unpretentious, unmasked, and free expression of internal experience (e.g., thoughts, feelings, and beliefs)."

Aware of consumers' propensity to seek authenticity in marketing and salespersons, the sales profession was beginning to shift to become more customer-needs focused. However, there was no previous study in the literature on personal selling that has explicitly examined the role of authenticity in personal selling. To fill this gap, Schaefer and Pettijohn (2006) conducted an empirical study to examine the relationship between authenticity and other important personal selling constructs, such as professional commitment and intention to stay in the profession. The authors collected useable data from 121 B2B salespersons from five international companies that located in the Midwest in the United States.

The results of the study are informative and underscore a number of important relationships amongst which are (1) a salesperson's authenticity is significantly related to sales performance for salespersons who are between the age of 25 and 34; (2) a salesperson's feelings of genuineness in their role may predict their performance and commitment to the sales profession; and (3) authenticity is positively related to affective professional commitment. Because authenticity appears to be a highly relevant construct for individuals in sales it is important that the Human Resource Departments in companies consider the construct in recruiting personnel for sales jobs. For universities, it is important that Human Resource Departments give a special consideration to the construct in recruiting persons for the positions as recruiting officers, admissions officers, and fundraising officers. Even though we cannot say that authenticity is less important in other roles, because the role of guidance counselors requires them to interact closely with students who often rely heavily on their advice, the position requires them to be genuine, authenticity may be considered as one of the top attributes in people recruited for those positions. Similarly, those who are the "face of the university" to potential donors cannot be seen to be less authentic.

Ferrell et al. (2007) contend that research on personal factors in personal selling and sales management tends to focus on the extent decision makers use teleological, compared to deontological, evaluations to resolve ethical issues; however, according to the authors there is no well-established framework to guide how such decisions are made. Therefore, drawing on sales and marketing ethics research and well-established ethical decision-making models in marketing, and the two major streams of research – individual and organizational factors, the authors developed a framework that includes organizational culture, ethical issue intensity, sales organization ethical climate or subculture (the variables that influence a sales-related ethical decision with the evaluation of outcomes) to provide an overview framework for understanding ethical decision making in selling and sales management. The goals of the framework are to (1) provide an understanding of existing research contributions; (2) demonstrate the usefulness of different research streams in advancing sales ethics research; and (3) delineate a foundation for critical evaluation and future research.

Other Relevant Constructs

Erevelles and Fukawa (2013) conducted a comprehensive study that covered a period of three decades on the use of the construct referred to in personal selling and sales management literature as affect which refers to an "internal feeling state" (Cohen et al., 2008) that captures emotion and mood and reflected on the theoretical frameworks of the construct and highlighted the managerial issues related to the construct in sales contexts. The authors observed a significant growth in the use of the construct and surmised that the growth may have been fueled by the realization that the study of traditional cognitive processes, by itself, has been inadequate for fully understanding many marketing phenomena.

Notwithstanding the increasing use of the construct in the area of marketing, Erevelles and Fukawa contend that

> identification, measurement, and classification of affective processes and outcomes in sales contexts may have hindered expansion of the body of research in the area. As a

result, critical affective processes in personal selling and sales management may not have been studied sufficiently thus far.

Thus, the authors call for further integration into personal sales management understanding of affective processes in fields such as psychology, neuroscience, and consumer behavior. This integration would help provide deeper insight in personal selling and sales management in increasingly hypercompetitive markets.

Peterson (2020) observed that self-efficacy, "the belief in one's capabilities to organize and to execute the courses of action required to produce given attainments" is the central construct in the social-cognitive theory of Bandura (e.g., 1977, 1982, 1986, 1997) and has been the subject of an impressive volume of research in several academic disciplines including business, education, medicine, music, and sports and for more than four decades has been one of the more important constructs in personal selling research. Given the large number of different scales used to measure self-efficacy in personal selling research and the associated meta-analytic studies, Peterson (2020) conducted an empirical examination of how nine self-efficacy scales that were used in personal selling research and included in the meta analytic studies on self-efficacy were conceptualized and measured.

The author concludes on the basis of his analysis that self-efficacy has not been conceptualized or operationalized in a consistent manner in personal selling research. As a result, much remains to be learned about the self-efficacy construct and its relationships to personal selling variables in general and sales performance in particular. Peterson (2020) therefore suggested that

> knowledge-generating research on the nature and scope of self-efficacy in the context of personal selling must be predicated on a reliable and valid measure of self-efficacy. Consequently, future personal selling research must resolve the practice of measuring self-efficacy in an ad hoc or opportunistic manner and devise a unified scale that meets theoretical and practical criteria.
>
> *(Peterson, 2020, p. 66)*

The lesson from these studies is that recruiters, fundraisers, and admissions officers play a unique selling role in a university. These officers, unlike other employees in a university, require not only special attributes but also different management approaches. Because factors which affect the roles that these individuals play change periodically, they will need to be trained periodically, if nothing else, to reinforce their ethical grounding which is vital to their success as well as the reputation of the university.

The Role of Third Parties

Because international students in state universities in the United States generally pay out-state tuition which is much higher than in-state tuition, as a sign of the times in which the funding model for many universities has changed, many universities, especially public universities, are turning to third-party recruiting agencies to recruit international students. According to the estimates by National Association for College Admission Counseling (NACAC) more than 20,000 third-party university students recruiting agencies operate worldwide (NACAC, 2014) and these agencies differ in terms of location, size, and student recruitment specializations. Using a third-party recruiting agency may not be a bad idea. In fact, the data in 2014 according to NACAC suggest that approximately one quarter of American institutions, or specific campus programs, contract with agencies to conduct international student recruitment.

However, the activities of some of the international student recruitment agencies have been the subject of considerable controversy in the United States. These controversies centered around the risks that they may pose to different stakeholders as a result of the way the agencies are compensated, that is, commission-based, and the propriety of institutions using per-capita commissions and payments for recruiting international students since some students might be unaware of the nature of the fees involved and the likelihood that some students could even be steered to an institution that pays a very high commission. In short, it must be noted that as independent agencies and not employees of a university, these student recruiting companies operate by their own rules. Because their unethical conduct could negatively impact the university for which they are recruiting, universities have to be careful and selective in selecting such recruiting agents.

Admission and College Fairs

Admission and college fairs are the equivalent of universities' trade fairs or trade shows. These fairs are jointly organized by several universities who send their admission officers and recruiters to represent them. Like trade fairs or trade shows, these admission officers and recruiting officers are a university's salespersons, hence are expected to give out brochures, catalogues, and other informational items about their respective universities. It should also be noted that participating in these fairs generates huge publicities for the respective participating universities. In the United States, HBCUs regularly host admissions and college fairs with a lot of fun fairs which generate a lot of publicity for them.

Embassies Abroad

Although education and political matters do not necessarily mix, it is becoming increasingly common for universities to use the embassies of their various countries to reach international students. In fact, it should not be a rarity for several universities to use the assistance of embassies of their home countries to jointly organize the equivalent of admissions fairs abroad.

Summary

Personal selling is an expensive but effective means of selling expensive and complex products. We discussed the evolution of personal selling and the impact of technology on the practice of personal selling. The chapter also discussed how personal selling can be used effectively in marketing universities, specifically, how personal selling can be used by a university's admissions and fundraising offices. The chapter also discussed the attributes that are needed in good personal sales people, and how personal selling relates to ethics. We specifically related the ethics of personal selling to Machiavellianism and deontological norms as well as authenticity.

Questions

1. What are some of the relevant personal selling attributes?
2. How has technology enabled personal selling?
3. When is it appropriate to use personal selling?
4. When do universities use personal selling?
5. What is a third-party recruiting agency?
6. Whom do they work for?
7. How can embassies abroad be helpful to home institutions in recruiting international students?

References

Brown, S.P., Cron, W.L., & Slocum, J.W. (1997). Effects of Goal-Directed Emotions and Salesperson Volitions, Behavior, and Performance: A Longitudinal Study. *Journal of Marketing* 16, 39–50.

Cant, M.C., & van Heerde, C.V. (2008). *Personal Selling*. Kenwyn, South Africa: Juta Academic.

Cohen, J.B., Pham, M.T., & Andrade, E.B. (2008). The Nature and Role of Affect in Consumer Behavior in Handbook of Consumer Psychology. In C. Haugtvedt, P. Herr, & F.R. Kardes, 297–348. New York: Lawrence Erlbaum.

Colon, G. (1998). Plug and Play: Executives Reveal the Secret to Simplifying Their Jobs and Boosting Their Reps' Performance: Technology. *Sales and Marketing Management* 150 (13 December), 64–67.

Dolliver, M. (2001). It's Popular, But Authenticity Isn't What It Used to Be. *Adweek Eastern Edition* 42 (27), 19.

Erevelles, S., & Fukawa, N. (2013). The Role of Affect in Personal Selling and Sales Management. *Journal of Personal Selling & Sales Management* 33 (1), 7–24.

Ferrell, O.C., Johnston, M.W., & Ferrell, L. (2007). A Framework for Personal Selling and Sales Management Ethical Decision Making. *Journal of Personal Selling & Sales Management* 27 (4), 291–299.

Frederickson, B.L. (2002). Positive Emotions. In C.R. Snyder & S.J Lopez (Eds.). *Handbook of Positive Psychology*, 120–134, New York: Oxford University Press.

Kahn, W. (1992). To Be Fully There: Psychological Presence at Work. *Human Relations* 45 (4), 321–349.

Koku, P.S. (2022). Revisiting Pfizer's DTCA of Lipitor Using Dr. Jarvik as a Spokesperson: Analyses under the Teleological and Deontological Theories of Ethics. *Journal of Global Marketing* 35(1), 99–114. https://doi.org/10.1080/08911762.2021.1943766.

Kotler, P., & Armstrong, G. (2017). *Principles of Marketing*. Upper Saddle River, NJ: Pearson Prentice Hall.

Lejfer, S.C. (1999). Bringing Business Intelligence to Sales Force Automation. *American Salesman* 44 (5) (May), 26–30.

Lewis, D., & Bridger, D. (2000). *The Soul of the New Consumer: Authenticity – What We Buy and Why in the New Economy* . London: Nicholas Brealey.

McClaren, N. (2000). Ethics in Personal Selling and Sales Management: A Review of the Literature Focusing on Empirical Findings and Conceptual Foundations. *Journal of Business Ethics* 27 (3), 285–303.

National Association for College Admission Counseling (2014). *International Student Recruitment Agencies: A Guide for Schools, Colleges and Universities*. Arlington, VA.

Peppers, D., & Rogers, M. (1998). Don't Resist Marketing Automation. *Sales and Marketing Management* 150 (9) (September), 32–34.

Peterson, R.A. (2020). Self-Efficacy and Personal Selling: Review and Examination with an Emphasis on Sales Performance. *Journal of Personal Selling & Sales Management* 40 (1), 57–71.

Powers, T.L., Koehler, W.F., & Martin, W.S. (1988). Selling From 1900 to 1949: A Historical Perspective. *Journal of Personal Selling & Sales Management* 8 (November), 11–21.

Rosen, M. (1999). Arming the Sales Force. *Insurance and Technology* 24 (2) (February), S4–S5.

Schaefer, A.D., & Pettijohn, C.E. (2006). The Relevance of Authenticity in Personal Selling: Is Genuineness an Asset or Liability? *Journal of Marketing Theory and Practice* 14 (1), 25–35.

Singhapakdi, A., & Vitell, S.J. (1991). Analyzing the Ethical Decision Making of Sales Professionals. *The Journal of Personal Selling and Sales Management* 11 (4), 1–12.

Spielberger, D., & Butcher, J.N. (2013). *Advances in Personality Assessment*, Vol. 9. New York: Routledge.

Swan, J.E., & Adkins, R.T. (1980–1981). The Image the Salesperson: Prestige and Other Dimensions. *Journal of Personal Selling & Sales Management* 1 (Fall/Winter), 48–56.

Taylor, T.C. (1993). Getting in Step with the Computer Age. *Sales and Marketing Management* 145 (3) (March), 52–59.

Thetgyi, O. (2000). Radical Makeovers: How Three Companies Use Strategic Planning, Training, and Support to Implement Technology on a Grand Scale. *Sales and Marketing Management* 152 (4) (April), 78–88.

Thompson, D.L. (1972). Stereotype of the Salesman. *Harvard Business Review* 50 (January–February), 20.

Verbeke, W., Belschak, F., & Bagozzi, R.P. (2000). The Adaptive Consequences of Pride in Selling. *The Academy of Marketing Science* 32 (4), 386–402.

Widmier, S.M., Jackson Jr. D.W., & Mccabe, D.B. (2002). Infusing Technology into Personal Selling. *Journal of Personal Selling & Sales Management* 22 (3), 89–198.

Winsted, K.F. (1999). Evaluating Service Encounters: A Cross-Cultural and Cross-Industry Exploration. *Journal of Marketing Theory and Practice* 7 (2), 106–123.

Wong (2010). For-Profit Colleges Encouraged Fraud and Used Deceptive Marketing, Watchdog Says. *ProPublica*. August 4. www.propublica.org/article/for-profit-colleges-encouraged-fraud-and-used-deceptive-marketing-watchdog-. Retrieved on June 1, 2021.

Wotruba, T.R. (1991). The Evolution of Personal Selling. *The Journal of Personal Selling and Sales Management* 11 (3), 1–12.

CASE #13 GOING TO THIRD-PARTY RECRUITERS

Universities are becoming increasingly aggressive in recruiting domestic and international students. One of the latest moves is to hire a third-party recruiter to recruit students from international countries. This case discusses the advantages and disadvantages of such a move.

Whereas private universities in the United States can and do charge the same tuition to every student regardless of their origin, state universities charge in-state students a lower tuition. In other words, state universities charge out-of-state and international students higher tuition. However, the "Dormant Commerce Clause" refers to the prohibition, implicit in the Commerce Clause, against states passing legislations that discriminate against or excessively burden interstate commerce. Of particular importance is the prevention of protectionist state policies that favor state citizens or businesses at the expense of noncitizens conducting business within that state.

In spite of the "Dormant Commerce Clause" states under the "market participation doctrine" (in *Hughes v. Alexandria Scrap Corp.*, 426 US 794 (US 1976)), which upheld a Maryland program that offered bounties to scrap processors to destroy abandoned automobile hulks are allowed to charge in-state students a lower tuition. In *Hughes v. Alexandria Scrap Corp*, the court held that

> The commerce clause of the Constitution (Art I, 8, cl 3) does not require inde-
> pendent justification for a state's entry into the market as a purchaser, in effect, of
> a potential article of interstate commerce, although the state restricts its trade to
> its own citizens or businesses within the state; nothing in the purposes animating
> the commerce clause forbids a state, in the absence of congressional action, from
> participating in the market and exercising the right to favor its own citizens over
> others.
>
> *(426 US 794, 96 S. Ct. 2488, 49 L. Ed. 2d 220 –*
> *Supreme Court, 1976, p. 822)*

In other words, besides using out-of-state and international students to internationalize
their campuses and local communities and broaden the worldview of their students and
enrich their experience, these students could also be used to generate higher revenue.
To this end, many state universities are becoming increasingly aggressive in recruiting
domestic out-of-state and international students. One of the latest moves is to hire a
third-party recruiter to recruit students, particularly from international countries.

According to NACAC, there are more than 20,000 recruiting agencies that operate
worldwide. These agencies differ in terms of location, size, and student recruitment
specializations. The utilization of the services of these agencies varies from country
to country. For example, even though their services are commonly employed by
institutions in Australia, the United Kingdom, and Canada, they are less often used by
universities in the United States and only one of every four institutions in the United
States use them.

There are several advantages and disadvantages to using third-party recruiters. Some
of the advantages include leveraging the experience of some of these organizations,
especially for institutions that are new to recruiting directly from outside their borders.
Other advantages lie in using agencies that are local and are located in difficult-to-
reach places. However, these advantages could also come with significant risks if the
"employing institution" is not careful. For example, there is the risk that commission-
based agencies could misinform students or "refer them to an institution based not upon
what is educationally and socially best for them but, rather, financially advantageous for
the agency."

According to NACAC, an American university that was audited in 2012 was found
to have significant problems linked to international student recruitment agencies that
the school used. The problems were harmful to the students and staff and damaged the
university's reputation so much so that the audit recommended the university terminate
all of its agency relationships. Furthermore, in 2014, a Canadian university was the subject of a C$24 million lawsuit, brought by a former agency partner of the institution.
Because of these kinds of legal, reputational, and financial risks that can arise from using
third-party recruiting agencies the NACAC suggests that a decision to use commission-
based agencies should be "supported by broader strategic planning, including an
assessment of the institution's current outreach practices and enrollment goals and an
examination of agency recruitment in comparison with complementary, or alternative,
strategies."

Questions

1. What is a third-party student recruiting agency?
2. What are some of the advantages in using a third-party recruiter?
3. What are some of the disadvantages in using a third-party recruiter?
4. Explain the "market participation" doctrine.

CASE #14 ADMISSIONS FAIR

Faced with increasing competition for students, universities are resorting to several time-proven business strategies to recruit students. This case discusses how college admission fairs, similar to job fairs, are being used to recruit students.

An admissions fair is sometimes referred to as an "open house" when it is held on campus and organized by only the host institution. To signal their significance, college admission fairs are often dubbed with names that sound grand such as the "National College Admissions Fair." College admission fairs are the universities' and colleges' equivalent of a trade fair or job fair. They are organized by either an umbrella organization such as the NACAC or by an independent group – a fraternity, sorority, or any such organization. These admission fairs bring together, under one roof at the same time, representatives, generally admission officers/staff from hundreds of universities. But are they now a dying breed?

As competition for students became more intense and recruiting costs kept increasing, universities that may otherwise be rivals resorted to collaborating and using industry and time-proven strategies such as employing trade fair-type approach to recruiting. A trade fair (also referred to as a trade show, trade expo – expo for exposition) is an organized exhibition in which companies in the same industry get to showcase and demonstrate their products, services, and innovations to industry partners and customers. It also offers companies the opportunity to study their rivals. While some trade fairs are closed to public, some are open to the public or take a hybrid form in which some days are closed to the public and some are not.

According to NACAC, college fairs started to become popular in the mid-1970s. Because the attending universities had to pay a fee to the organizers, organizing admission fairs have become a revenue generator for the organizers, and as a means for many universities to reach groups of students that they may otherwise not reach. Overtime, an industry has grown around college fairs as the size and form of the events have also changed. College admission fairs range from huge NACAC-sponsored events which hundreds of colleges and universities attend to smaller school-based fairs with only a dozen institutions represented. College admission fairs have also assumed several different models. Some fairs target students in specific segments, for example, students who are in the arts or underrepresented minority applicants, while others highlight international universities or schools specializing in the STEM fields. Though they have been effective in attracting a huge attendance, some people have become skeptical of their effectiveness in addressing students' needs exactly because of the huge attendance. They believe the size prevents personal attention.

College admission fairs have undoubtedly served a valuable role that has allowed many colleges and universities to market to a wide audience and encourage applicants to expand their postsecondary horizons. Indeed, for many graduating high school seniors, college admission fair is their first in-person encounter with a college representative. However, recent experimentations with virtual online admission fairs got a major boost from the recent pandemic (COVID-19) which caused many in-person events to migrate to a virtual environment. With the proliferation of the Internet, access to web content, webinars, virtual tours, videos and chat rooms, one wonders whether college admission fairs will soon be going the way of dinosaurs.

Questions

1. What is the NACAC and why has it come to play such a pivotal role in college admission fairs?
2. What are some of the advantages in having an organized college admission fairs?
3. What are some of the disadvantages?
4. Do you think college admission fairs are now irrelevant?

8

COMPETITION AND INNOVATIONS IN HIGHER EDUCATION

Introduction

We connect the dots between competition in higher education, globalization, and innovation in universities in this chapter. We first review the previous studies on competition amongst universities and discuss how it leads to innovation and globalization in higher education. We also discuss the concept of the Product Life Cycle (PLC) and how it enters into strategy formulation in higher education by treating both the university and its offerings as products at two levels that go through different phases in their life cycle. With careful management using the appropriate strategies, both the university and its programs will survive and thrive, but inappropriate strategy formulation can lead to the sad demise of the university or a program or both.

The Nature of Competition

Competition amongst living organisms (Darwin, 1859) and in the marketplace (Stigler, 1968) has been extensively studied. However, as observed by some scholars such as Stigler (1993) and De Fraja and Iossa (2002), competition amongst universities, where most of the research takes place, has ironically been less studied. However, the dearth of studies on universities does not mean that universities are immune from competition. Understanding how competition works in the marketplace in general and can work in the educational system in particular can prepare an individual to market a university, hence we first review a few studies related to competition in education to set the background on how it impacts or can impact marketing of universities.

Does Competition Destroy Ethical Behavior?

Commenting on the connection between ethical behavior and competition, Shleifer (2004) showed that conducts such as employment of children, corruption, excessive executive pay, manipulation of corporate earnings, and involvement of universities in commercial activities such as athletics (see Bok, 2003) which are generally described as "unethical" or a product

DOI: 10.4324/9781003160267-8

of "greed" are sometimes a consequence of market competition. Shleifer (2004) proceeded to distinguish between ethics and efficiency and explained that ethical norms evolved in some cases to sustain cooperative behaviors and support the successful function of social institutions.

However, it would be simplistic to jump to the conclusion that globalization of free market economy which has made competition keener around the world also leads to pervasive unethical behavior around the world. Shleifer (2004) offered two separate reasons for the earlier conclusion to be inaccurate:

> First, competition is the fundamental source of technological progress and wealth creation around the world. The same market forces that might encourage unethical conduct also motivate firms to innovate and create products leading to economic growth.
>
> As societies grow richer their willingness to pay for ethical behavior through government enforcement and private choice increases as well. As a consequence, both moral and regulatory sanctions work better leading to more ethical behavior.
>
> Second, as societies grow richer their views on ethical conduct change as well. Universalist ethics that emphasize cooperation and inclusion replace the more tribal and parochial beliefs.
>
> *(Friedman, 2004; Shleifer, 2004, p. 418)*

More questions than answers were generated by Shleifer (2004). For example, does competition undermine ethical behavior when suppliers and stakeholders have social preferences? Dewatripont and Tirole (2020) sought to answer this question in their unpublished paper. Using a theoretical model, the authors showed that under price regulation (health, schools, regulated professions, franchising), a higher price and competitive pressure compromise or boost ethics when cutting ethical corners increases or reduces demand. However, competitive pressure has no ethical impact when reduced ethics lowers cost and/or with market-determined prices. A more ethical firm commands a lower market share under price regulation, but not in a "low-morality market" with market prices. Finally, intense competition induces behavioral convergence among ethical types and/or corporate forms, to be better on the price front and the worse on the ethical front.

Previous Studies on Competition

Discussing the role of product differentiation in the nature of competition, Gabszewicz and Thisse (1986) went as far back to as the 1800 to discuss the work of some economists who had visited the topic of competition, for example, Bertrand (1883) who discussed the fragility of market equilibrium when competition arises among a few sellers. Hotelling (1929), on the contrary, believed that price instability would vanish when products are differentiated. In later examinations of the nature of competition, d'Aspremont et al. (1979) suggested that the possibility of price cycles will not completely disappear with product differentiation, instead differentiation only weakens the forces that lead to price instability. Gabszewicz and Thisse (1986) argued that vertical product differentiation and horizontal product differentiation do not operate in the same manner, and that a stable market outcome (including an endogenous product specification) arises more frequently with the vertical differentiation than with horizontal differentiation.

"Privatization" of higher education has gained currency in recent years (discussed in detail in Chapter 12). Currie and Vidovich (2000) argued that the word "privatization" is used to refer to "an ideological shift towards market principles such as competition, commercialization, deregulation, efficiency and changing forms of accountability." The term is, however, used in higher education to refer to different trends including the "creation of fully private institutions which operate without government financial support, to reforms in largely government-funded institutions operating in more of a quasi-market mode."

But where did this worldwide trend come from, and what does it hold for universities in the future? These are questions that Currie and Vidovich (2000) wanted to answer in their study. Citing reports of the World Bank and the Organization for Economic Co-operation and Development (OECD) (OECD, 1998), the authors suggested that these two institutions have been instrumental in nudging governments around the world to "change public policy based on the social good to one based on economic goals." These policy changes not only led to deregulation and privatization around the world, but also resulted in governments asking public sector organizations including universities to act like businesses. The impact of all these changes on universities mean, among other things, "creating 'leaner and meaner' decision making structures and processes in institutions and resulting in an intensification of academic work." Furthermore, the major impact of accountability in the way that it is being demanded "may lessen the quality of education for students and the quality of research for the community is the time it takes away from other important tasks academics perform."

Lamenting the dearth of theoretical studies on university system in which most researchers have a direct interest and despite its quantitative and qualitative importance, De Fraja and Iossa (2002) investigated competition between universities. The authors argued that given its importance and yet the considerably different manners in which the sector is organized in different countries, a sound understanding of the system is important as well as necessary to inform policies that are aimed at improving the performance of the sector.

It is important, however, to note that the market for universities is different from the market for other industries in three main respects:

1. The market for university education does not typically clear in the usual sense. Even though the potential exists for a market clearing price for university education, most systems nevertheless allocate places to students by administrative rationing.
2. The performance of a university (measured along the dimension of the quality of the teaching provided) depends positively on the ability of its own students.
3. The profit maximizing behavior typically assumed for large commercial organizations as well as for some not-for-profit private institutions is not likely to be a good proxy for the objective function of individual universities.

De Fraja and Iossa (2002) therefore developed a theoretical model that captures the three conditions outlined, assuming a hypothetical environment where two nonprofit universities compete by selecting the proportion of their funding devoted to teaching and research, the criteria for admission for their students, and where students choose and whether and where to attend university. The authors used the model to examine the "relationship between the cost incurred by students for attending a university located away from their home town and the equilibrium configuration that emerges in the game played by the universities." The study showed that (1) when student mobility cost is low, there is no pure Nash equilibrium strategy; and (2) when student mobility cost is high there are pure strategy equilibria; and (3) when student mobility cost is of an intermediate value, if equilibria exist, they are asymmetric.

Aghion et al. (2010) argued that competition is good for universities and that universities are more productive when they are both more autonomous and face more competition. Using survey data, the authors constructed indices of university autonomy and competition for both Europe and the United States and tested a series of hypotheses. The results showed that there are indeed strong positive correlations between the indices they constructed and multiple measures of university output.

To obtain causal evidence, Aghion et al. (2010) investigated exogenous shocks to US universities' expenditures over three decades. The exogenous shock came through the political appointment process, which was used to generate instrumental variables. The authors found that an exogenous increase in a university's expenditure generates more output, measured by either patents or publications, if the university is more autonomous and faces more competition. When variations over time were exploited in the "stakes" of competition for federal grants, the authors found that competition for US federal research grants by universities generated more output for a given expenditure when research competitions are high stakes. Drawing on these lessons Aghion et al. (2010) said that European universities could also benefit from a combination of greater autonomy and greater accountability which could come through increased reliance on competitive grants and enhanced competition for students and faculty (promoted by reforms that increase mobility).

Analyzing competition among universities and colleges for fee-paying students, Kim (2010) used a stylized theoretical model to analyze competition among need-blind colleges and universities that implement early decision admissions. An applicant's financial aid status cannot affect their likelihood of admission under need-blind admission system. In the need-blind model of competition a school can use early decision admissions as a screening mechanism to indirectly identify a student's ability to pay, while superficially maintaining a need-blind policy. The result of this model is that, in equilibrium, nonfinancial aid students are more likely to be admitted than financial aid students of comparable quality.

Globalization and Higher Education

Dill (2001) noted the changes in global economy that have impacted government policies around the world regarding higher education. The author observed that government policies around the globe are causing changes in the traditional modes of university organization and management leading to what is variously termed as "the marketization of higher education" or "managerialism" among others. According to Dill (1997) the most significant changes in government policy are those that have increased market competition within university systems and summarized the cause and effect of some of them as stated here:

1. As social demands for higher education have increased in the new global economy, many countries have adopted a policy of "massification" – of expanded access to higher education, but have provided less public support per student than in the past thus increasing competition for financial resources among universities as well as creating incentives for productivity improvements.

2. Governments in a number of regions such as South America and Asia have encouraged private higher education as a means of expanding access, thereby increasing competition in the traditional public sector for students and resources.
3. Governments are adopting quasi-market mechanisms for the allocation of resources to public sector universities, including incentive or performance funding, competitive allocation of research funding, and the introduction of tuition fees.
4. As a further step toward encouraging competition in the higher education sector, governments are also aligning accountability with control by delegating to the university level increased authority over inputs and decisions about resource use.

Because these changes have altered the nature of the rivalry among universities, both within and across states and nations, university leaderships have discovered that they need greater flexibility to compete effectively and are therefore seeking relief from traditional government regulations while governments at the same time want publicly funded universities to act in ways that are consistent with the social values of equity, efficiency, and academic quality. Formulating public policies that balance the competitive needs of the university sector with the public interest is not easy, and no "play book" has been provided. To fill this vacuum Dill (2001) designs a framework for analyzing the regulatory policy issues using examples from the United States and Europe.

Providing education services across national borders has become one of the fastest areas of international trade. According to the OECD report (OECD, 2002), about 2 million students were studying outside their countries in the 2000s; this number is expected to increase fivefolds in about 20 years while competition among universities for international students is also becoming intense. What is the impact this imposes on universities in Australia and New Zealand?

Using economic theory which suggests that competitive market forces will impact organizational efficiency, Abbott and Doucouliagos (2009) sought to examine the impact of competition on the efficiency of universities in Australia and New Zealand using panel data for the period 1995–2002 for Australia and 1997–2003 for New Zealand. The results of the analyses show that competition for overseas students has led to increased efficiency in Australian universities. However, competition for overseas students appears to have had no effect on efficiency in New Zealand. The authors suggest that the difference in the results might be explained by the difference in approaches used by universities in the two countries to recruit international students. Whereas universities in Australia tend to recruit international students from foreign countries, universities in New Zealand tend to recruit international students who are already present in New Zealand.

To cut costs, the public systems of higher education in many countries have resorted to providing financial incentives to cut duplicated programs, that is, same programs being offered at different institutions, in the name of funding system reform in Flanders (Belgium). The authors found that dropping duplicated programs at individual institutions tends to be socially undesirable, due to the students' low willingness to travel to other institutions and to the limited fixed cost and variable cost savings. Furthermore, the financial incentives offered to universities to eliminate programs may be ineffective, leading to both undesirable reform and undesirable status quo. The findings of the study illustrate the complexities in regulating product diversity in higher education, and even though it was conducted in Belgium only, the results, according to the authors, should serve as a word of caution for introducing different forms of decentralized financial incentive schemes.

Innovations at Universities

As indicated in the readings, competition leads to innovation and differentiation, but the issue is what types of innovation can a university have? The answer of course is many types: innovation can take place in different spaces within a university. However, innovation has to be planned in order for universities to fully harness the advantages that come with it. Naturally, the first place that innovations can occur in universities is through faculty research, but this type of innovation can be enjoyed generally only by research universities. Through scientific research, professors and other researchers in research universities can come out with either new, more efficient and cost effective ways of making an existing product or with an entirely new product.

There are at least three benefits that are associated with innovation through research. First, the university can use the innovation to get a lot of free media coverage (press releases, public relations, interviews with journalists, etc.). For example, a professor (Xiulin Ruan) at Purdue University in West Lafayette, Indiana, in the United States recently (in April 2021) discovered ultra-white paint that reflects 98% of sunlight (see www.purdue.edu/newsroom/releases/2021/Q2/the-whitest-paint-is-here-and-its-the-coolest.-literally..html. See also BBC's coverage of the news at www.bbc.com/news/science-environment-56749105, and Gill 2021). This invention was covered worldwide by different media.

Second, this type of media coverage can be easily converted into goodwill which the university can leverage into recruiting new students and faculty as well as in promoting the university to donors and legislators. It must be noted here that not only state or public universities have to deal with legislators, even private for profit or not-for-profit universities can deal with them in one way or the other. In some countries such as Italy, the government still pays, albeit, a small percentage of the operating budget for private universities.

Third, scientific innovations in universities such as the one discussed is generally patentable, as such it can be easily commercialized to generate revenue streams for the university. Furthermore, universities can use such innovations as a basis to establish and to promote a research park. This research park can be used to attract businesses which not only generate additional revenue for the university, but can also form a basis for other forms of alliances than can benefit students (e.g., in areas of employment, internships, and other arrangements that give them practical experience).

We must emphasize here that innovations in universities are not limited only to the scientific fields. They can take place in the field of arts, fine arts, business schools, and in curricular design. For example, a university can design its fine arts programs in such a way that there is collaboration with and connection to fine arts museums in the area. The curricula of the fine arts program could be designed in such a way that students in the program can either do internship with the museums or take some classes conducted with the museum's professional staff. Furthermore, an integral part of a performing arts program should be to regularly put on a show that is heavily advertised in the community. Similar to innovation in the sciences, but on different scale, a good execution of plays and exhibitions in the fields of creative arts can bring a lot of free media coverage and its associated goodwill to the university; this, as discussed earlier, can be leveraged for other purposes or to attain other objectives.

Several different courses and instructional formats could be used to make programs at a university more amenable to the needs of students. For example, eight-week semester programs could be used to select more ambitious students. Similarly, weekend and evening-only programs can be introduced for students who work full-time. Similarly, online programs can be introduced to make going to school more flexible. COVID-19 which forced many universities around the world to use the online and virtual formats has shown that these formats could be viable substitutes or complements to in-person classes. However, a unit that is going to use these formats must be sure to have the appropriate technology in place to deliver academically rigorous and no watered-down instructions or program. This of course means that it is not only the delivery technologies that must be current, but also the instructors who are recruited to teach in the programs are technology-savvy and are very comfortable teaching with those formats.

Study abroad programs are becoming quite popular now with internationalization (this is discussed in more detail in Chapter 11). These programs, amongst other things, are intended to give the participating students certain advantages, for example, improve students' confidence, give the participants a cultural and language immersion, expand their network, give them a worldview, and enhance their career opportunities. Designing a good study abroad program can give a university a competitive advantage in attracting students, if the program is properly exposed in the school's brochures as well as at their websites. Some universities such as Goucher College in Baltimore Maryland and Soka University of America in California not only emphasize the study abroad program but have also incorporated it into their curriculum. It is a graduation requirement (see www.usnews.com/education/best-colleges/articles/2019-03-22/3-benefits-of-studying-abroad).

Business schools can also be used as a pull to attract students. Even though liberal arts schools continue to play an important role in the market for education, it is not unusual for some students to spend at least the first year of their college education without having decided on a career or a major; some career-minded students decide even before graduating from high school on a career in business. Hence, such students use the presence of a good business school at a university as their criterion or at least one of the criteria in deciding on the university to attend.

As observed, because of the role business schools can play in student recruiting, it is important that such schools be well-equipped and appropriately advertised in a university's brochure and at its website. However, Byrne (2019) in his article in *Forbes* noted that enrollment in the MBA programs which used to be highly competitive in the leading business schools, around the world and particularly in the United States, is experiencing a significant decline. While we are not sure on the cause of this dip in enrollment which could be due to environmental factors and temporary, we can still see a space for business programs and business schools as recruiting vehicles of universities.

Innovations in business schools themselves or in business programs that could be used to market universities can take several forms. These may include customizing degree programs for the larger local companies that can enroll their employees as cohorts, offering of nondegree programs, developing certificate and flexible degree programs as well as having a renowned in-residency executive to conduct executive seminars. Business school degree programs can be designed to incorporate an obligatory requirement of an internship to graduate. Drexel University in Pennsylvania does this so well that it has become the school's national and international selling point.

Universities must also have active lifelong learning programs that can be used to pull senior citizens, some of whom may become potential donors. Finally, universities, particularly business schools, should maintain linkages with business community and solicit their input in developing new curriculum and programs. A good relationship with the local business community not only makes them relevant partners, but also the first to buy into the new programs that the university is offering.

The Product Life Cycle

How can Product Life Cycle (PLC) concept be applied in making a university more competitive? The PLC can be described or defined in a number of ways, but definition invariably captures the fact that it describes the course of the life of a product in five distinct stages from when the product was in development to the time it has been removed from the market. The five distinct stages involved in the PLC are the development phase, the introduction phase, the growth phase, the maturity phase, and the decline phase. Of course, the development phase takes place behind the scene and therefore not shown in the diagram, so the consumer gets to see only the last four stages (as shown in Figure 8.1). It must be realized that the decline phase does not always lead to a product being removed from the market, but it can also be repositioned to go through yet another life cycle.

The main idea behind the PLC is the recognition of the fact that because of competition and consumers' change in taste, no product can last forever. Certainly, different product categories have different life span – some last longer than others. Higher education as a product can be viewed with the same lens. However, the PLC concept can be applied to a university at two levels. First to the university as a whole as a service producer and second to the various programs or courses offered by the university.

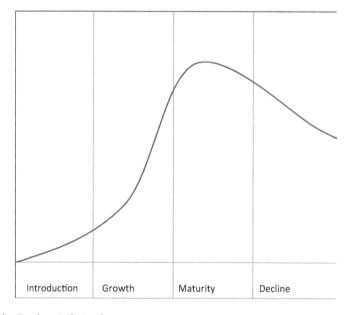

| Introduction | Growth | Maturity | Decline |

FIGURE 8.1 The Product Life Cycle

PLC at the University Level

Applying the PLC concept at the university level means that university leadership should be an innovator and visionary. Innovative leaders could see a university beyond a physical space (a collection of buildings at a particular location), students, staff, and instructors. The founding of the University of Phoenix, a for-profit university in the United States in 1976, designed to operate around the life of working folks is an extreme example, but represents the kind of innovative thinking that leadership of universities must engage to be competitive.

The traditional concept of a university as a physical space is slowly changing, as a result of competitive forces. One could argue that developing satellite campuses, offering of online courses (expedited by COVID-19), and having weekend degree programs are all examples of universities adapting to the changing competitive education environment. Universities that are nimble will do well, and those that are sluggish and continue to rely on old traditional models, especially the smaller less endowed private universities, will become vulnerable, fare less well in attracting students, for example, Morris Brown University in Atlanta (see www.ajc. com/education/morris-brown-timeline/) or even close (e.g., St. Catharine College, College of New Rochelle and Southern Vermont College to mention only a few), those that were tethering on the brinks financially such as Becker College in Leicester, Massachusetts, and Holy Family College, a private Catholic institution in Wisconsin, fell over the cliff due to COVID-19 (see Schermele, 2020).

Competition amongst universities does not necessarily mean the absence of cooperation, on the other it could also lead to formation of alliance between some universities for mutual gains. For example, some universities could have student exchange programs amongst themselves to allow students to experience a different school environment. Even if the universities are in the same city, they could have an arrangement in which certain courses (e.g., graduate courses) can be open for free to students from a rival institution across town. Also, schools can have cooperation between professors to work on scientific projects or even form a consortium that extends tuition waivers for the children of the faculty and staff to members of the consortium. One of the advantages of having such a consortium is that it allows those schools to attract faculty and staff that they could not have attracted solely on the basis of salary.

The PLC at the Program Level

Courses and programs must be viewed as a portfolio of offerings. Just as new products are added to the portfolio and obsolete or slow-moving ones are deleted, so must courses and programs be adjusted. Courses and programs such as Home Economics and Comic Art which attract very few students these days might be offered less often or even relegated to only schools that are resource rich and replaced by courses or programs in Aviation Administration, Business Analytics, Cyber Technology and/or Cyber Security that may now be more relevant and in demand. Furthermore, instead of eliminating less demanded courses completely (since for the sake of education that may not be desirable in of itself) an arrangement can be among public schools in one state so that only one or two of them offered courses in such programs, for example, Home Economics and the Classics.

It must be noted that just as distinct marketing strategies are designed and implemented in corporations for the distinct phases for product in its life cycle, so must it be in universities also. A program that is new may need a lot of promotion and advertisement in its introductory phase. In fact, the course could even be offered in the initial stages with enrollment figures that fall below the cut-off point, with time and promotion these figures should grow and less money will be spent on their promotion, and attention could be focused more on managing the program, for example, improving course content, etc.

With the passage of time, a program or course that is new today will become mature and might need to be tinkered with for repositioning purposes. Unlike the industry, few programs or courses in universities are removed from the market or do truly reach the declining phase, but they do happen particularly with electives, hence course/programs must be carefully monitored.

Differentiation of Universities

Differentiation is arguably a part of competition. In the market of many providers, the question is why, besides convenience, should consumers choose one university over the other? Certainly, a university must provide a consumer a reason to choose it over another university, hence the need for competitive differentiation among universities. Competitive differentiation is a cross-functional activity in which all the different components of a university try to "speak with one voice" in which the university tries to distinguish itself from other universities using such factors as customers' value, brand, tuition (price), and service. Clear and comprehensible statements based on all these four factors must be communicated to the various target audiences using the appropriate channels, as discussed in Chapter 7.

Statements addressing value must incorporate other statements that address the quality of education offered in the university at a given tuition. Sometimes statement on value may include the university's ranking which is also addressed in brand statements, and, of course, the quality of other services (such as the university's placement record of recent graduates) or even the average salaries of its recent graduates.

Competition is ever present in a free market; it never stops, hence a university's leadership must never stop strategizing.

Summary

In this chapter we have discussed how competitive forces result in innovation even in the market of higher education. We reviewed the concept of PLC and related it to innovation in universities at the level of programs and the level of university itself. We connected the dots between innovation and globalization of higher education which is discussed in much more detail later in Chapter 12.

Questions

1. How can you relate innovation in a university to competition?
2. What are some of the achievements of competition in the market for higher education?
3. How can a university use competition to market itself?
4. Does competition prevent universities from cooperating? Explain.
5. What are the five phases of a product life cycle?
6. Why is the development phase not shown in Figure 8.1?
7. Use the concept of a portfolio of offerings to explain a university's programs.

References

Abbott, M., & Doucouliagos, C. (2009). Competition and Efficiency: Overseas Students and Technical Efficiency in Australian and New Zealand Universities. *Education Economics* 17 (1), 31–57.

Aghion, P., Dewatripont, M., Hoxby, C., Mas-Colell, A., & Sapir, A. (2010). The Governance and Performance of Universities: Evidence from Europe and the US. Economic Policy Paper, January 2010 Printed in Great Britain.

Bertrand, J. (1883). Theorie mathematique de la richesse sociale. *Journal des Savants* 48, 499–508.

Bok, D. (2003). *Universities in the Marketplace: Commercialization of Higher Education.* Princeton, NJ: Princeton University Press.

Byrne, J. (2019). It's Official: The M.B.A. Degree Is in Crisis. www.forbes.com/sites/poetsandquants/2019/08/20/its-official-the-mba-degree-is-in-crisis/. Retrieved on August 20, 2021.

Currie, J., & Vidovich, L. (2000). Privatization and Competition Policies for Australian Universities. *International Journal of Educational Development* 20, 135–151.

Darwin, C. (1859). *The Origin of Species.* London: Murray John.

d'Aspremont, C.D., Gabszewicz, J. J., & Thisse, J.-F. (1979). On Hotelling's "Stability in Competition." *Econometrica* 47(5), 1145–1150.

De Fraja, G., & Iossa, E. (2002). Competition among Universities and the Emergence of the Elite Institution. *Bulletin of Economic Research* 54 (3), 275–295.

Dewatripont, M., & Tirole, J. (2020). The morality of markets and the nature of competition. https://www.tse-fr.eu/sites/default/files/TSE/documents/doc/by/tirole/morality_of_markets_181220.pdf

Dill, D.D. (1997). Higher Education Markets and Public Policy. *Higher Education Policy* 10 (3/4), 167–186.

Dill, D.D. (2001). The Regulation of Public Research Universities: Changes in Academic Competition and Implications for University Autonomy and Accountability. *Higher Education Policy* 14 (1), 21–35.

Friedman, B. (2004). *The Moral Consequences of Economic Growth.* New York: Knopf.

Gabszewicz, J.J., & Thisse, J-F. (1986). On the Nature of Competition with Differentiated Products. *Economic Journal* 96 (381), 160–172.

Gill, V. (2021). Whitest Ever Paint Reflects 98% of Sunlight. www.bbc.com/news/science-environment-56749105. Retrieved on October 1, 2021.

Hotelling, H. (1929). Stability in Competition. *Economic Journal* 39 (153), 41–57.

Kim, M. (2010). Early Decision and Financial Aid Competition among Need-Blind Colleges and Universities. *Journal of Public Economics* 94 (5–6), 410–420.

Morris Brown: A Timeline of the Life and Near-Death of an Institution. *The Atlanta Journal – Constitution* (Undated). www.ajc.com/education/morris-brown-timeline/. Retrieved on August 21, 2021.

Organisation for Economic Cooperation and Development (1998). *Redefining Tertiary Education.* Paris: OECD.

Organisation for Economic Cooperation and Development (2002). *Education at a Glance; OECD Indicators.* Paris: OECD.

Schermele, Z. (2020). Some Colleges Are Closing Permanently Because of the Coronavirus Pandemic. *TeenVogue.* www.teenvogue.com/story/colleges-closing-permanently-coronavirus-pandemic. Retrieved on August 22, 2021.

Shleifer, A. (2004). Does Competition Destroy Ethical Behavior? *The American Economic Review* 94 (2), 414–418.

Stigler, J. (1968). *Competition. The International Encyclopedia of the Social Sciences* 3, 181–186. New York: Macmillan and Free Press.

Stigler, S.M. (1993). Competition and the Research Universities. *Daedalus* 122 (4), 157–177.

CASE #15 A SEMESTER AT SEA (BASED ON THE US INSTITUTE FOR SHIPBOARD EDUCATION)

Universities are becoming creative in developing programs not only to attract students, but also to broaden students' outlook. This case discusses an innovative Semester at Sea program at Colorado State University.

With the ever-increasing cost of university education, people are beginning to question the value of college education. Those who favor college education argue that college education should be vocational and that college education is needed to broadly prepare a person for success in life, to make people more engaged and enlightened, and capable of thinking critically, communicating clearly, and ultimately being a well-rounded global citizen. On the contrary, those who argue that college education is unnecessary point to the fact that it does not necessarily make graduates work-ready, that is, in most cases it does not necessarily equip graduates with skills for the job market.

It seems both camps have a valid point, but more importantly, it seems college education can be made to satisfy both camps. Students can acquire lifeskills and learn how to be global citizens in the global village that is getting increasingly smaller while going college, and still be able to develop analytical and critical thinking skills for their careers. For that purpose, some universities have created study abroad programs that expose their students to other cultures and to other parts of the world. One such example is the Semester at Sea program at Colorado State University.

The Semester at Sea program is a unique study abroad program in which students don't really leave their home – a ship. The program was founded at Colorado State University in 1963 and administered by the Institute for Shipboard Education (ISE) at the university. As a large public university with a good reputation and accreditation, the Semester at Sea program is well-recognized and about 600 students participate in the program during each academic year. The program offers between 70 and 72 courses at level 100 and level 200 across a wide range of disciplines including but not limited to psychology, human development, Spanish, anthropology, history, religion, philosophy, and business in one semester. Every course has an in-country Field Class built into it, and all students are required to take a Global Studies course. A student can earn between 12 and 15 credits from Colorado State University while being exposed to 10–14 countries across multiple continents and cruising over 20,000 nautical miles.

The program is open to students from any university (i.e., to even those who may not be enrolled at Colorado State University). Because the program is administered by a recognized university and at lower levels, students from other schools should have no problems transferring their courses. Depending on the type of room that a student occupies, tuition and board for the Semester at Sea could run from about $26,000 to $32,000 per student. It is also open to lifelong learners (i.e., adult nondegree seekers) and with books, immunizations, personal programs, visas, and airfare, one can expect to pay $35,000–$41,000 for the full program.

Even though the semester is on the high seas, it still inculcates in its students the spirit of volunteering and offers its students the opportunity to volunteer in many of the field programs. For instance, in one case, students spent eight hours in a day's program cleaning a beach in the Island of Mauritius and in the process got to learn about marine habitats and how to protect and sustain them.

While the program seems to be fairly successful as evidenced in student enrollment and safety given its extremely low rate of incidents, the uncertainties around the world these days give one some concerns. For example, the COVID-19 pandemic led to the cancellation of the scheduled Fall 2020 class, and the Spring 2020 class had to avoid some countries altogether. The Semester at Sea can boast of a list of famous guest lecturers including but not limited to Indira Gandhi, Mikhail Gorbachev, Anwar Sadat, Nelson Mandela, and Desmond Tutu. If imitation is the best flattery, then we can say that the Semester at Sea Program is being flattered because similar programs are being organized, for example, the Sea|Mester's academic credits are sponsored by the University of South Florida; the University of Virginia and the University of Miami are also affiliated with separate and independent programs.

Questions

1. Is the Semester at Sea a good marketing program for a university?
2. What value does the Semester at Sea program create for its students?
3. Does the Semester at Sea program add any value to the university?
4. Are the benefits from the program worth the inherent risks?

CASE #16 BUSINESS ANALYTICS?

To continue to attract students, some old programs are replaced, repackaged, or rebranded. This case discusses one of such instances in which a course in business analytics was introduced in a local university.

Many business schools can, at the least, get credit for practicing what they preach. They preach and teach innovations and instill in their students that a good business is the one that satisfies the needs of its customers. So, business schools must try to satisfy the needs of their customers – students and businesses in the marketplace by being current in their course offerings, that is, teach and offer courses that equip their students with the skills that the market place currently needs. To do this, many business schools periodically survey businesses in their service areas and conduct curriculum review – a process which leads to the introduction of new courses and elimination of some old ones.

In a recent curriculum review, the faculty of the department of information technology at Hope University's business school realized that their courses needed to be revamped to meet the needs of the market place. Drastic changes had occurred in the market with regard to the use of technology and data, and their course offerings had not kept pace with the changes, hence change needed to be made. Changes can be done in two ways. The first and easy way is to introduce a new course as an elective and simply promote it hoping that enough students will take it. The second and more difficult way is to introduce the new course and make it a required course for students majoring in information technology. This is a more difficult approach because the number of credit hours required to graduate must remain the same, so requiring a new course means a current required course must be dropped from the list of required courses. Furthermore, professors sometimes become rather protective of the courses they teach; hence another problem becomes whose "goat is going to be goaded," in other words, whose course is going to be eliminated?

One thing that clearly stood up in the data collected and in the national trends is that businesses in the market now use more data and technology than ever before. They are using the data and models to help them in decisions on scheduling, pricing, inventorying, etc., hence the decision was made to initially introduce a course in **marketing analytics** as an elective (an easier decision), even though some people on the faculty strongly felt that it should be made a requirement. It was decided that the issue would be revisited later.

Business analytics is the science of using data to build mathematical models that help decision-making processes and create value for companies or organizations. It is relevant in nearly every field. It can be used in business, medicine, technology, retail, or real estate. Business analytics has many individual components such as data mining, data visualization, descriptive analytics, predictive analytics, etc., that work together to provide insights for decision makers.

Even though the practice has now caught the attention of everyone, it is really not new. Business analytics has been used in the industry since the nineteenth century when management science practices were instituted in the industry by Frederick Taylor. For example, it was said that Henry Ford measured the time that it took to add each component part on to a vehicle that was being made in his newly established assembly line for making the model T in 1908. However, business analytics began to command more attention in the late 1960s when computers were used in decision support systems.

Question

1. What is "business analytics"?
2. Do you think business analytics as a course to be studied is a fad or a legitimate part of a curriculum?
3. How does the concept of PLC apply to introducing a course in the university?
4. How does introducing a new course relate to university marketing?

9
NAMES AND NAME CHANGE – UNIVERSITY BRAND MANAGEMENT

Introduction

Part of marketing is communicating using symbols. In this chapter we focus on name as a communication symbol that is used, besides structural changes, to communicate in a world of information asymmetry organizations' insiders' superior information to the market. We show in the chapter that universities similar to corporations can also communicate to their audiences using similar strategies. We also review the relevant literature on name change and signaling theory and discuss some real-life examples.

What Is in a Name?

"What's in a name? That which we call a rose by any other name would smell just as sweet" is a line that William Shakespeare used in his play *Romeo and Juliet* to convey the notion that the naming of things is irrelevant. But is it? Name is one of the rare topics that has been studied by scholars across several disciplines, from biblical studies to English and physics, and anything in between, and the overwhelming consensus is that whereas Shakespeare must have been poetic in Romeo's declaration of love for Juliet, there is certainly more to name than its functionality for identification. For example, Moa Bursell (2012) studied 45 individuals with Middle Eastern backgrounds in Sweden who changed their foreign-sounding surnames to more Swedish-sounding or neutral surnames and found that these individuals have a positive earnings progression compared to individuals who keep their foreign-sounding names.

Similarly, Cotton et al. (2008), in a study that examined how the uniqueness and ethnicity of first names influence affective reactions to those names and their potential for hire, concluded that common names were seen as least unique, best liked, and most likely to be hired. Unusual names were seen as most unique, least liked, and least likely to be hired. Russian and African-American names were intermediate in terms of uniqueness, likeability, and being hired, but significantly different from common and unique names, but not significantly different from each other. The authors concluded on the basis of the study that the name that an individual

DOI: 10.4324/9781003160267-9

carried has a significant impact on how they are viewed, and conceivably, whether or not they are hired for a job.

So, what is the connection between names and brands? Typically, a brand is a name, term, design, symbol, or any other feature that is used to identify and distinguish the seller's good or service from those of competitors. Brands are used in different facets of commerce for recognition and more importantly, to create and store value referred to as brand equity for the product and company. Names and brands are also used to communicate a product's or company's attributes. A brand name can literally "make or break" a product or brand.

Take the case of *Nova*; General Motors learned this when it named one of its Chevrolet brands *Nova,* which in Spanish means "it doesn't go" (see Kotler, 1994, p. 423). Guess what happened to the brand? It had to be withdrawn from the market as sales were spectacularly poor. After all who would buy an automobile that the maker claims "does not go"? A further example of the power in a corporate name was evidenced in a study conducted by Allegheny Airlines before changing its name to USAir. The executives of the then Allegheny Airlines learned to their surprise from marketing research that most air travelers, "based on name alone, indicated that they would prefer to fly 'USAir,' which was at the time not even in existence, to flying with the existing Allegheny Airlines" (Koku, 1997a; *Wall Street Journal*, 1980).

Psychologists and sociologists have also shown through the study of semiotics and symbology that names and symbols evoke attention and evince desired responses (see Mowen, 1995, pp. 717–719; Solomon, 1992, pp. 58–60) as such corporations are beginning to examine the names they use or have chosen to use. As a result of studies commissioned by companies on names, and structural changes such as mergers and acquisitions, some companies are choosing to rename themselves. What are the effects of these name changes on companies? If the effects are positive can universities also do the same? To answer these questions, we review the literature on corporate and university name change. However, because many corporate name changes implicate signaling theory, we first give a simple overview of signaling theory here.

Signaling Theory

Signaling theory is used to explain behaviors that are aimed at reducing information asymmetry between two parties that can benefit from the reduction (Spence, 1974). Michael Spence, a 2001 Noble Laureate in Economics, succinctly used signaling theory in his work (1973) to explain why potential more productive job applicants in the labor market might distinguish themselves to potential employers through the acquisition of more education. Implicit in the model is the assumption that acquisition of rigorous education is not inexpensive, hence nonproductive potential employee would acquire less of it.

Connelly et al. (2011) provided a review of the theory in an article in the *Journal of Management*. Signaling theory, the authors asserted, is useful for describing behavior in a world of information asymmetry in which parties (individuals or organizations) have access to different levels of information. Typically, the sender who is in possession of insider information must choose whether and how to communicate or send that information (or signal), and the other party, the receiver, the target of the communication must also choose how to interpret the signal.

Instances of signaling in business include situations such as top executives increasing ownership stakes in their firms which communicates the intent with the capital markets that diversification strategies are in the owner's best interests (Goranova et al., 2007). Differently, when a college football coach visits high schools in expensive luxury vehicles that are emblazoned with the university's logo, it is intended to communicate to prospective recruits that the university that is trying to recruit them is resource-rich (Turban & Cable, 2003), and when the leadership of a newly established company in an Initial Public Offering (IPO) stacks their board with a diverse group of prestigious directors, they are probably sending a message to potential investors about the firm's legitimacy (Certo, 2003).

Similar to Connelly et al. (2011), Karasek III and Bryant (2012) also presented a review of the past and the present use of signaling theory and prognosticated on its future. The authors presented how signaling is used in our everyday lives by the way people carry themselves, speak, and interact. They also presented how organizations use signaling in their advertisements, recruiting, and annual reports, and suggested future areas of research using the theory.

Talking further about how signaling is used in everyday life, Martin (2015) showed that even academic disciplines are amenable to name change and that "solid state physics" transitioned to "condensed matter physics" in order to make the subject more acceptable. Whitmarsh (2009) also showed that politicians choose between the terminology "climate change" or "global warming" depending on their political persuasions because studies have shown that "global warming" evokes more concern than "climate change."

Corporate Name Change

There is a long stream of research on corporate name change that investigates the impact of name change on consumers' perception and on the companies' financial performance. Some of the name changes were structural due to mergers and acquisitions while others were strategic rebranding decision or involved the use of signaling theory. How did you receive the news when Facebook, one of the largest social media companies in the world, in the midst of a major controversy sparked by a whistle blower in the United States in October 2021 suddenly announced a name change from Facebook to Metaverse or Meta for short? You can see Paul (2021) and Rodriguez (2021) for detailed discussions.

In one of the earlier studies on strategic name change Horsky and Swyngedouw (1987) suggested that a company's name like the quality of its products or the quality of its technical services is generally closely tied to its image. Therefore, changing a company's name is a major policy decision that may have been contemplated by many companies, even though only some of them may have actually implemented or in other words gone through with a name change.

Because these changes are not inexpensive, Horsky and Swyngedouw (1987) investigated whether changing a company's name can improve its financial performance, and if so what types of firms are likely to benefit from the process. Using a sample of 58 companies – with data obtained from 1981 to 1985 from the Center for Research in Securities Prices (CRSP) tapes – the event study technique, and signaling theory, the authors analyzed the financial performances of the companies after a name change has been implemented. The results of the study showed that most of the firms that undertook the name change performed much better financially after the change relative to before the change, and companies that produced industrial goods were more likely to benefit from the change. The authors used signaling theory to explain their findings and suggested that the name change was to communicate an inside information to the market.

Even though the Internet became a popular means of commerce in the mid-1990s in the midst of the dotcom bubble, no study had investigated the effect of corporate name change in this area of e-commerce during this period. Arguing that much could be learned from investigating corporate name in this area (i.e., name changes involving dotcom), Cooper et al. (2001) investigated the effect of corporate name change on Internet-related dotcom companies using the event study technique. The sample which was selected during 1998 and 1999 consisted of 95 firms.

The results showed that the "dotcom" effect produced approximately 74% cumulative abnormal returns for the ten days surrounding the announcement day. Furthermore, the effect does not appear to be transitory and there was no evidence of a postannouncement negative drift. The authors therefore concluded that a mere association with the Internet seems enough to provide a firm with a large and permanent value appreciation during the dotcom bubble.

Following on Cooper et al. (2001) in studying name change signal in the area of e-commerce, Mavlanova et al. (2012) argued that e-business environment is a prime area of information asymmetry because buyers cannot physically evaluate the quality of products that they buy and are also unable to easily assess the trustworthiness of sellers. Cognizant of this fact, sellers need to communicate product quality through website signals.

Using signaling theory, the authors developed a three-dimensional framework to classify website signals. Cooper and his colleagues empirically tested the framework with a comparative content analysis of websites from a sample of online pharmacies. The results showed that sellers who sold low-quality products were more likely to use easy-to-verify, less costly signals and used fewer signals than do sellers of high-quality products. On the contrary, sellers of high-quality products used costly, difficult-to-verify signals and displayed more signals. These signals provide information to online buyers and regulatory institutions in charge information that could be used to evaluate an online retailer.

Why do you think a high-quality online retailer would use costly signals and what do you think would happen if an online retailer of high-quality products used less costly signals?

Does Every Name Change Work?

Muzellec (2006) asserted that brand names are a fundamental marketing and strategic devices and that two decades previously, a corporate name was simply a trade name that described the industry in which the producer was and a service or a product the seller produced. However, companies' increasing awareness of the importance of corporate reputation has led them to actively treat corporate names as brands instead of merely as trade names. This together with other structural reasons, such as mergers and acquisitions, has led many to change their names. The newly designed corporate names are now intended to evoke a set of core values such as life, competence, unity, vision, and performance. However, this trend towards names that evoke common values as a means to brand the corporations could make it difficult for companies to effectively differentiate themselves from one another, which is the fundamental objective of branding. Thus, the author advises corporate leadership to be cautious with name changes.

"Do consumers care what name a brand possesses?" Alternatively, does a brand name provide equity in its own right? Even though the academic literature generally regards the brand name as central to consumer brand equity, very little research has been conducted to support this assumption. Round and Roper (2010) set out to answer this question using a series of 25 semistructured qualitative interviews which were carried out with consumers to explore the functions performed by brand name for established products and services.

To isolate the brand name element this study focused on global marketing–induced brand name changes. The results of the study indicate that majority of the corporate-led functions do provide brand name equity in their own right, and the concept of consumer brand name equity for established products and services can be justified. Furthermore,

> a material proportion of the equity from a brand name was determined by the consumer and that many consumers had created their own associations for the brand name, positive and negative, independent of and different from those driven by the corporation.
>
> *(Round & Roper, 2010, p. 938)*

Wu (2010) noted that corporate name changes are more common than people think, and that about 30% of companies listed on CRSP tapes have changed their names since 1925. While most of the name changes were the result of structural changes such as mergers and acquisitions, there have been many instances where the name changes occurred without any structural event. What might be precipitating these name changes, one would ask?

In an empirical study consisting of 1,041 name changes that occurred in the absence of any corporate event between 1980 and 2000, Wu (2010) investigated the relation between the different types of corporate name changes, the reputational concerns that precede them, the important corporate events, and performance changes that follow them. The results suggest that generally a firm adopts a radically different name to disassociate itself from a poor reputation, take on the name of a well-recognized brand, change its name to associate with a good reputation, or make a minor change in its name by adding or deleting a part of its name that identifies it with a particular product to accompany a narrower business focus or a broader business focus. The results also showed that, except for radical name changes, significant organizational upheaval follows most corporate name changes. Thus, the strength of the firm's subsequent economic performance is tied to changes in the business direction that the type of name change foreshadows.

Focus on the Services Industry

Koku (1997a) argued that because services are different from manufactured goods, investigating the effect of corporate name change that did not focus on services industry alone must have missed capturing attributes that make the services industry different, hence previous studies of corporate names such as Horsky and Swyngedouw (1987) or Karpoff and Rankine (1994), which did not focus on only services such as banks, suffered from either selection bias or aggregation bias. Having made this argument, Koku (1997a) examined the effect of corporate name change in the services industry only.

To accommodate multiple announcements which are often made together with the name change, the author used trend analysis of Price/Earnings ratios (P/E ratios) instead of the traditional event study technique. The results of the study showed that on average, corporate name change signaling is an effective strategy for firms in the services industry to communicate improved standards or to signal a clean break from the past. Furthermore, the name change effect is larger for companies that made multiple announcements (e.g., made other announcements such as the appointment of a new CEO together with the name change or within a few weeks of the name change). Why do you think using multiple signals seems to lead to bigger name change effect?

Do you think cities and destinations also signal? Yes, they do; while a few may use name change signaling, others may do so by projects that they invest in. In one of the few studies in this area, Zenker and Beckmann (2013) investigated how the city of Hamburg in Germany signaled a change in its image by investing large sums of money in "flagship projects," not only to develop the city as such, but also to change perceptions of the city's brand toward a more desired image. To effect a change, the city of Hamburg invested €575 million to build a new symphony hall (Elbphilharmonie), and €400 million to develop the International Architectural Fair. The city was also considering candidature for the Olympic Games in 2024–2028. To evaluate the success of these expenditures in branding the city, Zenker and Beckmann (2013) employed the improved version of Brand Concept Map approach and an experiment that had a sample size of 209. The results of the study showed that different flagship projects have different image effects for the city brand.

University Name Changes

Koku (1997b) observed that an interesting phenomenon had swept across American university campuses in the 1980s in which many universities changed their names. Examples include Tuskegee Institute, a well-known HBCU in Tuskegee, Alabama, which changed its name Tuskegee University amid a lot of rancor, and the University of Southwestern Louisiana, Lafayette, Louisiana, which changed its name to the University of Louisiana. After reviewing signaling models and the signaling literature in economics and finance, Koku (1997b) suggested that changing a company's name to send a signal and to broaden consumer appeal is a common business practice that was being adopted by universities in the United States in an attempt to increase enrollment numbers.

The author suggested that signaling through name change is an expensive and controversial practice when used by universities. It invariably pits one camp of alums who would like to maintain tradition and keep the old name against another that welcomes the change and sees it as progress. Because the divide amongst alums could negatively impact the university in several ways such as "boosting" the school for recruits and on donations, Koku (1997b) thought the phenomenon was interesting and sought to examine its effect on enrollment figures. Using a sample of 140 schools which changed their names and a type of event analysis technique that considered the name change as an event, the author examined preevent and postevent enrollment figures while checking similar universities that did not change their names. The results according to the author showed that only 7% of the sample enjoyed incremental change in postevent enrollment (significance level at 5% two-tailed test). After explaining why name change alone would not be enough to impact enrollment figures, the author advises university administrators who would use the name strategy for enrollment purposes to be careful.

What Do All These Mean?

The articles reviewed in the previous section, particularly Koku (1997b), show that a university is like a company and its name can be viewed as a brand name. Alternatively, a university can have a collection of brand names, similar to a large automobile manufacturer. Because the leadership of a university could have useful information about the value/quality of the university that outsides may not necessarily have, a university similar to companies can use its name including a name change to signal this private information to its target audiences. However, it must be noted that name change (rebranding) per se does not confer a magical transformation on to a university, instead the name change should come with or accompany the necessary changes otherwise it will be ineffective.

You should by now be asking yourselves what prevents other companies or universities from using name change signaling if advantages are associated by the name changes? Well, implicit in the name change signaling are some realistic assumptions. First, signaling is expensive, so changing a university's or a company's name is not an inexpensive process. Second, there is a cost associated with lying, that is, sending "false" signal or signaling falsely, and this cost outweighs the benefits. Third, multiperiodicity is assumed, that is, based on the fact that every company generally wants to be in business forever, of course, unless they are a fly-by-night company, cheating in one period will be punished during the next period, thus there is no incentive to cheat.

Because in addition to names, logos and symbols are also used to communicate, universities must be careful in choosing their colors, mascots, and logos. Every communication "device" must be used to send the same message otherwise there would be a conflict or contradictions which could create confusion for the target audience.

Summary

This chapter in a way deconstructs a name and suggests that there is more to a name than meets the eye. It reviews the relevant literature on name change in the corporate world and of universities, and of signaling theory and suggests that names, particularly name changes, can be used to communicate or signal inside information to outsiders in a world of information asymmetry. To universities, name changes can be a little more controversial than in the corporate world because some alums might want to keep tradition and retain the old name while some of them might be interested in progress and want a new name. Invariably one party is pitted against the other. Besides evidence from the only study that we are aware of that has examined name change of universities as a strategy to improve enrollment suggested that it is not very effective, nonetheless, the option is there and can be used under the right circumstances, though university leadership must use this option cautiously.

Questions

1. What is signaling?
2. Why would signaling be irrelevant under perfect information?
3. Why can name change be a signal?
4. What is structural name change?
5. Why is a corporate name change less controversial than a university's?
6. Do you think name change signaling works?
7. Name two universities that have change their names and discuss the circumstances surrounding the name change.

References

Bursell, M. (2012). Name Change and Destigmatization among Middle Eastern Immigrants in Sweden. *Ethnic and Racial Studies* 35 (3), 471–487.

Certo, S.T. (2003). Influencing Initial Public Offering Investors with Prestige: Signaling with Board Structures. *Academy of Management Review* 28 (3), 432–446.

Connelly, B.L., Certo, S.T., & Ireland, R.D. (2011). Signaling Theory: A Review and Assessment. *Journal of Management* 37 (1), 39–67.

Cooper, M.J., Dimitrov, O., & Rau P.R. (2001). A Rose.com by Any Other Name. *Journal of Finance* 56 (6), 2371–2388.

Cotton, J.L., O'Neill, B.S., & Griffin, A. (2008). The "Name Game": Affective and Hiring Reactions to First Names. *Journal of Managerial Psychology* 23 (1), 18–39.

Goranova, M., Alessandri, T.M., Brandes, P., & Dharwadkar, R. (2007). Managerial Ownership and Corporate Diversification: A Longitudinal View. *Strategic Management Journal* 28 (3), 211–225.

Horsky, D., & Swyngedouw, P. (1987). Does It Pay to Change Your Company's Name? A Stock Market Perspective. *Marketing Science* 6 (4), 320–335.

Karasek, III, R., & Bryant P. (2012). Signaling Theory: Past, Present, and Future. *Academy of Strategic Management Journal* 11 (1), 91–100.

Karpoff, J.M., & Rankine, G. (1994). In Search of a Signaling Effect: The Wealth Effects of Corporate Name Changes. *Journal of Banking and Finance* 18 (6), 1027–1045.

Koku, P.S. (1997a) Corporate Name Change Signaling in the Services Industry. *Journal of Services Marketing* 11 (6), 392–408.

Koku, P.S. (1997b) What Is in a Name? The Impact of Strategic Name Change on Student Enrollment in Colleges and Universities. *Journal of Marketing for Higher Education* 8 (2), 53–71.

Kotler, P. (1994). *Marketing Management: Analysis, Planning, Implementation, and Control.* Upper Saddle River, NJ: Prentice Hall.

Martin, J.D. (2015). What's in a Name Change? Solid State Physics, Condensed Matter Physics, and Materials Science. *Physics in Perspective* 17 (1), 3–32.

Mavlanova, T., Benbunan-Fich, R., & Koufaris, M. (2012). Signaling Theory and Information Asymmetry in Online Commerce. *Information & Management* 49 (5), 240–247.

Mowen, J.C. (1995). *Consumer Behavior*, 4th ed. Englewoods Cliffs, NJ: Prentice-Hall.

Muzellec, L. (2006). What Is in Name Change? Re-Joycing Corporate Names to Create Corporate Brands. *Corporate Reputation Review* 8 (4), 305–321.

Paul, K. (2021). Facebook Announces Name Change to Meta in Rebranding Effort. www.theguardian.com/technology/2021/oct/28/facebook-name-change-rebrand-meta. October 28, 2021. Retrieved on November 25, 2021.

Rodriguez, S. (2021). Facebook Changes Company Name to Meta. www.cnbc.com/2021/10/28/facebook-changes-company-name-to-meta.html. October 28, 2021. Retrieved on November 25, 2021.

Round, D.J.G., & Roper, S. (2010). Exploring Consumer Brand Name Equity Gaining Insight through the Investigation of Response to Name Change. *European Journal of Marketing* 46 (7/8), 938–951.

Solomon, R.M. (1992). *Consumer Behavior: Buying, Having, and Being.* Boston, MA: Allyn & Bacon.

Spence, M. (1974). Competitive and Optimal Response to Signals: An Analysis of Efficiency and Distribution. *Journal of Economic Theory* 7, 297–332.

Turban, D.B., & Cable, D.M. (2003). Firm Reputation and Applicant Pool Characteristics. *Journal of Organizational Behavior* 24 (6), 733–751

Wall Street Journal (1980). The Name Game. July 7, p. 13.

Whitmarsh. L. (2009). What's in a Name? Commonalities and Differences in Public Understanding of "Climate Change" and "Global Warming." *Public Understanding of Science* 18 (4), 401–420.

Wu, Y. (2010). What's in a Name? What Leads a Firm to Change Its Name and What the New Name Foreshadows. *Journal of Banking & Finance* 34 (6), 1344–1359.

Zenker, S., & Beckmann, S.C. (2013). Measuring Brand Image Effects of Flagship Projects for Place Brands: The Case of Hamburg. *Journal of Brand Management* 20, 642–655.

CASE #17 WHAT'S IN A NAME?

(Based on Tuskegee University, United States)

This case discusses rebranding of Tuskegee Institute with a name change to Tuskegee University. It discusses the controversy that accompanied such a seeming simple act.

Changing one's name to signify a change in one's direction is not new. This practice goes to as far back as the biblical days. The Bible has accounts of Simon having to change his name to Peter when he became a follower of Jesus, and Saul one of the persecutors of Christians changing his name to Paul when he converted to Christianity. Women in many cultures in contemporary society change their maiden names to their husband's name when they get married signal, among other things, their community and other possibly interested suitors that they are no longer available. Even Shakespeare, perhaps unknowingly, stepped into name and name changing "game" when he declared "Rose by any other name would smell just as sweet." But is that really the case? Then why all the fuss about name changes? Perhaps, Shakespeare was not entirely correct because names and symbols seem to matter. They have meanings, they evoke feelings and signify things.

Changing the name of an existing organization is not an inexpensive process. Besides the fractures and controversies that it causes, there are also financial costs that range from thousands of dollars to millions depending on the size of the company. Rebranding which comes with a name change entails several activities such as customer research, brand audit, naming and tagline, corporate stationary, website, brand identity, and logos. Name change of companies is less controversial than name of universities as the latter entails disinvesting a lot of emotions of alumni groups. Against this backdrop, Tuskegee Institute decided to change its name in 1985.

Tuskegee Normal Institute was founded on July 4, 1881, by the State of Alabama's House Bill #165 which authorized the establishment of Negro Normal School in Tuskegee. This bill was championed by one Mr. George Campbell, a former slave owner who was introduced in the Alabama Senate by one Mr. W.F. Foster as a favor to one Lewis Adams, a former slave, tinsmith, and community leader who helped Mr. W.F. Foster's reelection to the Alabama Senate by securing him the support of Black voters in Macon County, Alabama.

With the passage of the bill, $2,000 appropriation, for teachers' salaries, was authorized by the legislation and a board of commissioners was formed to get the school organized. There was no land, building, or teachers, but only state legislation authorizing the school. The board sent word to Hampton Institute in Hampton, Virginia, another school for Blacks, which was looking for a teacher for Tuskegee Institute. That was when Mr. Booker T. Washington was chosen not only to teach, but also to serve as principal. He was the principal of the school from July 4, 1881, until his death in 1915. Initial space and building for the school were provided by Butler Chapel AME Zion Church not far from the school's present site; however, the campus was moved to "a 100-acre abandoned plantation," not far from the school's initial site, which has become the nucleus of the school's present site.

Under Mr. Booker T. Washington, the school attained its institutional independence in 1892. The Alabama Senate again through legislation granted authority to Tuskegee Normal and Industrial Institute to act independent of the state of Alabama, making the school a private institution. Booker T. Washington remained as the head of the institution and led it to prominence amongst Black tertiary institutions which came to be known as Historically Black Colleges and Universities (HBCU) until his death in 1915. He was succeeded by Robert R. Moton as president of Tuskegee from 1915 to 1935. Under Morton's leadership, the schools donated land for the creation of the Tuskegee Veteran's Administration Hospital which was opened in 1923. Robert Moton was succeeded in 1935 by Dr. Frederick D. Patterson who supervised the establishment of the institute's veterinary medicine program. Today, nearly 75% of Black veterinarians in the United States are Tuskegee Institute's graduates.

Dr. Benjamin F. Payton became the fifth president of the school in 1981 and initiated a process to change the name of the institution from Tuskegee Institute to Tuskegee University in 1984. His rationale was to remove ambiguity and signal the stakeholders and the international countries from which the school draws many students that the school was indeed a full-fledged university. It must be noted that in some countries outside the United States, the term "institute" in educational communities is used to refer to polytechnic institution which are not full-fledged universities.

The name change process at Tuskegee Institute, though well-intentioned, generated a lot of controversy and divisiveness amongst its alums. While some factions supported the name change and saw it as "progress" and an act that was long overdue, others called for the dismissal of President Payton, and some even withheld financial and nonfinancial support from the university, until "it was clear that the name Tuskegee Institute would remain," their press release stated. In 1985, the process was completed and the name of the school was officially changed from Tuskegee Institute to Tuskegee University.

Questions

1. Why do some institutions change their name?
2. Are the basic reasons for changing the name of a corporate the same as those for changing the name of a school?
3. Process-wise, which one do you think is easier, corporate name change or changing the name of a university? Why?
4. Do you know any other academic institution that has changed its name? What are the reasons behind the name change?

CASE #18 SIGNALING THROUGH THE HIRING OF A UNIVERSITY PRESIDENT

This case discusses how the hiring of a university president can be used as part of a marketing strategy not only to send a signal to the stakeholders, but also to attract donors.

A president of a university is the chief executive officer of the university and reports to a board of trustees, or a board of directors, or a board of regents, depending on the university's structure. While the hiring process of a president in a public university might differ slightly from that of a private university on issues of transparency and public disclosure of the process, there is no doubt that the president of a university is an important individual in the life of a university, as such due diligence and care must be exercised in hiring one.

As a university's leader, the president is expected to collaborate with a wide range of internal and external stakeholders in defining a clear vision and setting the direction for an institution. The president is expected to operate seamlessly at two levels – at the macro and micro levels. At the macro level, the president serves as the champion of the university's reputation, articulates the strategic goals and messages of the university in order to build broad support for and ownership of the university's aspirations among its many constituents, including faculty, partners, staff, students, alumni, the university's board, the foundation, local communities, government, business, and industry leaders statewide, the media, and the general public.

Furthermore, still at the macro level, the president is expected to lead the institution in the acquisition of resources, focusing particularly on the development and implementation of initiatives to attract new sources of financial support as well as set priorities for future private fundraising campaigns. At the micro level the president is responsible for the development of a comprehensive and responsible budget that would be used to advance the institution's strategic goals and priorities. The president is also responsible for overseeing both human and financial resources in a manner that ensures accountability. The president is expected to be good at change management, be affable and yet firm, and have a good appetite for details and getting results.

Finding a person who embodies all these characteristics is not an easy task. A new university president's previous track records are generally a good indication of the direction in which they will take a university. It will tell the stakeholders whether the incoming president is a consensus builder and yet firm and results orientated. It will tell the stakeholders how good the incoming president is at fundraising or initiating new programs. This is why hiring a new university president can send a useful signal to the university's stakeholders.

The opportunity to hire a new president came up at Hope University, a small university, in 2008, and the board of trustees decided to hire an agency to search for talents. The three previous presidents were locals giving people the mistaken view that being local trumped everything else such as the ability to do the job well. Critics claimed that hiring locally was equivalent to inbreeding. To put a stop to those kinds of unfounded gossips, the search process was made transparent and representatives from all the stakeholders – students, faculty, staff, alums, and the local government served on the search committee.

The CVs of the top four candidates who were asked to make public presentations in the school's auditorium on four separate dates were published at a portal created specifically for the purpose on the school's website. Written comments were invited from the public after each candidate's presentation.

The two top candidates were again invited back to campus for public questions and answers session. The search process ended after 12 months. In the end a Harvard graduate who came thousands of miles away was chosen as president in 2009.

Questions

1. What kinds of signals can a newly hired president send and to whom?
2. Does hiring a new university president present a marketing and branding opportunity?
3. Are the expectations of a university president making it difficult to find one?
4. Are the expectations of a president realistic?

10

THE EDU*SCAPE*

The University Experience

Introduction

Several important innovations have been incorporated in service delivery since 1981 when the servicescape model was introduced, hence it makes sense to update the model to reflect those changes. This chapter reviews the literature on some of the important changes that have been made to the model; it also argues that universities are a part of the services ecosystem and therefore applies the servicescape model to them in what we call the Edu*scape*.

What Is Edu*scape* and How Can It Be Used in University Marketing?

Edu*scape* is a term we coined to describe application of servicescape to universities. Servicescape is a term introduced to services marketing by Booms and Bitner and later popularized by Bitner (1992) with the introduction of servicescape model. Servicescape is referred to as "the environment in which the service is assembled and in which the seller and customer interact, combined with tangible commodities that facilitate performance or communication of the service" (Booms & Bitner, 1981), or the "design of any physical location where customers come to place orders and obtain and obtain service delivery" (Wirtz & Lovelock, 2018).

It can be seen from these definitions that the term servicescape can also be applied to universities as "sellers" or providers of education. The servicescape of a university as with any retailer encompasses the physical structures and surroundings (buildings, parks, lawns, plants, flowers, etc.) and the intangibles (school spirit, ambience, colors, color, décor, etc.). The question we have to answer though here is how can universities market themselves effectively using servicescape? To answer this question, we first review a few of the relevant literature on services.

DOI: 10.4324/9781003160267-10

Application of Servicescape in the Business World – The Hospitality Industry

Wakefield and Blodgett (1996) built on Bitner's (1992) servicescape framework which encompasses customers' behavioral responses such as approach/avoidance, spending money, and repatronage intentions to examine the effects of such features as facility aesthetics, layout accessibility, electronic equipment, seating comfort, and cleanliness on customers' perception of quality of a servicescape in leisure service settings and hypothesized that such features will have a positive effect on customers' perception of quality.

In the results of the analyses based on data from 3,600 consumers in a football setting, 600 from a minor league baseball setting, and 100 each from three different casinos with LISREL VII (Jöreskog & Sörbom, 1990) software showed that the five elements of servicescape investigated had different effects on consumers' perception of quality. For example, electronic equipment and displays had no significant effect on perceived quality in the minor league baseball, but a significant effect on quality perception in the football and casino. Aesthetic appeal of the facility architecture and décor, as well as the facility layout accessibility and cleanliness have a positive effect on the perceived servicescape quality in all three leisure service settings (i.e., baseball, football, and casinos). Furthermore, the study found that seating comfort had a significant effect on perceived servicescape quality in only the two sports settings, but had no effect on quality in the casino setting. On the whole the results of the study suggest that servicescape does have a significant impact on leisure service customers' repatronage intentions and on the length of time they desire to stay in the leisure service.

But does servicescape have any effect on restaurant patronage? Following previous studies such as Foxall and Greenley (1999), Cronin (2003), and Foxall and Yani-de-Soriano (2005) who suggested that servicescape may have strong influence on customers, Harris and Ezeh (2008) sought to conceptualize, operationalize, and test a multidimensional and more social view of servicescape as well as the direct and moderated linkages between servicescape and loyalty intentions.

To accomplish their objectives, Harris and Ezeh (2008) developed a total of 11 hypotheses (9 testing direct effects and 2 testing moderating effects). Data were collected from 271 restaurant patrons in the United Kingdom who were considered eligible and analyzed using the SPSS 12 package for Windows. The results of the analyses support five of the nine hypotheses which posited direct linear relationship between elements of servicescape and consumers' loyalty. The study found no support for relationship between factors such as music, aroma, credibility, competence, and consumer loyalty; however, the authors surmised that the absence of a statistically significant relationship between those four factors and consumer loyalty may have been due to the data aggregation procedure employed in the study.

With regard to moderating effects, music, competence, and credibility which were found to be nonsignificant in their linear relationships with loyalty intentions were found to be significant as moderating factors, and aroma which was initially found to be nonsignificant in direct effects was found to be significant in the total model. For practitioners the results of this study suggest that they could improve consumers' positive intentions to be loyal by carefully and judiciously managing a range of servicescape variables.

Similar to Wakefield and Blodgett (1996), two and a half decades later, scholars continue to apply the servicescape model to different facets of the hospitality industry and address such questions as what is the effect of serviescape on the quality of life of patrons? Lee and Chuang

(2021) noted that it was necessary to reexamine the effects of the various dimensions of servicescape in the hostel industry as the general market environment and consumers' needs in the hotel industry were changing at a rapid pace. For example, the wellness movement showed that customers prefer to stay where they feel happy (Mettler, 2016), while Pine and Gilmore (1998) showed that hotels that used to offer only traditional amenities were quickly undergoing changes in which they refocused on creating distinctive experiences through designing and staging as evidenced in the implementation of biophilic designs to create an environment where customers feel happy and their inner "fulfillments flourish" (Pratt, 2015).

In the midst of all these changes in hotels, Choi and Kandampully (2019) observed that because customers experience various environmental stimuli during their hotel stays, for effective hotel design and management purposes, it is important to assess the overall effect of a hotel and to identify the effect of the various environmental stimuli on guests. Besides delighting guests, hotels do offer a differentiated atmosphere that is intended to create favorable customers' evaluations and employ significant level of environmental cues to distinguish themselves from competitors. However, the effects of these expanded servicescape on customer evaluations have not been well-studied.

To contribute to filling this knowledge gap, Lee and Chuang (2021) investigated the effects of an expanded servicescape on customers' evaluations, including customer satisfaction, quality of life, and customer loyalty, in the context of the hotel industry. Using data from 294 individuals collected online by Qualtrics, the authors developed and tested a number of hypotheses on expanded servicescape elements and quality of life and loyalty. The results of the study showed that all four dimensions of the servicescape positively influenced customer satisfaction; however, only physical and natural dimensions (ambience and fascination) showed positive effects on customers' quality of life. The results further showed that both satisfaction and quality of life enhanced customer loyalty. The authors argued that because providing a distinctive customer experience is critical to fostering customer loyalty, it is important that hotel managers understand how various environmental cues can be used to enhance customer experience and customer loyalty.

How do consumers translate servicescape into quality? Even though servicescape (physical facilities of a service company) has been extensively studied, the effect of servicescape on quality perception has been inadequately captured in previous studies. To fill the research gap, Reimer and Kuehn (2005) conducted a comprehensive examination of the impact of the servicescape on perceived quality using the corrected version of the SERVQUAL scale (see Parasuraman et al., 1988, 1991; Brady et al., 2002) with structural equation modeling to capture the indirect effects. The authors obtained data (n =1,267) from two service industries (banks and restaurants) from the German-speaking part of Switzerland. The results of their analyses were insightful and show that servicescape plays a greater role in customers' perception of quality than shown in the majority of previous studies. In the words of the authors,

> The servicescape is not only a cue for the expected service quality, but also influences customers' evaluations of other factors determining perceived service quality. Thus, the servicescape has a direct and an indirect effect on perceived service quality, which leads the servicescape to have a high overall effect. The results also show that the servicescape is of greater importance in determining customers' evaluations of the expected service quality in a hedonic service compared to a utilitarian service.
>
> *(Reimer & Kuehn, 2005, p. 787)*

The Effect of Servicescape on Employees

While the effect of servicescape on customers is well documented in the literature (Bitner, 1992; Bone et al., 1999) the same cannot be said about the effect of servicescape on employees, leaving one to still ask whether there is any connection between servicescape and employee attitudes and job satisfaction? According to Parish et al. (2008) the answer to this question is yes, based on the review of previous studies in environmental psychology and social interactions (Sundstrom & Sundstrom, 1986; Wineman, 1982; Wall & Berry, 2007). However, Parish et al. (2008) argued that previous studies were limited in scope and did not show the pathways through which servicescape affects the attitudes of employees nor how attitudes generate outcomes that are beneficial to the service firms.

The authors addressed these deficiencies by developing and testing a model that considered the effect of three elements of servicescape (pleasantness, safety, and convenience) on service workers' job stress and job satisfaction and subsequently their commitment to the organization and referral intentions. The model was tested through a quasi-experiment with longitudinal data collected from nurses using the 7-point Likert-type scale. The data were collected in three distinct rounds at different time intervals with sample sizes of 235 (49%), 207 (43%), and 264 (55%) respectively. The results of the analyses show that the physical workplace does have an effect on the service workers (hospital nurses) studied. However, the results are not generalizable because the study was limited to only the nurses in a particular hospital.

Social Servicescape and Cyberscape

The past two decades have witnessed a tremendous growth in consumers' use of the Internet which necessitated the expansion and application of the servicescape model beyond physical space. According to Tombs and McColl-Kennedy (2003), there is considerable evidence that supports the assertion that environmental variables do have substantial influence on consumer behavior in service settings (Baker et al., 1992; Bitner, 1992; Grewal & Baker. 1994). Nevertheless, research seemed to have focused only on the effects of the physical elements ("atmospherics"), ignoring the social aspects (customers and service providers) of the environment. To refocus the direction of research, Tombs and McColl-Kennedy (2003) first reviewed the extant literature in four major streams of research. Can you guess which streams they are? Why did you choose the streams you have chosen?

Well, the streams reviewed by Tombs and McColl-Kennedy (2003) are (1) previous marketing (servicescapes); (2) environmental psychology (approach–avoidance theory, behavior setting theory); (3) social psychology (social facilitation theory); and (4) organizational behavior (affective events theory). On the basis of the literature review, the authors developed a new conceptual model which they referred to as the "Social servicescape." This new model, the authors argued, reflects the social environment and purchase occasions dictated by the desired social density which influences customers' affective and cognitive responses, including repurchase intentions. Tombs and McColl-Kennedy argued further that customers play a key role in influencing the emotions of other customers, either positively or negatively, and to the extent that this largely determines whether some customers intend to return to the service setting requires that this interaction too be reflected in the new model (social servicescape).

However, expanding servicescape to social servicescape still falls short in capturing all the developments that have taken place with the introduction of mega online stores such as Amazon and Ali Baba, and such platforms as Lyft, Uber, Didi, etc. What do you think is missing? Williams and Dargel (2004) carefully reviewed Bitner's (1992) seminal paper on servicescape which posited that the physical surroundings of an establishment can be used to facilitate organizational as well as marketing goals. The authors acknowledged previous attempts by researchers such as Wakefield and Blodgett (1996), Sweeney and Wyber (2002), and Tombs and McColl-Kennedy (2003) to either extend or adapt Bitner's (1992) servicescape model to different settings.

Williams and Dargel (2004) indeed credited Bitner's (1992) model being useful to businesses in general, particularly to services industries because of their unique characteristics to wit "their intangibility and perishability, the inseparability of production and consumption, and heterogeneity in delivery quality," hence e-businesses, whether offering products or services, ultimately share many of the same characteristics of service industries. Some of the similarities according to Williams and Dargel (2004) lie in the fact that the benefits derived by consumers using e-commerce do not reside solely in the products purchased, which could have been purchased anywhere, but rather in the intangible benefits derived from interactions with the websites. Some of these benefits according to Williams and Dargel are saving time, enjoying convenience, and reducing the risk of dissatisfaction and this is made possible with enhanced availability of information on the Internet.

Following these arguments, Williams and Dargel (2004) adapted Bitner's model to incorporate encounters in "cyberspace" where the key characteristics of the service "product" are present using constructs of "flow" from motivational psychology (Csikszentmihalyi, 1975; Hoffman & Novak, 1996; Rettie, 2001). The result of the conceptual model developed by the authors suggests two important points. First, the need to focus the target site's content at a particular group of users in cyberspace. Second, there is also the need to offer vividness to provide depth of sensory information when designing cyberspace. Similar to physical space, Williams and Dargel (2004) concluded, stimuli may be planned and designed in cyberspace to engender approach behavior.

How do you see Williams and Dargel's (2004) arguments and adaption to servicescape being applied to education? Think especially about the era of COVID-19. Does it change when COVID-19 is considered in the mix of things?

Other Adaptations

Rosenbaum and Massiah (2011) proposed an expanded model of servicescape by pointing out the weaknesses in the original servicescape framework proposed by Bitner (1992). According to the authors, the model as conceptualized by Bitner (1992) consisted of only three types of objective, physical, and measurable stimuli which could be controlled "to enhance or constrain employee and customer approach/avoidance decisions and to facilitate or hinder employee/ customer social interaction" (Parish et al., 2008). The environmental stimuli were consolidated into the following three dimensions:

1. Ambient conditions.
2. Spatial layout and functionality.
3. Signs, symbols, and artifacts.

However, according to Rosenbaum and Massiah, Bitner's framework was based on research in environmental psychology (Barker, 1968), which was in turn based on work in ecology which modeled how living organism responds to stimuli in unison (Stokols, 1977; Grayson & McNeil, 2009). However, this model on its own had weaknesses, as such it is not surprising that Bitner's model inherited those weaknesses too.

To rectify this deficiency and to develop the expanded model of servicescape, Rosenbaum and Massiah undertook an extensive review of the literature on a variety of topics on servicescape in marketing and outside marketing. On the basis of the review of literature, the authors suggested that a servicescape does not comprise only objective, measurable, and managerially controllable stimuli, but also subjective, immeasurable, "which are often managerially uncontrollable social, symbolic, and natural stimuli, which all influence customer approach/ avoidance decisions and social interaction behaviors." The authors also suggested that how customers respond to social, symbolic, and natural stimuli are often the "drivers of profound person–place attachments. Thus, government institutions (e.g., schools, hospitals) can improve people's lives by creating natural servicescapes that have restorative potential."

Cosmopolitan Servicescape

What is cosmopolitan servicescape and how does it work? Figueiredo et al. (2021) suggested in their article which appeared in the *Journal of Retailing* that the purpose of cosmopolitan servicescape is to put the ideology of cosmopolitanism into servicescape and to support "cosmopolitan consumers performing their cosmopolitan competence." The authors extended the concept of servicescape through an ethnographic examination of Red Rooster Harlem, a restaurant, which is considered cosmopolitan by providing space to consumers to encounter different cultures through the application of different cultural resources that "shift out in time, place, and identity."

By applying an analytical lens grounded in the cultural understanding of retail spaces to Red Rooster Harlem, the authors showed that "cosmopolitan servicescapes juxtapose cultural resources to create incongruent meanings, promote heteroglossia, and appeal to different levels of cosmopolitan competence." Furthermore, cosmopolitan servicescapes "use decoding cues to facilitate cosmopolitan engagement and recognition cues to frame the environment as cosmopolitan." The authors have by their work contributed to the literature on themed retailing servicescape, a much overlooked niche, by providing retail managers a strategy to attract cosmopolitan consumers.

Servicescape in Universities

It is evident from the review of literature that servicescape model is being adapted and applied to the different facets of services industry, and even though, as we have alluded in the abstract to this chapter, universities are also services, only few studies have focused on applying the servicescape model to universities. One of the few that focused on competition for students in higher education using servicescape was conducted by Theron and Pelser (2017). The authors noted that the landscape of higher education in South Africa, like in other countries around the world, has undergone dramatic changes during the past two decades. Some of the changes in South Africa's system of higher education were caused by a change in the country's governance system (in 1994), the demand for free education, and the emergence of private universities during this period. The universities managed student commitment in a challenging environment which was characterized by poverty, high dropout rate, and high unemployment amongst graduates with a battery of tools.

Theron and Pelser (2017) observed that even though the literature on how universities managed student commitment documented a variety of ways including instructor commitment (Dachner & Saxton, 2015), financial aid (Strauss & Volkwein, 2004), and academic integration (Beck & Milligan, 2014), no study has been done on the other means maintaining students' commitment, such as the role of a university's physical elements (a university's virtual presence and the appearance of a university's infrastructure and signage). To close this research gap, Theron and Pelser set out to investigate the effects of physical element attributes on student commitment. From the existing servicescape literature, the authors identified a number of antecedents of physical elements that could have a possible effect on students' commitment. In addition to the traditional servicescape (Bitner, 1992), the authors incorporated the "social servicescape" (Tombs & McColl-Kennedy, 2003) and the virtual servicescape.

The social servicescape model includes such variables as purchasing occasions (service context), social density (physical elements), displayed emotions of others, customers' affective responses (internal), and customers' cognitive responses (behavioral intent or actual behavior), and the virtual servicescape referred to variously as "cyberscape" (Williams & Dargel, 2004), "e-servicescape" (Hopkins et al., 2009), or "e-scape" (Koering, 2003), with virtual servicescape being defined as "the purposeful design of web environments to generate positive effects in visitors to enhance favourable customer responses" (Dailey, 2004).

Theron and Pelser (2017) analyzed data collected from 290 students from a multicultural South African university. The results of the analysis showed that both physical element dimensions and "virtual servicescape" contribute significantly to influencing the overall student commitment. However, contrary to popular belief, the study revealed that social servicescape did not have a significant impact on student commitment. This study undoubtedly has important implications for the marketing of universities.

The choice of university like any consumption choice is driven primarily by two factors, the rational and the emotional. The rational factors include such considerations as career prospects (Maringe, 2006) and distance from home (Briggs, 2006), while the emotional factors are more subjective and include such factors as the institution's "atmosphere" (Pampaloni, 2010). As a backdrop, we note that a combination of factors such as an increase in tuition and the number of UK students wanting to study abroad have resulted in an increased competition amongst universities in the United Kingdom for students which is also referred to as the marketization of higher education (Gibbs, 2001). These changes brought discussions of students' choice of a university to the fore.

While there have been active discussions on the subjective, emotional, and sociological factors that influence students' choice of a university, only a few studies have conducted in-depth investigation of what constitutes these feelings. Because the provision of university education is a service, albeit a complex service (Hemsley-Brown & Oplatka, 2006), the four key characteristics of services that are present are intangibility, inseparability of production and consumption, heterogeneity, and perishability (Zeithaml et al., 1985). On the basis that the concept of physical servicescape (Bitner, 1992), though frequently applied to retail settings, is equally applicable in a nonretail setting (Rosenbaum & Massiah, 2011), Winter and Chapleo (2017) sought to use the serviescape model to conceptually explore the emotional factors driving students' choice of a university.

The authors conducted in-depth interviews with 24 prospective students who attended university open days at two UK universities. A decision was made to interview only prospective students because they had yet to make a commitment and that elements of a university servicescape could equally trigger avoidance or approach behaviors. To ensure the validity of the data gathered, the authors during the interviews explored participants' reflections and experiences at all open days they had attended, not just the open day when they were recruited.

The results of the study provide an interesting insight into the use of servicescape in the marketing of universities. They show that websites and prospectuses play an important role in creating a significantly positive impression of the university servicescape in encouraging attendance at an open day. However, the written and visual impressions provided by the website and prospectus lose their significance once the prospective student attends the open day, hence the need to "fit in" the actual university environment experienced at the open day. It is interesting to note that participants in the study indicated the "need for a sense of belonging during" the open day as an important driver of their decision-making process. This "self-reference" is consistent with the social and socially symbolic dimensions of the servicescape model adopted. The simple takeaway of this study is that "impressions" do really matter in university marketing.

The Tools of Servicescape in Universities

In addition to the physical structures, also at the disposal of universities are such tools as technology quality of instruction, intramurals clubs, sororities and fraternities, school anthem, school colors and school spirit, competitiveness, logos, and honor code amongst several others. Although it is not our intention to exhaustively discuss how a university would use these tools, we wish to briefly refer the reader to articles we have reviewed that touch on these variables.

Technology: Technology is now incorporated in the servicescape model as argued by Williams and Dargel (2004) and discussed earlier. Universities can therefore actively use their technology not only to recruit prospective students, but to also market the university's brand. This can be done by showcasing the university's technologies both at its website and on its open day activities. This is particularly important to technological universities such as Carnegie Mellon University or the Massachusetts Institute of Technology that stake their "claim to fame" on technology.

Quality of Instruction: This is equivalent to service quality in retailing and plays a very important role in the marketing of universities and in recruiting students. Students could be invited to sit in some classes if they want to, so that they can "sample" instructional quality, if they choose, but more importantly faculty's research and discoveries must be publicized. These can be used as a proxy for teaching quality and the worldview or cosmopolitanism that the university stands for (see Larsen & Bean, 2021).

Intramurals, Sororities, and Fraternities: These can be used by universities to address their social servicescape as discussed by Tombs and McColl-Kennedy (2003).

School Anthem, School Colors: These are a good way of portraying a university as a united front that is collectively engaged in a single mission – spreading knowledge. They can also be used as evidence of school spirit, and the inclusiveness that obtains on campus.

Competitiveness and Honor Code: These are useful in portraying the university as serious in its scholarship. It separates universities that are serious about scholarship from those that are not so serious. It sends subtle messages to prospective students about the academic environment or the seriousness with which academic work is taken.

Logos: They portray more than tradition. Besides serving as a means to distinguish one university from the other, they serve as a symbol of the university's mission in abbreviation. They are used to constantly remind outsiders of what a university stands for.

Summary

This chapter reviews the concept of servicescape introduced by Booms and Bitner (1981) as "the environment in which the service is assembled and in which the seller and customer interact, combined with tangible commodities that facilitate performance or communication of the service" and the several different adaptations of the model to fit several different contexts in the services industry. Because universities are also primarily a service provider we argue that the model applies to them also and coined the term Edu*scape* to refer to the application of servicescape to universities. The chapter also discusses how the concept could be used in the marketing of universities.

Questions

1. What is servicescape?
2. How does the concept apply to marketing universities?
3. How does a university's use of open house fit in the servicescape model?
4. How can a university's anthem be used as marketing variable?
5. Can the presence of fraternities and sororities on campus be used to market a university?
6. How can a university's technology be used to its marketing advantage?
7. How can a university's staff (not faculty) be used to market the university as a part of its Servicescape?

References

Baker, J., Levy, M., & Grewal, D. (1992). An Experimental Approach to Making Retail Store Environmental Decisions. *Journal of Retailing* 68 (4), 445–460.

Barker, R.G. (1968). *Ecological Psychology: Concepts and Methods for Studying the Environment and Human Behavior.* Palo Alto, CA: Stanford University Press.

Beck, H.P., & Milligan, M. (2014). Factors Influencing the Institutional Commitment of Online Students. *The Internet and Higher Education* 20, 51-56.

Bitner, M.J. (1992). Servicescapes: The Impact of Physical Surroundings on Customers and Employees. *Journal of Marketing* 56 (2), 57-71.

Brady, M., Cronin, J., & Brand, R. (2002). Performance-Only Measurement of Service Quality: A Replication and Extension. *Journal of Business Research* 55 (1), 17–31.

Briggs, S. (2006). An Exploratory Study of the Factors Influencing Undergraduate Student Choice: The Case of Higher Education in Scotland. *Studies in Higher Education* 21 (6), 705–722.

Bone, P.F., & Ellen, P.S. (1999). Scents in the Marketplace: Explaining a Fraction of Olfaction. *Journal of Retailing* 75 (2), 243–262.

Booms, B.H., & Bitner, M.J. (1981). Marketing Strategies and Organization Structures for Service Firms. In J. Donnelly & W.R. George (Eds.), *Marketing of Services*, pp. 47–51. Chicago, IL: American Marketing Association.

Choi, H., & Kandampully, J. (2019). The Effect of Atmosphere on Customer Engagement in Upscale Hotels: An Application of SOR Paradigm. *International Journal of Hospitality Management* 77, 40–50.

Cronin, J.J. (2003). Looking Back to See Forward in Services Marketing: Some Ideas to Consider. *Managing Service Quality: An International Journal* 13 (5), 332–337.

Csikszentmihalyi, M. (1975), *Beyond Boredom and Anxiety*. San Francisco, CA: Jossey-Bass.

Dachner, A.M., & Saxton, B.M. (2015). If You Don't Care, Then Why Should I? The Influence of Instructor Commitment on Student Satisfaction and Commitment. *Journal of Management Education* 39 (5), 549-571.

Dailey, L. (2004). Navigational Web Atmospherics: Explaining the Influence of Restrictive Navigation Cues. *Journal of Business Research* 57 (7), 795-803.

Figueiredo, B., Larsen, H.P., & Bean, J. (2021). The Cosmopolitan Servicescape. *Journal of Retailing* 97 (2), 267–287.

Foxall, G.R., & Greenley, G.E. (1999). Consumers' Emotional Responses to Service Environments. *Journal of Business Research* 46 (2), 149–159.

Foxall, G. R., & Yani-de-Soriano, M.M. (2005). Situational Influences on Consumers' Attitudes and Behaviour. *Journal of Business Research* 58 (4), 518–525.

Gibbs, P. (2001). Higher Education as a Market: A Problem or Solution? *Studies in Higher Education* 26 (1), 85–94.

Grayson, R.A.S., & McNeil, L.S. (2009). Using Atmospheric Elements in Service Retailing: Understanding the Bar Environment. *Journal of Services Marketing* 23 (7), 517–527.

Grewal, D., & Baker, J. (1994). Do Retail Store Environmental Factors Affect Customers' Price Acceptability? An Empirical Examination. *International Journal of Research in Marketing* 11 (2), 107–115.

Harris, L.C., & Ezeh, C. (2008). Servicescape and Loyalty Intentions: An Empirical Investigation. *European Journal of Marketing* 42 (3/4), 390–422.

Hemsley-Brown, J., & Oplatka, I. (2006). Universities in a Competitive Marketplace – A Systematic Review of the Literature on Higher Education Marketing. *International Journal of Public Sector Management* 19 (4), 316–338.

Hoffman, D., & Novak, T.P. (1996). Marketing in Hypermedia Computer-Mediated Environments: Conceptual Foundations. *Journal of Marketing* 60 (3), 50–68.

Hopkins, C.D., Grove, S.J., Raymond, M.A., & La Forge, M.C. (2009). Designing the E-Servicescape: Implications for Online Retailers. *Journal of Internet Commerce* 8 (1-2), 23-43.

Jöreskog, K.G., & Sörbom, D. (1990). *LISREL VII: Analysis of Linear Structural Relationships by the Method of Maximum Likelihood: User's Guide*. Mooresville, IN: Scientific Software.

Koering, S.K. (2003). E-scapes: The Electronic Physical Environment and Service Tangibility. *Psychology & Marketing* 20 (2), 151-167.

Lee, S.A., & Chuang, N-K (2021). Applying Expanded Servicescape to the Hotel Industry. *Journal of Hospitality & Tourism Research* 22(2), 213-233.

Maringe, F. (2006). University and Course Choice. Implications for Positioning, Recruitment and Marketing. *International Journal of Educational Management* 20 (6), 466–479.

Mettler, L. (2016). How Hotel Rooms Are Evolving for Today's Wellness Traveler. https:// travel.usnews. com/features/how-hotel-rooms-are-evolving-for-todays-wellness-traveler

Pampaloni, A. (2010). The Influence of Organizational Image on College Selection: What Students Seek in Institutions of Higher Education. *Journal of Marketing for Higher Education* 20(1), 19–48.

Parasuraman, A., Berry, L., & Zeithaml, V. (1991). Refinement and Reassessment of the SERVQUAL Scale. *Journal of Retailing* 67 (4), 420–450.

Parasuraman, A., Zeithaml, V., & Berry, L. (1988). SERVQUAL: A Multiple-Item Scale for Measuring Consumer Perceptions of Service Quality. *Journal of Retailing* 64 (1), 12–40.

Parish, J.T., Berry, L.L., & Lam, S.Y (2008)., The Effect of the Servicescape on Service Workers. *Journal of Service Research* 10 (3), 220–238.

Pine, B., & Gilmore, J. (1998, July–August). Welcome to the Experience Economy. *Harvard Business Review*. https://hbr.org/1998/07/welcome-to-the-experienceeconomy.

Pratt, M. (2015, March 25). 5 Trends Shaping Today's Hospitality Industry. *Building Design + Construction*. www.bdcnetwork.com/blog/5-trends-shaping-todayshospitality- Industry.

Rettie, R. (2001). An Exploration of Flow during Internet Use. *Internet Research: Electronic Networking Applications and Policy* 11 (2), 103–113.

Reimer, A., & Kuehn, R. (2005). The Impact of Servicescape on Quality perception. *European Journal of Marketing* 39 (7/8), 785–808.

Rosenbaum, M.S., & Massiah, C. (2011). An Expanded Servicescape Perspective. *Journal of Service Management* 22 (4), 471–490.

Stokols, D. (1977). Origins and Directions of Environment-Behavioral Research. In D. Stokols (Ed.), *Perspectives on Environment & Behavior*, pp. 5–36. New York: Plenum,

Strauss, L.C., & Volkwein, J.F. (2004). Predictors of Student Commitment at Two-Year and Four-Year Institutions. *Journal of Higher Education* 75 (2), 203-227.

Sundstrom, E., & Sundstrom, M.G. (1986). *Work Places*. Cambridge: Cambridge University Press.

Sweeney, J.C., & Wyber, F. (2002). The Role of Cognitions and Emotions in the Music-Approach-Avoidance Behaviour Relationship. *Journal of Services Marketing* 16 (1), 51–69.

Theron, E., & Pelser, A. (2017). Using Servicescape to Manage Student Commitment towards a Higher Education Institution. *South African Journal of Higher Education* 31 (5), 225-245.

Tombs, A., & McColl-Kennedy, J.R. (2003). Social-Servicescape Conceptual Model. *Marketing Theory* 3 (4), 447-475.

Wakefield, K.L., & Blodgett, J.G. (1996). The Effect of the Servicescape on Customers' Behavioral Intentions in Leisure Service Settings. *Journal of Services Marketing* 10 (6), 45–61

Wall, E.A., & Berry, L.L. (2007). The Combined Effects of the Physical Environment and Employee Behavior on Customer Perception of Restaurant Service Quality. *Cornell Hotel and Restaurant Administration Quarterly* 48 (1), 59–69.

Williams, R., & Dargel, M. (2004). From Servicescape to 'Cyberscape'. *Marketing Intelligence & Planning* 22 (3), 310-320.

Wineman, J.D. (1982). Office Design and Evaluation. *Environment and Behavior* 14 (May), 271–298.

Winter, E., & Chapleo, C. (2017). An Exploration of the Effect of Servicescape on Student Institution Choice in UK Universities. *Journal of Further and Higher Education* 41 (2), 187–200.

Wirtz, J., & Lovelock, C. (2018). *Essentials of Services Marketing*, 3rd ed. Upper Saddle River, NY: Pearson Prentice Hall.

Zeithaml, V., Parasuraman, A., & Berry, L. (1985). Problems and Strategies in Services Marketing. *Journal of Marketing* 49 (2), 33–46.

CASE #19 FUN AND ACADEMICS ARE NOT INCOMPATIBLE

This case discusses the extent to which a university goes to create a distinctive ambience on campus for learning.

Universities of the olden days had a reputation for being cold, austere, and rigorous. The university catalogs contained black and white pictures of libraries and classrooms with chalkboards partially revealing a formidable looking mathematical equation. If there were pictures of students in the catalog, they were either in the libraries with books or in classrooms with lecturers in front of the class teaching. Such was the impression that universities wanted to create. Is that still the case? What has changed?

The situation is now much different. There are hardly any catalogs to speak of these days, instead all the information that potential students need on a university are available at the university's website, and instead of austere pictures that forebode mental discipline, pictures at the website show students having fun. They could be playing Golf Frisbee or Volley Ball in the sand. If the pictures should people in the library or in a science lab, they are shown smiling and seemed to be (actually) having fun studying. Colleges/universities are now prepared to show that they are about balance; while it is important to take one's classes seriously, it is equally necessary to let down one's hair and have fun during one's undergraduate years.

So what has changed? In a response to this question, one commentator said that "deregulation has happened." In the current environment, governments all over the world are cutting back on their appropriations for public universities and are asking the universities to make up the shortfall on their own. Furthermore, private universities are now allowed to operate in countries (particularly in emerging countries) where until recently only the government could run a university. Public universities are encouraged to come up with programs for which they could charge the so-called "market rate." These have resulted in an environment where universities have to compete amongst themselves for students. As a result of these competitions, schools are no longer afraid to show that a campus is just not strictly for learning, and even having some fun while learning could be a good thing. Schools can now proudly feature the dual principle of "work hard, play hard" mentality that many students seek. Some of the fun activities such robotic competition in which students build robots to undertake the most complicated maneuvers within five minutes or the three-minute dissertation competition could also be fun.

"So, a university campus could be mistaken for Club Med," commented an observer, "and the residence halls look like hotels," he continued. At Hope University, to make up for the shortfall in funds from the government which it needs to construct new residential facilities, the university entered into an income-sharing partnership with a private real estate development company to build the facilities and collect a percentage of the revenue that would be generated thereof for the next 30 years. Moreover, competition for students makes the schools compete with each other to show who is more student-friendly or whose facilities are more student-oriented. The well-manicured lawns and endless list of cultural and extra curricula activities are all part of the package in creating an ambience that is welcoming and study-friendly. It is therefore not surprising when Hope University states on its website that it is "Five minutes as the crow flies from the beach"!

Questions

1. What has caused the change in how universities project themselves?
2. Would advertised fun on campus sway you to choose a university over the other?
3. Can students have fun when learning also?
4. What is the marketing and branding lesson in all this?

CASE #20 THE COLLEGE MARCHING BAND (SOUTHERN UNIVERSITY AND A & M COLLEGE, UNITED STATES)

To create a unique school spirit, some universities developed award-winning marching bands which perform at the school's football games and at other major activities. This case discusses "The Human Jukebox," the award-winning marching band at a small HBCU in Louisiana.

There are very few occasions in a university's life in the United States when school spirit is displayed beyond what is shown at football games. School spirit is the sense of identity and community shared by members of an educational institution be it elementary schools, high schools, community colleges, or universities. Members of an educational institution often manifest spirit in the exhibition of school colors, in dress and decoration, in attendance at athletic events, or at graduation ceremonies. School spirit is displayed verbally in the form of chants, cheers, or songs, and visually through schools' marching bands and school mascots.

While some schools use the school's choir, chorale, or marching band as goodwill ambassadors, for HBCUs, school spirit is fiercely portrayed through their marching band. In fact, so integral is the marching band intertwined with their school spirit that there is even an annual marching band contest organized amongst them for the bragging rights of being judged the best HBCU marching band of the year. However, contest between marching bands is not limited to HBCUs alone; in fact, marching band contests are held every year amongst high schools and universities at regional and national levels. Besides serving as school's goodwill ambassadors, many marching bands perform at pep rallies, during football games and during half-time breaks at football games.

Being a member of a school's marching band comes with its rewards and sacrifices. It gives members more than in-classroom school learning experience. Marching band members get the opportunity to develop important leadership skills and discipline. They learn and exercise uniformity of both musical and visual performance, carriage, bearing, style, focus, and relying on each other. Perhaps, the most important lesson in being a marching band member in college is in time management as a lot of time is invested in rehearsals and preparations.

The marching band of Southern University and A & M College (known for short as Southern University) in the city of Baton Rouge in the State of Louisiana in the United States is legendary in its right. Southern University was founded in 1880 as a public historically black land-grant university, and Southern University's marching band was formed in 1947 by Mr. T. Leroy Davis who continued to serve as the band's director from its inception until 1964. Mr. Davis was credited for helping organize the first Southern University Band Festival and Band Day and was well-known for his contributions and achievements in the world of music.

So legendary are the talent and performances of the Southern University's marching band that it has been nicknamed the "Human Jukebox." The band has been recognized for its powerful sound, soulful arrangements, extensive song catalog, and entertaining showmanship, and has been consistently recognized as one of the best marching bands in the nation by *USA Today*, NCAA, ESPN, and *Time*. In addition to having been invited, thus far, to perform at perform at four presidential inaugurations (first at President Ronald Reagan's in 1981, followed by President Bill Clinton's inaugurations in both 1993 and 1997, and in President Biden's in 2021), the band was one of the 20 bands from all over the world (from such countries as Denmark, Costa Rica, Mexico, and Japan) invited to perform at the 131st Rose Parade in Pasadena, California. The band has also performed in movies and in a Superbowl half-time performance.

While there is no doubt that the band teaches its members incredible discipline, a marching band in other schools, for example, Florida A & M, a rival HBCU school, have been rocked by scandals associated with initiation hazing. In the case of Florida A&M, a student died in a 2011 incident which led to criminal cases against some of the band members. However, the Human Jukebox continues marching on (visit https://tournament ofroses.com/events/about-rose-parade/#participants to discover more about each band).

Questions

1. Does a university's marching band play any valuable marketing role?
2. What role does school spirit play in university marketing?
3. Should marching band members be rewarded for their role and time?
4. How does a marching band serve as a school's goodwill ambassador?

11

INTERNATIONALIZATION OF UNIVERSITIES

Introduction

Internationalization of higher education is a concept or an idea that has gained currency in the world of higher education, especially in the midst of a move to privatize or deregulate higher education. But what does internationalization of higher education actually mean? As it turns out, the term seems to mean different things to different people in different countries or context. This chapter reviews the concept and the literature from different parts of the world on what internationalization of higher education means. The chapter draws the reader's attention to marketing opportunities that internationalization of higher education can mean to different universities.

Internationalization of Higher Education

What does internalization of higher education or university mean? Why internationalize, what are the costs and benefits associated with internationalization? How can a university use internationalization to market itself? These are a few of several important questions that the various stakeholders of internationalization of universities ask. We will, in this chapter, answer these and other questions using a few of the many published papers and books on the subject.

The internationalization of higher education was defined by Knight (2004) as "the process of integrating an international, intercultural or global dimension into the purpose, functions or delivery of post-secondary education" (cited in Bucker & Stein, 2020). However, the phrase "internationalization of higher education," as later observed by Knight (2014), has become commonplace and is used to "describe anything and everything remotely linked to the global, intercultural or international dimensions of higher education and is thus losing its way" (p. 76).

Bartell (2003) without actually defining what internationalization of higher education means noted that universities worldwide have been under intense pressure from several quarters to adapt to the unprecedented postindustrial environmental changes that are taking place in the social, technological, economic, and political arenas. Even though calls for universities to adapt to the changing environments seem to be coming from disparate sources

DOI: 10.4324/9781003160267-11

(see Readings, 1996; Sporn, 1999; Ellingboe 1998 cited in Bartell, 2003) there seems to be an agreement that universities also need to change (Mittelman, 1996; Skolnikoff, 1994; Marsella, 2001). What is a logical way through which this change could be implemented with the least disruption? To offer guidance, Bartell (2003) investigated the process of internationalization of universities and draws on Sporn's (1996) organizational culture typology to develop a framework that the author hoped would assist in the process of internationalization of universities.

According to Bartell (2003) internationalization of universities is akin to an organizational adaptation process that "requires its articulation by the leadership while simultaneously institutionalizing a strategic planning process that is representative and participative in that it recognizes and utilizes the power of the culture within which it occurs." Furthermore, both the collegial process and executive authority are necessary for a university to bring about substantive, integrated, university-wide internationalization that is needed. Bartell used examples from cross-disciplinary global clusters and dual degree programs, including the required study abroad component that some universities have instituted as an "indication of the attention given to the relationship between the institution's culture and the strategy to advance the internationalization process." Furthermore, Bartell argued that for the process to move smoothly, it would require the identification and understanding of the variety of approaches to internationalization of universities in relation to their external environments, the internal cultures, and the functioning structures. Putting all these factors together in a framework, Bartell (2003), similar to Hayden et al. (2000) and Wiley (2001), called for a flexible approach to an internationalization process that will work well for all the stakeholders.

Similar to Bartell (2003) but from a slightly different angle, Qiang (2003) observed that higher education has become a real part of the globalization process of "cross-border matching of supply and demand," and as a result, higher education can no longer be viewed in a strictly national context. On the basis of this observation, Qiang calls for a broader definition of internationalization to "embrace the entire functioning of higher education and not merely a dimension or aspect of it, or the actions of some individuals who are part of it." On the basis of this argument, Qiang unlike Bartell (2003) provided the meaning and definition of the term as well as a conceptual and organizational framework of internationalization of higher education.

According to Qiang (2003) while there are many convincing arguments for the internationalization of higher education, the two primary arguments are: (1) The fact that academic and professional requirement for graduates, these days, reflect the demands of globalized economies and societies, higher education must provide the requisite preparations, academic and otherwise, and these include, but are not limited to, multilingualism and social and intercultural skills and attitudes. Furthermore, the level of specialization in research and the size of the minimum investments that are required in certain fields of research and development require collaborative efforts and intensive international cooperation. (2) International students have become a significant source of institutional revenue and national economic interest. Furthermore, the engagement of new information and communication technologies in the delivery of education and the involvement of private enterprises in this area have blurred national borders and the role of national governments in education.

Hence, because of its complexity, different entities have attached different meanings to the term internationalization. To some, it is an "aim itself," while to many entities and in many other settings, it is viewed as a means to achieve a wider goal, for example, quality improvement, and restructuring and upgrading of higher education systems and services (Van der Wende, 1997). Even though it is clear from interpretations that the "key element in the term is the notion of between or among nations and cultural identities," the different interpretations of the term have led to different approaches to its implementations. Qiang (2003), upon a careful review of the literature, identified four main approaches to internationalization, namely the activity approach, competency approach, ethos approach, and the process approach.

The Activity approach advances activities such as curriculum and pedagogy, student/faculty exchange, technical assistance, and exchange of international students.

The Competency approach emphasizes the development of skills, knowledge, attitudes, delivery, and values in students, faculty, and staff.

The Ethos approach emphasizes creating a culture or climate that values and supports international/intercultural perspectives, the presence of diverse viewpoints, and initiatives.

The Process approach stresses integration or infusion of an international/intercultural dimension into teaching, research, and service through a combination of a wide range of activities, services policies, and procedures.

Qiang also identified four separate rationales which are used to support the different approaches, and three main stakeholders of the internationalization process. The four rationales are the political rationale, the economic rationale, the academic rationale, and the cultural and social rationale.

The political rationale according to Qiang "relates to issues concerning the country's position and role as a nation in the world, e.g. security, stability and peace, ideological influence, etc."

The economic rationale refers to

> objectives related to either the long-term economic effects, where internationalization of higher education is seen as a contribution to the skilled human resources needed for international competitiveness of the nation, and where foreign graduates are seen as keys to the country's trade relations, or the direct economic benefits, e.g. institutional income and net economic effect of foreign students, etc.

The academic rationale "includes objectives related to the aims and functions of higher education."

The cultural and social rationale "concentrate on the role and place of the country's own culture and language and on the importance of understanding foreign languages and culture."

The three stakeholder groups identified by Qiang (2003) are the government sector, the education sector, and the private sector. The author uses the approaches, the rationales, and the stakeholder groups identified to develop a holistic framework of internalization that recognizes the fact that internationalization polices are based on a mixture of rationales that affect country and situational contexts. In the end the Qiang surmised that internationalization is not linear, but a cyclical process that needs reinforcement and reward which will lead to a renewed "awareness and commitment."

Mok (2007), on the one hand, argues that the rise in the knowledge economy which has generated new global infrastructures such as information technology has played a major role in information technology's rise to prominence. For its part, information technology has changed not only the socioeconomic context that has resulted from globalized economy, but has also the nature of knowledge, its acquisition, and research. Information technology is also restructuring higher education and its reach.

Critically reflecting on education reforms in Asia that resulted from globalization, Mok (2007) discusses the changing university governance models and the strategies that higher education systems in Asia have adopted in making themselves more globally and internationally competitive. The author also discusses issues and problems that have resulted from internationalization of universities in Asia, particularly when Asian societies primarily follow wholesale the Anglo-Saxon paradigm when internationalizing their universities.

In terms of problems, Mok (2007) suggests that educational restructuring and reforms that were taking place in Asia were significantly influenced by the Western public management–oriented doctrines and neoliberalist ideologies and practices. Furthermore, even though Mock accepted the proposition that Europe and the United States are more advanced than their Asian counterparts as far as "higher education institutions in general and academics in particular" are concerned, he suggests that careful thoughts be given to issues such as the extent and ways that good practices "borrowed" from the West "could really integrate well" into the educational systems in Asian countries.

Mock concludes that Asian countries that are engaged in the internationalization of their education systems must appreciate the importance of mutual understanding and respect for their own "cultures and traditions and develop, reinvent, and promote our systems to enable others to understand, master, and appreciate diversities of cultures and traditions." Then they can have a genuine knowledge reproduction. Furthermore, Asian countries must commit themselves to developing alternative academic paradigms for promoting cross-cultural understanding and cross-national policy learning which internalization entails.

Bucker and Stein (2020) observed that Knight (2014) did not call for the redefinition of the term "internationalization of education"; however, he called for a reconsideration of the fundamental values upon which the definition stood. A similar point was also made by de Wit (2014). So, what does internationalization of higher education actually mean? To answer this question, Bucker and Stein (2020), almost two decades after Bartell (2003), examined the definitions offered by three leading higher education professional associations, National Association for Foreign Student Advisers (NAFSA), the International Association of Universities (IAU), and the European Association of International Education (EAIE) using critical discourse analysis of dominant discourses around internationalization. The approach used by Bucker and Stein is generally used by scholars to de-naturalize the assumptions and ideas in discourses where a discourse refers to how language is used "to define, categorize, and explain our social world, becoming the basis for establishing identities, justifying action, and creating social structures" (Chabbott, 2003). The use of discourse as observed by other scholars creates truths that are used not only to explain "the social world," but also to create reality (Foucault, 1980).

The results of the analyses showed that all three major associations rely on similar definitions that emphasize international students, student and scholarly mobility, and curricular exchange. Interestingly, these definitions give little attention to "the ethics of international engagement, particularly across unequal relations of power." The authors therefore concluded by posing numerous questions that administrators and faculty who are engaged in internationalization should consider in order to elicit deep conversations about what internationalization of higher education means particularly with regard to global inequality, ethical responsibilities, and enabling alternative possibilities.

The Globalist, Internationalist, and Translocalist Models of Internationalization

Reviewing the history of internationalization of education, Chan and Dimmock (2008) observed that while the term internationalization was not new, its use in education system, however, was relatively new. Reviewing the history of the use of the term in the education system, the authors noted that the term "international education" was generally used in pre-1980 years and is still being used in the United States (de Wit, 2002). Even though the term "international education" refers to an academic discipline involving the comparative study of educational systems around the world in the context of the field of "comparative education" (Cambridge & Thompson, 2004), it is more generally used in the internationalization of education to refer to "international characteristics" such as "international-mindedness and open-mindedness, second language competence, flexibility of thinking, tolerance and respect for others" that are desirable in a global economy and therefore taught to students (Hayden et al., 2000; Wiley, 2001).

Evidenced in organizations such as the Fulbright and Institute of International Education (IIE) programs in the United States, international education is viewed to a certain degree and promoted as a beneficial tool to achieve mutual understanding and peace among nations (Knight, 1997). However, the term international education has also been used to denote education delivered across national borders by international schools which may or may not promote multicultural education (Cambridge & Thompson, 2004). It now appears that universities worldwide are adopting strategies of internationalization in pursuit of competitive advantage locally and internally. However, the real motives behind internationalization and how universities go about the internalization process remain unclear. So, what do you think internalization of higher education means?

To shed more light the real motives behind internationalization and how universities go about the internalization, Chan and Dimmock (2008) conducted two case studies: one was conducted in the United Kingdom while the other was conducted in Hong Kong. The authors noted that by 2008, the term "internationalization" was liberally used by universities that had international aspirations of one form or the other. Because the liberal use of the term shows that the concept was undefined at the time, it was shaped and differentiated by institutional, national, and international contexts in which it was used. Delving more into the concept and its meaning for higher educational institutions, the authors proposed the use of two models, "internationalist," "translocalist," and a third model "globalist" which is a hypothetical model in their case studies.

According to Chan and Dimmock (2008), the internationalist model of internationalization accepts the "old internationalization" or "archaic universalism" of the earliest universities as described by Scott (1998), which Cambridge and Thompson (2004) referred to as "founded upon international relations with aspirations for the promotion of peace and understanding between nations" (p. 173). The translocalist model embraces a more nationalistic view of internationalizing. It acknowledges the importance of internationalization of education; however, "the role and position of the institution within the home country or motherland is placed on a higher plane" (Chan & Dimmock, 2008, p. 201). On the contrary, according to the authors' hypothesis, globalist model is

> based on more unilateral benefits of national or institutional self- interests. It describes some international schools and possibly higher education institutions offering

transplanted national education while eschewing intercultural understanding, open-mindedness, or mutually beneficial international and inter-institutional cooperation.

(Chan & Dimmock, 2008, p. 201)

With these interpretations, Chan and Dimmock (2008) concluded based on their case studies that none of the three models of internationalization in reality fits "the crux of university internationalization well and that three models capture different aspects of realities of the importance of international, national and institutional contexts, as well as available opportunities and parameters of choice in decisions relating to internationalization." In reality, the three models overlap.

Paradoxes and Responsibilities of Internationalization

Similar to other researchers on internationalization (Cambridge & Thompson, 2004; Chan & Dimmock, 2008), Kubota (2009) observed that many universities around the world are engaged in internationalization efforts as globalization advances. However, according to American Council on Education's (ACE) 2008 report on "Mapping Internationalization on US Campuses" (Green et al., 2008), internationalization still remained a low priority in many US universities as of 2008. Drawing on his own experiences in teaching in two universities (one in the United States and the other in Canada), Kubota (2009) observed that in spite of the ACE report, internationalization was a major initiative that was being implemented through academic integration of global issues and used to raise a university's international profile by increasing international student enrollment.

Kubota (2009) also noted that an integral aspect of internationalizing of higher education is developing language and cultural competency, and even though the benchmarks in ACE's report for measuring internationalization include measures for academic offerings which entailed "questions related to foreign language learning, such as whether a foreign language is required for admissions and graduation, how many foreign languages are offered, and whether academic credits are granted for study abroad," there was no question that dealt with the extent to which academic support was provided to international students according to their linguistic and cultural needs. Thus, insufficient attention to academic English to support international students whose first language was not English which was not only witnessed by the author in the universities in which he taught but also evidenced in the absence of a question on language support in the ACE's report, Kubota (2009) argues

signifies the paradoxes of the current internationalization initiatives that are heavily influenced by market-driven neoliberal and neocolonial politics supporting free trade in services, competition, and Anglo dominance of language, culture, and academic knowledge, which ultimately hinders the development of translingual and transcultural competency in foreign languages for English-speaking students promoted by the 2007 report by the Modern Language Association.

(MLA Ad hoc Committee on Foreign Languages, 2007; Kubota, 2009, p. 612)

Discussing the paradoxes and responsibilities posed to foreign language professionals by the gap in internationalization efforts, the author examines two critical questions regarding internalization. First, why is there a need to internationalize higher education, and second how have the current internalization initiatives come into being? In answering these questions, Kubota (2009) concludes that fostering "translingual and transcultural competence" is part and parcel of the academic and social/cultural dimensions of internationalization, hence equal weights must be given to those as they are being given economic and political rationales.

Given this background, we now review internationalization of higher education as viewed in the literature in different parts of the world.

Views on Internationalization of Education from Other Developed Countries

(Views from Portugal)

How do scholars from other countries view internationalization of higher education? As noted, the role of higher educational institutions as producers and diffusers of knowledge through formal learning processes has never been more important worldwide as the economies around the world are undergoing transformational changes. However, these global economic changes are also changing higher educational systems around the world. One of the common changes is the transition from elite education systems to mass education systems (Neave, 1996). This transition has also brought a substantial financial burden to the already strained public budget in many countries and states; as a result, the relationship between the state and higher educational institutions has shifted – the direct state-controlled coordination in many countries has been replaced by a more recurrent state-supervised coordination (Neave, 1996). Most "state universities" are now being granted fairly high degrees of autonomy in which they are being asked to be more "responsive, accountable and proactive" (Horta & Vaccaro, 2008). As observed by McGuiness (2002), with the mediation of governments, markets have become the primary driving force behind innovations and entrepreneurial activities in universities worldwide.

Against this backdrop Horta (2010) analyzed the role of the state in the internationalization of national prominent universities in a "catching-up country," specifically Portugal. By examining the changes that have taken place in the higher educational system, going to as far back 60 years, the author took a longitudinal analytical approach, looking at the importance of state-led science and higher education internationalization initiatives in Portuguese universities. Horta noted that globalization or the participation of most prominent Portuguese universities in the global framework brought its challenges. For example, most of the universities thrusted onto the global stage suddenly "realized that their undisputed dominance in the national higher education system was minimized in the global higher education system" (Marginson, 2006). Thus Horta's (2010) objective was to discuss the appropriate approach to internationalizing universities in "catching-up countries" such as Portugal, that is, whether Portugal or any other "catching-up country"

> should be merely preparing national universities to compete globally by fostering institutional competitiveness at national level, typical modus operandi of a state supervision model – or whether further public policies and funding are necessary to integrate and better prepare these universities to compete and cooperate at global level?
>
> *(Horta, 2010, p. 64)*

From the analyses, the author concludes that the state has an important role to play in the internationalization process of universities. This role can be played in several ways, by supporting the "build-up of institutional knowledge capacity" and by rewarding internationally oriented scholarly activities. Even though the author could not identify any university that emerged to national prominence that could compete with globally ranked research universities as a result of implementing these public policies, nonetheless Horta (2010) deems the implementation of such policies as useful for the true internationalization and integration of the Portuguese universities in the global higher education system.

Views from Germany

Wahlers (2018) reviews the internationalization of universities in Germany which he notes has been in practice since World War II. Wahlers observed that the concept of internationalization at German universities, which has resurged since the late 1980s, has historically been based on the idea of cooperation and partnership which emerged post-1945. This idea is based on the belief that only a Germany that was firmly rooted in Europe and the world could be internationally accepted and economically successful. Therefore, in Germany, the political support for the exchange of students and researchers embedded in international university partnerships is rather strong. This unwavering political support in the 1990s led to several binational initiatives including the Franco–German University and the Sino–German College for Graduate Studies which are both predicated on trust-based cooperation for the purpose of promoting cultural exchange and understanding between peoples.

Wahlers (2018) stated that the education programs of the European Union which require the full integration of student mobility into regular study programs have provided additional impetus for cooperation between universities and internationalization of universities. However, the "normal" competition between universities within the system in Germany has intensified the effects of globalization and has led to more domestic competition instead of cooperative approach. Ironically, it was the same European dimension which provided the impetus for a global competitive approach, especially when European education ministers in 1998 established the goal of "creating a competitive and internationally attractive European Higher Education Area aiming to gain a sizeable share in an expanding worldwide market of globally mobile students and researchers."

Competition to attract international students to German universities has been very successful. From 158,000 in 1997, the international student population increased to approximately 358,000 in 2017 (about 12% of all students). Success in attracting international students to Germany has created its own problems though. Because the students generally have to take preparatory language and content courses together with other ongoing support, having international students entails more than financial expenses. However, the presence of international students in Germany offers valuable contributions to the host country in achieving a truly "international classroom" in the universities. The question is which way should Germany take, with concerns over the increasing cost of having international students, and yet recognizing the contributions of having international students in the country? Already, the newly elected state government in North Rhine–Westphalia, Germany's most populous state, has announced its intention to introduce tuition fees for students from countries outside the European Union. Under the proposed arrangement the universities will only keep 20% of the fees collected and forward the remaining 80% to the government. Whether this will be acceptable or workable is yet to be seen.

Views from the United States

With Wahlers (2018) commenting on the "German way of Internationalization," it is only a matter of time before one starts asking about the state of affairs of internationalization in American university also, as the United States is one of the leading proponents of internationalization of universities.

Brajkovic and Helms (2018) indirectly answered this question by analyzing the 2016 Mapping Report published by the ACE's Center for Internationalization and Global Engagement's (CIGE). The CIGE's report which is published every five years evaluates the current state of internationalization at American colleges and universities. It analyzes progress and trends and identifies future priorities. The six key areas which comprise the CIGE's Model for Comprehensive Internationalization are as follows:

- Articulated commitment.
- Administrative structures and staffing.
- Curriculum, "cocurriculum," and learning outcomes.
- Faculty policies and practices.
- Student mobility.
- Collaboration and partnerships.

According to Brajkovic and Helms' (2018) analyses, the CIGE's report was mixed. It showed that gains have been made in certain areas while progress was slow in others. Such areas as institutional support for internationalization in terms of both administrative structures and staffing and financial resources experienced gains. Similarly, articulated commitment to internationalization in mission statements and strategic plans which were supported by specific policies and programming that operationalize broad ideals were more common than in the previous five years. Furthermore, the report indicated that the greatest gains seemed to be made by two-year institutions, while doctoral granting institutions seem to have plateaued on some aspects of internationalization. The results also show that for many institutions, "internationalization efforts are still focused first and foremost on the external; student mobility in both directions and international partnerships," while on-campus internationalization efforts are viewed as less important. Interesting, only about one-half of the institutions have reported active efforts toward curriculum internationalization. Furthermore, progress seemed to have slowed in American institutions with regard to faculty policies and support; recognition of faculty contributions to internationalization needs to be revamped in order to expedite things in these areas, observed the authors. What is your view on Brajkovic and Helms' (2018) assessment?

Views from Developing Countries

Most scholars trace the current phenomenon of internalization of universities to around three to four decades ago. However, Mohsin and Zaman (2014) in an interesting paper in which they review the history of internationalization of higher education traced the practice to as far back as 445 BC when the Sophists were itinerant teachers (Welch, 1997). Nonetheless, Mohsin and Zaman (2014) agreed with other scholars that the modern-day phenomenon of internationalization of higher education seemed to have taken root in the early 1990s under different terminologies such as student exchange programs, study abroad programs, etc. (Marden & Engerman, 1992).

The authors argued that with globalization, every research university has become part of a worldwide network, as such internationalization has become a major strategic priority for universities that want to internalize their institutions and connect their organizations, students, and their faculty to a world that has become globalized. A survey of the leaders of 115-member universities of the IAU conducted in 2010 cited by the authors revealed that the vast majority of the leaders believed that internationalization is of utmost importance, and the number of higher education institutions that have moved from an ad hoc to a planned approach toward internationalization has increased.

However, internationalization of universities within the context of their local environments is a complex issue that requires a methodical approach. Hence studies such as those conducted at the Center of Studies of Higher Education (CSHE) at Nagoya University (Japan) that are studying this issue in the Japanese university context and Queen's University (Canada) that developed "Critical Perspectives in Cultural and Policy Studies" project in 2004 to foster international collaboration among international collaboration among researchers, teachers, and students are going to play useful roles.

Mohsin and Zaman (2014) conclude that internationalization is no longer being considered solely as "the international mobility of students and teachers; rather, this process is now acknowledged as an important component of higher education policy at both the institutional and the national level." Despite the positive consequences, internationalization does have several challenges that prevent the attempts of several institutions, particularly in developing countries to become truly global institutions. According to the authors it would take several steps such as an institutional commitment, administrative structure, and planning and strategies to face the challenges of internationalization. This being the case, many universities are unable to become global institutions because of the academic and economic barriers that they cannot by themselves remove. Thus, assistance from the governments in developing countries is necessary.

Abbas et al. (2015) who also reside and teach in universities in developing countries tried to capture the perspective of academics who live and teach in universities in those countries of internationalization of higher education in their 2015 piece. As with other researchers on the topic, the authors observed that internationalization of universities has increased significantly in to scope, volume, and complexity during the past two decades, but viewed as a worthwhile endeavor that is beneficial for students, universities, and other stakeholders. Abbas and his colleagues attributed the reason many universities have embraced internationalization to the desire to increase their range and functions partly to meet the need for the universities to become competitive on a global scale and to increase their revenue (Henkel, 2005). Viewing the operations of universities in developing countries through a complex web of forces of globalization, internationalization of universities, the impact of World Trade Organization's (WTO) control over higher education, and the assurance of quality standards for high ratings, the authors presented the challenges, opportunities, and threats faced by the higher education sector in a developing country such as Pakistan.

Abbas et al. (2015) noted that in the context of Pakistan, internationalization of higher education amongst other things has transformed the landscape of higher education in which education appears to no longer as a public good, but as a product that can be bought and sold like other products in the market. The result of this is the increase in the number of private universities in Pakistan form 22 in 2000–2001 to 69 in 2013–2014, an increase of 47 (over 200%) in 13 years. While this change makes university education more easily accessible to many, meeting the quality assurance requirements for the QS (world) ranking which includes meeting the following seven required criteria at varying levels poses a challenge to many institutions in developing countries:

- International faculty.
- International research collaborations.
- International scholars.
- International scholar support.
- Inbound exchange students.
- Outbound exchange students.
- Transnational diversity.

According to the authors, even though meeting these challenges is hard, they represent opportunities for universities in developing countries to develop creative and innovative strategies.

The Way Forward and Why?

It is clear from the literature that internationalization of universities as a worldwide phenomenon is here to stay; the important question then is how can one university use its internationalization program as a competitive advantage over another? The answer to this question lies in the extent to which a university is internationalized. While many universities are internationalized, they have done so at varying degrees and varying degrees of commitment. In some universities, a foreign language requirement and a required semester abroad is the approach they have adopted, while some emphasize faculty and student exchange programs. Others yet emphasize collaborative research between their faculty and faculty in other universities abroad. Each university may have a sound rationale for its approach and herein lies the marketing opportunity. Whatever the approach that a university is adopting, it must be communicated to the university's stakeholders and promoted to prospective students; otherwise it is as good as having no internationalization program.

Summary

We have in this chapter covered the different definitions of internationalization of higher education and its implication to higher educational institutions in different parts of the world. Because internationalization of higher education intertwines with privatization of higher education in some fashion, the chapter paves the way to the discussion of privatization of higher education in the next chapter.

Questions

1. What does internationalization of higher education mean?
2. Name three marketing opportunities that internationalization of higher education can create for a university.
3. What are some of the advantages of internationalization of higher education?
4. What are some of the challenges that some universities face in their attempt to internationalize?

References

Abbas, S.G., Muhammad Tariq Yousafzai, M.T., & Khattak, A. (2015). Internationalization of Universities: Challenges, Threats and Opportunities for Third World Countries. *The Dialogue* 10 (4), 378–389.

Bartell, M. (2003). Internationalization of Universities: A University Culture-Based Framework. *Higher Education* 45 (1), 43–70.

Brajkovic, L., & Helms, R.M. (2018). Mapping Internationalization on US Campuses. *International Higher Education* 92, 111–113.

Bucker, E., & Stein, S. (2020). What Counts as Internationalization? Deconstructing the Internationalization Imperative. *Journal of Studies in International Education* 24 (2), 151– 166.

Cambridge, J.C., & Thompson, J.J. (2004). Internationalism and Globalization as Contexts for International Education. *Compare* 34 (2), 161–175.

Chabbott, C. (2003). *Constructing Education for Development: International Organizations and Education for All.* New York: Routledge.

Chan, W.W.Y., & Dimmock, C. (2008). The Internationalization of Universities – Globalist, Internationalist, and Translocalist Models. *Journal of Research in International Education* 7 (2), 184–204.

de Wit, H. (2002). *Internationalization of Higher Education in the United States of America and Europe: A Historical, Comparative, and Conceptual Analysis.* Westport, CT: Greenwood Press.

de Wit, H. (2014). The Different Faces and Phases of Internationalization of Higher Education. In A. Maldonado-Maldonado & R.M. Bassett (Eds.), *The Forefront of International Higher Education: A Festschrift in Honor of Philip G. Altbach,* pp. 89–99). Dordrecht, The Netherlands: Springer Science & Business Media.

Ellingboe, B.J. (1998). Divisional Strategies to Internationalize a Campus Portrait: Results, Resistance, and Recommendations from a Case Study at a U.S. University. In J.A. Mestenhauser & B.J. Elllingboe (Eds.), *Reforming the Higher Education Curriculum: Internationalizing the Campus,* pp. 198–228. Phoenix, AZ: American Council on Education and Oryx Press.

Foucault, M. (1980). *Power/knowledge: Selected Interviews and Other Writings, 1972–1977.* New York: Pantheon.

Green, M.E., Luu, D., & Burris, B. (2008). *Mapping Internationalization on U.S. Campuses: 2008 Edition.* Washington, DC: American Council on Education.

Horta, H., & Vaccaro, A. (2008). ICT, Transparency and Proactivity: Finding a Way for Higher Education Institutions to Regain Public Trust. In A. Vaccaro, H. Horta, & P. Madsen (Eds.), *Transparency, Information and Communication Technology – Social Responsibility and Accountability in Business and Education,* pp. 227–240. Charlottesville, VA: Philosophy Documentation Center.

Hayden, M.C., Rancic, B.A., & Thompson, J.J. (2000). Being International: Student and Teacher Perception from International Schools. *Oxford Review of Education* 26 (1), 107–23.

Henkel, M. (2005). Academic Identity and Autonomy in a Changing Policy Environment. *Higher Education* 49 (1–2), 155–176.

Horta, H. (2010). The Role of the State in the Internationalization of Universities in Catching-up Countries: An Analysis of the Portuguese Higher Education System. *Higher Education Policy* 23 (1), 63 – 81.

Knight, J. (1997). Internationalization of Higher Education: A Conceptual Framework. In J. Knight & H. de Wit (Eds.), *Internationalization of Higher Education in Asia Pacific Countries*, pp. 5–20. Amsterdam: European Association for International Education (EAIE).

Knight, J. (2004). Internationalization Remodeled: Definition, Approaches, and Rationales. *Journal of Studies in International Education* 8 (1), 5–31.

Knight, J. (2014). Is Internationalisation of Higher Education Having an Identity Crisis? In A. Maldonado-Maldonado & R.M. Bassett (Eds.), *The Forefront of International Higher Education: A Festschrift in Honor of Philip G. Altbach,* pp. 75–87. Dordrecht, The Netherlands: Springer Science & Business Media.

Kubota, R. (2009). Internationalization of Universities: Paradoxes and Responsibilities. *Modern Language Journal* 93(4), 612–616.

Marden, P.G., & Engerman, D.C. (1992). International Interest: Liberal Arts Colleges Take the High Road. *Educational Record* (Spring) 73 (2), 42–46.

Marginson, S. (2006). Dynamics of National and Global Competition in Higher Education. *Higher Education* 52 (1), 1–39.

Marsella, A.J. (2001). Essay: Internationalizing the Psychology Curriculum. Psychology International 12 (2), 7–8.

McGuiness, A.C. (2002). Linking Strategic Planning and Budgeting and Organizing for Change. Boulder, CO: National Center for Higher Education Management Systems.

Mittelman, J.H. (Ed.) (1996). *Globalization: Critical Reflections.* Boulder, CO: Lynne Riener.

Mohsin, A., & Zaman, K. (2014). Internationalization of Universities: Emerging Trends, Challenges and Opportunities. *Journal of Economic Info* 1 (1), 1–9.

Mok, K.H. (2007). Questing for Internationalization of Universities in Asia: Critical Reflections. *Journal of Studies in International Education* 11(3/4), 433–454.

Neave, G. (1996). Homogenization, Integration and Convergence: The Cheshire Cats of Higher Education Analysis, in V.L. Meek, L. Goedegebuure, O. Kivinen, and R. Rinne (Eds.), *The Mockers and the Mocked: Comparative Perspectives on Differentiation, Convergence and Diversity in Higher Education,* pp. 26–41. London: Pergamon Press,.

Qiang, Z. (2003). Internationalization of Higher Education: Towards a Conceptual Framework. *Policy Futures in Education* 1 (2), 248–270.

Readings, B. (1996). *The University in Ruins.* Cambridge, MA: Harvard University Press.

Skolnikoff, E.B. (1994). Knowledge without Borders? Internationalization of the Research Universities. In Cole, J.R., Barber, E.G., & Graubard, S.R. (Eds.), *The Research University in a Time of Discontent,* pp. 337–343. Baltimore: Johns Hopkins University Press.

Sporn, B. (1999). Current Issues and Future Priorities for European Higher Education Systems. In P.G. Altbach & P.M. Peterson (Eds.), *Higher Education in the 21st Century: Global Challenge and National Response.* New York: Institute of International Education, Report No. 29, pp. 67–77.

Van der Wende, M. (1997). Missing Links: The Relationship between National Policies for Internationalization and Those for Higher Education in General. In T. Kälvemark & M. van der Wende (Eds.), *National Policies for the Internationalization of Higher Education in Europe,* pp. 10–38. Stockholm: National Agency for Higher Education.

Wahlers, M. (2018). Internationalization of Universities: The German Way. *International Higher Education* 92, 9–11.

Welch, A.R. (1997). The Peripatetic Professor: The internationalization of the Academic Profession. *Higher Education* 34 (3), 323–345.

Wiley, D. (2001). Forty Years of the Title VI and Fulbright-Hays International Education Programs: Building the Nation's International Expertise for a Global Future. In P. O'Meara, H.D. Mehlinger, & R.M. Newman (Eds.), *Changing Perspectives on International Education,* pp. 11–29. Bloomington, IN: Indiana University Press.

CASE #21 TAKING UNIVERSITY EDUCATION TO THE MARKET

This case discusses the current trend in which universities locate campuses abroad. It discusses Lancaster University's approach to establishing a campus in Accra, Ghana, West Africa.

The beginnings of Lancaster University, United Kingdom, started with an announcement to its effect in the House of Commons on November 23, 1961, and the formation of two planning groups who were charged with the responsibility of seeing to it that the university becomes a reality. The university's founding vice-chancellor, Charles Carter, assumed his position on April 1, 1963. On September 14, 1964, Her Majesty the Queen approved the university's Charter and Statutes, and its first group of students were admitted in October 1964. Her Royal Highness Princess Alexandra was installed the University's Chancellor in November 1964, and remained in that position until December 2004.

The first transition in the university was transfer of departments from Lancaster to Bailrigg which took place between 1966 and 1970, at the same time as when the first four colleges were being established to enable students to come into residence, a process which began in 1968. The university was committed to teaching and research from the outset and has attained much success later by building on earlier initiatives in the areas of the environment, low temperature physics, and the study of the creative arts. What started in 1964 with a few students now boasts of over 12,000 undergraduate and graduate students and from nothing has attained world-class ranking in less than seven decades.

Internationalization of campuses and universities (which can mean several different elements) started during the past three decades, and several universities are taking several different approaches (sometimes simultaneously) to internationalize. Some universities like Lancaster have opted to expand abroad through a partnership with an independent entity such as Transnational Academic Group (TAG). The question of the appropriateness of a public university entering into relationship with a private entity to undertake a common venture is an unsettled one that has entered the public debate since governments around the world have started cutting back on appropriations for universities and have liberalized the ownership of universities by the private sector in addition to encouraging formation of Public Private Partnership (PPP).

TAG was cofounded in 2007 by Zafar Siddiqi with a view to develop human capacity in emerging markets. In addition to Lancaster University's campus in Ghana, TAG also owns and operates Curtin University's Dubai campus and South Africa–based African Business News (ABN) training in partnership with the Australian Institute of Management in Western Australia.

Lancaster University Ghana, a product of the partnership between the TAG and Lancaster University in the United Kingdom, was launched in Accra Ghana in 2013 with a stated mission of providing world-class education and opportunities to students across the African continent. Its students do not only have access to over 130,000 online journals and e-resources, but also have the opportunity to visit the United Kingdom and participate in exchange programs throughout the year and at the end of their studies graduate with a Lancaster University degree.

With a steady increase in enrollment, the school in Accra has just moved to a new location. Currently, construction of new facilities is underway which when completed, according to the university officials, will expand the university's capacity to hold about 3,000 students and 300 staff. The completed campus will have such facilities as smart classrooms, a modern library, prayer room for Muslims, on-site hostel accommodation for students, multipurpose sports complex, and a cafeteria.

Questions

1. Are you surprised by the approached used by Lancaster University to expand to Ghana? Why? Why not?
2. What are possibly the marketing and branding opportunities in this program?
3. Does a school like Lancaster risk its academic reputation by expanding globally using a third party?
4. Is Lancaster's approach to expanding to Ghana an example of the type of PPP that is being encouraged around the world?

CASE #22 SHOULD IT BE A PHD BY RESEARCH OR WHAT? QUESTIONS ON INTERNATIONALIZATION

This case discusses some of the questions on internationalization that administrators grapple with. It focuses on whether a school should introduce the PhD by research only or the PhD by coursework program.

Internationalization of university education which took on a new favor in the mid-1990s was generally embraced in many quarters as the perceived benefits including collaboration among faculty across national borders and the equivalence of university degrees which enhanced easy mobility of labor. However, these benefits also brought university administrators new headaches that they happily did not have to deal with previously. One of such problems encountered in Hope University (a fictitious name) is to decide on the nature of its PhD program.

Hope University, like most universities, in the midst of liberalization and internalization of higher education is growing its enrollment figures and expanding its offerings at the same time. One of the decisions that is currently under discussion is the nature of its proposed PhD program in management. There was a considerable discussion initially on whether the PhD program should be called a PhD in management which offers specialization in the various subject areas such as finance, marketing, strategic management, accounting, information technology, etc., or whether it should be called a PhD in business administration but offer the same specializations.

A decision was made to call the program a PhD in business administration, and the next step in the decision-making process though proved to be more vexing. The issue is whether the program should be a PhD by research as being offered by some of the local universities or a PhD by coursework as offered in US business schools? After heated discussions influenced mostly by where a speaker had obtained his/her PhD, the committee in charge of planning the program decided to list the advantages and disadvantages inherent in each option. However, it was first made clear that the PhD by coursework does not mean that no research is required, rather research for dissertation is done only after the student has finished and passed all the courses and a comprehensive exam which is administered after the coursework part of the program has been completed. The coursework would take anywhere between two and three years to complete.

It was early on decided that the doctorate that was being considered was a research and not a practitioner degree. Hence, the issue of whether the degree should be a PhD or a DBA was moot at this point. It was also noted that while differences in the discipline (the field of study, e.g., whether it is the sciences or the humanities) mattered, these discussions were being encouraged for only the business discipline.

Some of the advantages for students enrolling in PhD by research program were listed as follows:

1. Might take shorter time to complete the research as students don't need to complete any coursework.
2. If students can complete the research faster, they can extract portions from their thesis to write and publish some articles.
3. Students will have publications before they graduate, since the requirement for graduation is to have a number of publications from their thesis.
4. Might be more suitable for students who have done research before and already have preconceived ideas on what they want to write their dissertation on.
5. Could be less stringent than the PhD by coursework.

The advantages of a PhD by coursework and research were listed as follows:

1. Is a more structured program, that is, students are guided by some courseworks before final research for the dissertation.
2. Suitable for students who don't know how to conduct research and did not conduct research for the master's or haven't done any rigorous research before. Hence, suitable for MBA degree holders.
3. Suitable for students who did not have any preconceived research topic.
4. Some coursework can strengthen the student's knowledge/understanding as they have almost totally forgotten what they have studied during their master's.
5. Might better prepare students for academic work that involves some teaching since serving as a teaching/research assistant is generally a part of the PhD by coursework program.

Questions

1. Which university marketing opportunity does the PhD by research offer, if any?
2. Which university marketing opportunity does the PhD by coursework offer, if any?
3. What is the difference between a DBA and a PhD in business?
4. Which one would you opt for, if you had to choose between a PhD by research in business administration or a PhD in business administration?

12

THE EXPANSION OF PRIVATE UNIVERSITIES

Introduction

The argument for the privatization of state-owned enterprises to achieve efficiency and effectiveness is often made in transition and developing economies even though it has not necessarily been borne out by empirical evidence. This argument, over the past decades, has spilled over into the educational arena as well where proponents of the market model for public education have been rather vocal and contend that it will foster competition among providers and lead to delivery of better services at the same or lower cost than providing them through traditional public schools.

Whether privatization of university education leads to a more efficient use of public resources is still being debated; however, our focus in this chapter is on the marketing opportunities that privatization of universities has generated in both developing and advanced economies. We will accomplish this by looking at how privatization of higher education is being done or has been done in different countries around the world and the marketing windows the process offers both public and private institutions.

The History of Private Universities in Latin America

While we can begin looking at the history of privatization of university education at any region or country for that matter, we thought it would be interesting to start with Latin America because of its rich history of private universities and because we can take a "snap shot," as it were, at several countries in the region simultaneously and independently.

In evaluating the performance of private universities in Latin America (about 20 different countries including Columbia, Chile, Mexico, and Brazil), Levy (1985) first made some general comments regarding the state of higher education. According to Levy, because of their spectacular growth, expectations of universities in the developing world is high, and not being able to meet those expectations, universities in developing countries are much maligned. There is nowhere this is more evident than in Latin America where most of the frustrations according to Levy are over the inability of universities to "solidify independent

DOI: 10.4324/9781003160267-12

national identities, promote democracy, spur economic productivity, or reduce social inequalities." However, because most of the criticisms were against public universities, formidable alternatives emerged, a major one being private universities. From marginal existence in the 1930s private universities now account for about 33% of student enrollments. Private universities are compared with the public universities that are characteristically linked to different models of development.

With the exception of Japan and the United States, the majority of countries in the developed world (excluding the communist world) relies almost exclusively on public institutions to perform the task expected of education. Most of the developing nations (Africa, Middle East, and parts of Asia) also seem to have opted for public-based models. However, several Asian nations now rely heavily on private higher education, and many other nations, in the developing as well as developed worlds, are also establishing private universities. Some others are introducing or augmenting some characteristics of private systems (e.g., tuition) within their public universities.

Discussing the longitudinal data that have been accumulated on university education in Latin America, the author observed that there was no private university in Latin America until the 1880s, with Colombia and Chile being the only exceptions, and less than 3% of the total Latin American enrollments were in the private sector by as late as the 1930s. This figure jumped to approximately 14% in 1955 and to about 20% by 1965. It went up to 30% in 1970, and about 34% by 1975 where it seemed to have plateaued. These figures are slightly distorted though because Brazil with massive private sector exerts a lot of weight on the total figures, nevertheless, the broader argument remains the same. There is yet another argument about what is actually considered a "private university." This is so because some might argue that private higher education is not really a new phenomenon in Latin America and that colonial universities were church universities which are private.

However, Levy (1985) argues that even though the colonial universities were church universities, they were also state universities. Why? Considering the various criteria (juridical ownership, founding authority, governance, finance, and mission), most colonial universities were actually a complex mixture of private and public. "For example, Argentina's only colonial university (the University of Cordoba, 1614) was created and owned by the state, but run largely by the Jesuits with papal authorization," and it was the public university structure that strongly emerged when the church-state partnership finally weakened as a result of independence movement in Latin America.

On the basis of the data, Levy identified three different major waves of growth in private universities in Latin America that led to distinguishable private subsectors. The first noticeable wave consisted of Catholic universities, which were created in reaction to the secularism of the public universities. This wave swept through a fairly large swath of Latin America including such individual countries as Argentina, Bolivia, Brazil, Chile, Ecuador, Panama, Paraguay, Peru, and every Central American nation except Costa Rica. The second wave of private universities according to Levy (1985) could be called "secular elite," or "elite" which emerged because of dissatisfaction of elite actors with the public sector. In this case the desire for class privileges, conservatism, or just academic tranquility and prestige were the most important factors. The third wave was neither elitist nor nonsecular institutions with nonselective admission standards. This wave represents a preoccupation to get job training and to avoid leftist politicization. It is basically a reaction to the perceived inadequacy of public universities.

With more data analyses, Levy concludes that private universities are meeting their goals, but this success is based on their ability to choose desired tasks and excluding others in order to satisfy their own constituencies.

> Thus, even if they fulfill their goals better than the public universities fulfill theirs, they need not be regarded as superior. Rather, they could be considered more limited institutions, fulfilling their functions well largely because they leave other, often tougher, functions to the public sector.
>
> *(Levy, 1985, p. 457)*

If Levy's assessment is correct, what marketing opportunities has privatization created in Latin America for both public and private universities?

From Argentina

Unlike Levy (1985) who examined the history of private universities in about 20 Latin American countries in one fell swoop, Marcelo (2012) "zeroes in" on Argentina as one of the largest economies in Latin America (World Bank, 2012). The author in a brief research note explains why the private university sector in Argentina continues to lag those in other Latin American countries. While enrollment in private universities in Latin America account for almost one-half of all enrollees, in Argentina they account for merely one in every five enrolled students, according Marcelo. Why is this the case and is it likely to change?

It would appear that the low enrollment in private universities in Argentina is not attributable to market forces, but to political acts by the state that was intent on holding its monopoly over university education. According to Marcelo (2012), attempts to break the state's monopoly over university education in Argentina were vehemently opposed by the political structure until the late 1950s with the first private university being established in Argentina in 1959. By the end of the 1960s, enrollment in the private sector tertiary education accounted for about 20% of students enrolled in universities. Nevertheless, the private sector was not permitted to play a major role in university education. It was not viewed as a complement to the state's efforts nor as part of a systemic design, instead it was merely tolerated.

In Argentina the public sector was the main absorber of new students, unlike other developing countries such as Tanzania (in East Africa; see Ishengoma, 2007), it and remained committed to retaining this position through such policies as deciding in 1973 to keep the doors of the national university open for all qualified secondary school graduates, and in effect allowing no new private universities to open. Interestingly, the government continued to hold monopoly over higher education in Argentina, even during periods of fiscal crises in the 1980s when the "exhausted state was begging for funds." Even though the laws that kept the doors of public universities open were reversed in 1989, the harm was already done and Argentina would become one of the few Latin American countries to experience a decline in enrollment in private universities.

Marcelo (2012) in his observations noted that the implementation of neoliberal political/economic policies in the 1990s which saw a wave of privatization of higher education around the world brought a new opportunity for expansion/participation of the private sector in tertiary education in Argentina as well. As a result, 20 new private universities were founded between 1989 and 1995, and for the first time in the history of Argentina, the number of private universities outnumbered the number of public universities (48–40). These newcomers brought heterogeneity to a system that was dominated in enrollment by the public side (86% in 1995). However, as soon as the door seemed to open, it quickly shut again with the opening of the National Accreditation Agency (CONEAU) in 1996. CONEAU's job was to approve the application of new private universities, but this agency became a barrier to the founding of private universities instead of a facilitator, according to Marcelo. It rejected 9 out of every 10 applications through a strict enforcement of the requirements, and from 2000 to 2009, only 12 private universities were allowed to enter the market, and only 3 since 2005.

By the end of 2009, 60 private institutions enrolled only 20% of all university students in Argentina. This percentage is similar to the percentage of student enrollment at the end of the 1960s (18%). However, it is important to note that even though enrollment of new students in private universities was at 20% by the end of 2009, this represents a 6% increment over the past decade, an indication that the public might be appreciating the quality of education offered by the private institutions. Not to be outdone by the private sector, the public universities started to widen their academic offering and expanding their reach through satellite campuses. Thus, the state is still not disposed to give up its role of main demand absorber.

Marcelo (2012) concludes that sadly Argentina has a debatable but strong dual barriers to private higher education growth – by implementing public policy regulations on the private sector and through an expansive or even lax policy within the public side, particularly concerning the opening of new institutions. From Argentina, let us now take a look at some countries in Europe.

The Private Universities of Bulgaria

As a transition country that was part of the Union of Soviet Socialist Republics (USSR), Bulgaria's private university offers an interesting window into the privatization of higher education. Slantcheva (2005) in a short essay provides a review of the landscape of private universities in Bulgaria and discusses their achievements and challenges. The author notes that the presence of nonstate actors in Bulgarian higher education became possible only after the fall of the communist regime in 1989. The first private universities appeared in 1991, amidst skepticism, following the passage of a law on academic autonomy. However, private universities in Bulgaria have, over the past decade, managed to establish themselves as a separate and distinct sector of the Bulgarian higher education landscape. Of the 247,000 students who are educated at 42 universities and 46 colleges in Bulgaria in 2004, 11.3% of them enrolled in private universities which according to Slantcheva is evidence to the public's acceptance of private universities.

Even though they grew quickly in Bulgaria, the growth rate of private universities in Bulgaria was paltry compared to their growth rate in other postcommunist countries such as Romania or Poland where they account for approximately 30% of student enrollment. The Bulgarian parliament recognized five private universities (Varna Free University, New Bulgarian University, Burgas Free University, the American University in Bulgaria, and Slavic University in Sofia) between 1991 and 1995; however, Slavic University in Sofia was closed by a parliamentary order in 1999 because of administrative irregularities.

Private universities in Bulgaria differ in structure, particularly in finances, from one another as well as from public universities. For example, Free Universities of Varna and Burgas rely primarily on local support and tuition fees to operate while New Bulgarian University and the American University in Bulgaria are heavily dependent on financial support from foreign donors. The common challenge faced by all the private universities in Bulgaria in the 1990s was the legal vacuum in which they operated until 1999 even though the 1995 higher education law created requirements for the establishment of other private institutions. Other challenges came from the National Accreditation Agency that is supposed to verify every program in the new institutions; however, the verification standards used by the agency were based on inflexible public university models passed down from the communist era. Also, the strong public distrust of private universities, with the exception of the American University in Bulgaria, because of the high tuition fees that they charge as well as the nontraditional programs and courses that they offered created problems.

In spite of the difficulties and challenges, private universities in Bulgaria have achieved several successes. They were the first in the country, in the early 1990s, to use the bachelor's-master's-doctoral degree structure. This degree structure was officially introduced into the Bulgarian higher education in 1995 only as an effort to harmonize the entire system with European higher education structures, but the public universities were late in adopting the structure. The private university sector was also responsible for introducing such programs as liberal arts degrees and courses based on credit and semester system.

Once considered a place for students who failed to gain entry to state institutions of higher education, Bulgarian private institutions have managed to gain legitimacy by being able to defy the persistent "government tendency to treat them more as an *addition* to the existing higher education system" instead of as an *alternative* to it.

The Italian Experience

Unlike Bulgaria, Italy is not one of the transition countries (moving from planned economy to free market economy) and yet Italy's experience with privatization is unique. Hunter (2010) provides us with an analysis of the Italian experience with privatization of higher education based on the study of three nonstate universities. Privatization of higher education in Western Europe in general and Italy in particular is a little different from the rest of the world. Instead of experiencing an explosion in the growth of private higher education institutions, private universities have largely remained on the peripheral with little or no attraction to researchers.

Hunter posits that even though the term "privatization" of higher education is used worldwide since the phenomenon is global, the meaning of the term is not necessarily the same in every country and it is shaped by a country's position, policy, and by the nature and purpose of the emerging private higher education. In Italy, for example, the term "private" refers exclusively to "nonstate" or "free" higher education institutions that operate within the Italian regulatory framework as nonprofit organizations (Hunter, 2010).

According to the author, unlike in other parts of the world, the persistence of a highly centralized and uniform model of higher education which was established at the time of Italian unification has resisted societal pressures for decentralization and diversification. And even though the Italian constitution provides conditions for private universities, currently, only 28 nonstate universities exist alongside 61 state universities. The majority of nonstate institutions have been established within the recent decades in response to growth and variety in demand that have been only partially met by the state. While the nonstate institutions represent about 25% of the Italian higher education sector, they are significantly smaller in terms of enrollment, and hold only approximately 10% of the total student population.

The characteristics of nonstate institutions in Italy are influenced by their ownership which fall into three general categories – the religious ownership or affiliation (primarily Roman Catholic), the local authority institutions, and the business groups or individuals (including the recently founded distance education providers). These ownership types influence the institutions' mission, disciplines, and target groups. Even though nonstate universities are governed primarily through the national regulatory framework, they are essentially self-funding institutions that rely almost exclusively on revenues generated from tuition. However, acknowledging their contribution to the public good, they receive a small contribution from the state's higher education budget that averages at around 14% of their budget.

In Italy, because of their funding structure, the nonstate universities have less financial accountability; however, they are heavily regulated by the national legislation for the hiring of tenured academics and through the requirements for legal validity, as such their discretionary behavior is significantly curtailed or reduced. They have only minor margins of greater autonomy than their state counterparts. Because the accreditation process of nonstate universities ensures that they have the same quality and standards as their state counterparts, but without funding, there is little room for nonstate universities to deviate. Under heavy financial pressure, some are transforming from nonstate status to state status. However, according to Hunter (2010) as the distinction between private and public higher education blurs, the Italian nonstate universities that are successful in exploiting their "privateness" have the potential to embody the best examples of privatization of higher education.

From Europe we can transition to the continent of Africa (specifically, to sub-Saharan Africa) where growth in nonstate universities, for several reasons, have been phenomenal. First, the governments in many African countries, faced with resource constraints, could not expand the capacities of the existing state universities. Second, growth in the college-going segment of the population of the various sub-Saharan African countries has resulted in an increased demand for university education. Third, nowhere in the world more than in Sub-Saharan Africa university education is truly viewed as a ticket out of poverty, hence the demand for it continues to grow with every family pushing someone in the family to obtain a university education and come back to assist them out of poverty.

Views from Tanzania, East Africa

Ishengoma (2007) discusses the implications of a surge in enrollment in private universities in Tanzania and the related issues of academic quality. The author notes that at attaining its independence, a deliberate decision was made by the government to control access to scarce resources such as education to ensure equal access by all socioeconomic groups. This program was implemented together with the nationalization and government control of all major means of production which included private educational institutions owned by Christian missionaries and other religious organizations, with the exception of Roman Catholic seminaries and one tertiary educational institution.

According to Ishengoma, the demand for university education in Tanzania is high; however, the (public) higher education sector remained elitist. Take, for instance, in 2006–2007, out of the 15,185 who passed the matriculation exam and were thus eligible for admission into the University of Dar es Salaam (Main Campus), the premier public university, only 7,049 applicants (less than 50%) were admitted. The low admission into public universities resulted in the growth of demand-absorbing private higher education sector in Tanzania.

The author noted further that approximately only 1% of the relevant age group in Tanzania enjoyed the benefit of a tertiary education in as recently as 2000; however, there were as of 2007, 21 private universities and university colleges (note that the term "university college" is used in the United Kingdom and in its former colonies to refer to the university that is not autonomous, that is, relies on another university, a full-fledged university to award the university college's degrees) that were registered by the Tanzania Commission for Universities (TCU). Out of the 21, only 4 of the private universities received *Certificates of (Full) Accreditation* from the TCU by 2007 (World Bank, 2003). The demand for higher education globally and the inability of state universities to accommodate this demand have often been cited as one of the reasons for the phenomenal growth of private universities (Levy, 2006). However, the situation might be different in Tanzania where some of the universities may have been founded to meet special manpower requirements. This objective has now transitioned into a race, so to speak, as competition among the major religious denominations was to "establish higher education institutions as one of their strategies to consolidate their spheres of influence among their followers."

In addressing the issue of instructional quality in private universities in Tanzania, Ishengoma (2007) analyzed the qualifications of the leadership (the vice-chancellors) of the universities. He argues that the academic qualifications and ranks of the vice-chancellor (chief executive) in any institution of higher learning positively or negatively impacts the provision of "quality of higher education in terms of the leadership style in which these institutions are governed" because in the author's words, "Quality democratic academic leadership also influences the practice of academic freedom by the faculty and institutional autonomy." On this metric the author showed that 33.3% of the vice-chancellors/provosts in private universities held master's degrees and 55.5% held doctorates. Furthermore, 44.4% of the heads of these institutions are of the rank of a professor compared to public universities and colleges where 10 out of 11 vice-chancellors/principals held doctorates, and all the 11 (100%) were either full or associate professors with vast academic leadership experience.

According to Ishengoma (2007), "the fact that one-third of the vice-chancellors/ provosts in Tanzanian private universities have master's degrees and that only 44.4% have attained the academic rank of professor has implications for the quality of academic leadership in these institutions." Implied in the author's argument is that a private university whose vice-chancellor is a full professor or an associate professor "is more likely to oversee the enforcement of rigorous academic standards, and hire the most qualified academic staff." While the argument does not necessarily disqualify a nondoctorate holder from being a vice-chancellor's or holding a senior academic position in a private university, the point being made is that it would be desirable to hire a highly qualified person for those positions as done in the public universities in Tanzania.

On the faculty (instructional) level, Ishengoma (2007) observed that there was no comprehensive data; however, information obtained from six of the private universities (31.5% of all private universities)

> shows that in the academic year 2005–2006, these universities employed in total 2 full professors; 10 associate professors; 24 senior lecturers; 45 lecturers; 14 assist-ant lecturers; and 11 tutorial assistants. Full professors accounted for 1.8% of all the teaching staff in 6 private universities.

Furthermore, according to the author, anecdotal evidence suggests that the majority of the faculty in private universities is of the rank of lecturers and assistant lecturers, with a negligible number of senior lecturers, associate professors, and full professors. One of the reasons offered by the author for the paucity of qualified academics (senior academics) in the private universities in Tanzania is because "these institutions mainly employ part-time faculty or retired or retrenched civil servants on a three-year or one-year contract terms, renewable at the discretion of the employer." With job insecurity, many qualified academics would hesitate to take up positions in the private university sector in Tanzania and this has a negative impact on the academic quality.

A further indictment of private universities in Tanzania is that their expansion of student enrollment is constrained by the fact that the majority of these institutions still operates from rented premises in urban and semiurban areas, and are not able to undertake large-scale construction of new educational facilities because of their limited financial resources. Their generally inadequate and dilapidated infrastructure and depleted resources are such that they cannot expand through growth in enrollments. Enrollment expansion which is not accompanied by expansion of educational facilities negatively impacts on the quality of education. According to the author,

> The surge of private higher education institutions in Tanzania and in the neighbouring East African countries has resulted in quality problems in these institutions, recently necessitating a regional workshop of the three countries under the auspices of the Inter-University Council of East Africa (IUCEA). At this regional workshop, the IUCEA was urged "*to delve into the problem of the mushrooming of bogus universities and the proliferation of fake degrees*" and "*bogus providers of higher education.*" *A Quality Assurance Handbook for University Education in East Africa* is being developed by the IUCEA in collaboration with the German International Academic Exchange Program (DAAD).
>
> *(Ishengoma, 2007, p. 105)*

From Tanzania we "visit" Kenya, Tanzania's neighboring country, for another experience with privatization of higher education in sub-Saharan Africa.

Views from Kenya, East Africa

Even though Kenya might be close geographically to Tanzania, the educational experience as far as the private university educational sector is concerned is very different. Mwebi (2012) noted that similar to Tanzania, access to university education in Kenya was for a long time an exclusive preserve of a selected few who managed to pass highly the then Kenya Advanced Certificate of Education and now Kenya Certificate of Secondary Education. However, unlike

Tanzania, control over public universities in Kenya was not through a national government's policy to control access to limited resources. The competitive nature of the examinations locked out many candidates who qualified from pursuing university education, and the emergence of private universities has created a reprieve of sorts that was long overdue for students who qualified, but failed to get admission into public universities because of space limitations. They could join the private universities. However, concerns have been raised in certain quarters about the characteristics of students admitted and the quality of education provided in private universities in Kenya.

To contribute to the discussions, the author investigated private universities in Kenya, specifically with regard to student characteristics, access factors, quality of education, and completion rate to find answers to questions relating to the factors that influence access, determine the relationship between access factors and enrollment, establish perceptions of stakeholders on quality of education provided, and determine completion rate for the 2007–2008 academic year cohort. The saturated sampling technique was used to select 21 Academic Registrars (AR), 21 Deans of Students (DS), 21 Student Leaders (SL), and the stratified random sampling technique was used to select 1,225 students and 148 lecturers. The production function theory was used to guide the study, and data were collected using questionnaires and in-depth interviews. The descriptive, ex post facto, and correlational analyses were conducted.

The results of the analyses revealed that the minimum entry qualifications of students admitted by private institutions was a C+ in Kenya Certificate of Secondary Education and there were more females (58.23%) than males (41.77%). The majority (52.47%) of the students was below 24 years of age, and most of them enrolled in the faculties of education, business, and computing science which accounted for over 70% of total enrollment. The following were identified as the major factors which influenced their choice:

- Newspaper advertisements.
- Reasonable cost of the programs.
- Strict graduation schedules.
- University academic resources.
- The variety of programs.
- Preuniversity programs.
- Campus visits (open house).
- Visits to high school by university recruiters.
- Colorful graduation ceremonies.
- Television ads.
- Good public relations

The major stakeholders perceive the quality of students from private universities in Kenya to be high; however, they rated the quality of physical facilities, teaching and learning materials, and administrative services as low. Mwebi (2012) estimated the completion rate of the student cohorts studied to be very high (96.80%); however, the study provided no basis to compare this rate to the completion rate from public universities.

In the end, the study concluded that students admitted into the private universities did meet the requirements to be admitted to public universities in Kenya, and their school choice was mostly influenced by such factors as access to advertisements in the print and electronic media. As expected, the study recommended that private universities in Kenya improve their infrastructure including physical facilities, teaching and learning materials, and administrative services. It appears the problems of infrastructure faced by private universities in Kenya are similar to those faced by private universities in Tanzania.

Views from Malawi, East Africa

Illustrating the reach of privatization of universities that has swept the world, Kajawo (2019) studied Malawi, a small landlocked country with a population of 19 million (Malawi government, 2018) in Southeastern Africa formerly known as Nyasaland under the British colonial rule.

Kajawo (2019), like other researchers, observed that privatization of higher education has been well-accepted worldwide including Malawi. However, no study has investigated how well private universities are performing in a small developing country such as Malawi. Given the large difference in resources that state and private universities have in Malawi, it is likely that there is a gap in how well these two sectors meet their goals of providing similar and equal quality of education, hence the author sought to examine how the accreditation policies, resources such as financial, human, and physical were contributing or affecting the performance of private universities as well as the challenges private universities face in Malawi.

Access to university education in Malawi, as in many other African countries, was very difficult in 1990s. Consider the fact that even in the mid-2000s less than 1% of those who were eligible could enroll in a university in Malawi (World Bank, 2009). To ease the financial pressure on the government to provide more funds for university education, the government of Malawi in 2006 decided to implement a higher education liberalization policy which permitted the founding of private universities. Four private universities were founded by 2009 (World Bank, 2009), but this number increased to 18 by 2017 while the number of state universities increased from 2 to 4. Is the rapid growth in private university education a good thing for the country? After all, one would argue that, all else being equal, the greater the number of Malawians who obtained university education, the better trained and skilled they would become to build the economy. However, what happens if these university-educated graduates did not receive properly training in the universities?

To evaluate how well these private universities are performing, Kajawo (2019) drew on Bertalanffy's systems theory (see Weckowicz, 1989) and conducted an extensive review of the literature on higher education and privatization of higher education in Malawi, and examined six private universities located in the Blantyre City in Malawi using mixed methods research approach and the descriptive convergent parallel design. A total of 152 persons were interviewed using questionnaires and face-to-face meetings. The results of the analyses revealed that most people felt that private universities have made higher education accessible to many Malawians who would not have been able to gain access otherwise. However, the quality of education being offered in the private universities was questionable partly because most of them relied solely on tuition fees for revenue and did not have adequate financial resources to hire qualified faculty and staff and to provide the necessary technological infrastructure. However, because these institutions are playing an important role in absorbing qualified high school graduates who would not otherwise gain access to university education, the study recommends that the government increase its monitoring role to ensure that the minimum instructional quality is met and even give financial assistance to the private institutions given the role they play in creating a public good. The author also encouraged private institutions themselves to explore other means of generating revenue and some of the universities should consider merging in order to have stability.

The problems with private institutions in Malawi seem to be similar to those in Tanzania and Kenya. How can these institutions improve their financial resources? You would have noticed that even though Kenya, Tanzania, and Malawi are sub-Saharan African countries, they are in the East of Africa, hence to have another viewpoint, we travelled to Ghana, in the west of the sub-Saharan region of Africa.

Experiences from the Private Education Sector in Ghana, West Africa

The overarching question is whether the experiences of private universities in Ghana, West Africa, are different from the experiences in East Africa. With the proliferation of private higher educational institutions all over the world, particularly in developing countries where the states do not have enough resources to rigorously monitor quality (see discussions on private higher education in Malawi, Kajawo (2019)), one wonders to what extent the private institutions themselves are self-policing as far as ensuring high quality education is concerned. To answer this question Ntim (2014) investigated quality issues in higher private institutions in Ghana. The author's objectives were twofold. First, to determine whether quality assurance culture was embedded in the emerging private universities in Ghana within the context of national policy on Higher Education. Second, to assess the extent to which consumers of education, especially students, are a part of the process of ensuring quality education in private institutions.

Ntim (2014) asserts that formal education has been recognized as one of the critical factors for socioeconomic development, as such governments alone could not continue to "monopolize" higher education. He cited Africa, as an example, of where the quality of education in general and of higher education in particular has been identified as a key factor that will allow the continent to succeed in global competition. This recognition in Africa has therefore led to the "de-monopolization of higher education from the government" which started in the mid-1990s and allowed the participation of the private sector in higher education.

The participation of the private sector in the ownership and operation of universities, however, in developing countries such as Ghana meant that education consumers (students, parents, guardians, etc.) must be protected from unintended consequences of privatization, and steps must be taken to ensure that they receive the best value in terms of the quality of education for the money that they pay. This led to the demand for structures and institutional processes that support quality assurance in private universities in Ghana.

To identify institutional processes and structures that support the development of an internal quality culture in the emerging private universities in Ghana, the author first defined quality culture as "a way of continuously aiming to improve and do better," using processes (activity), inputs (information, materials), resources (people, equipment, space), and control (quality monitoring system) to produce outputs (products and/or services). The author surveyed 120 respondents who were selected through a purposive sampling method from 30 of the 55 private universities in Ghana.

The questionnaire used collected data in three parts. Part 1 collected personal data on the respondents, part 2 collected data on the personal vision on the goals of a university. This was done with an adapted version of the Attributes of the Intelligence Scale (Okagaki & Steinberg, 1993), and part 3 collected data on the academic/administrative/students' perception of quality assurance culture practices, and comprised five subparts. The 120 respondents comprised members of a full range of the internal composition of a university – from senior administrators, full professors, lecturers, secretaries, to students.

The results of the study indicate that private universities in Ghana are embedding quality assurance culture as demanded by the national policy on higher education. Even though the results showed that 45% of respondents admitted to the absence an official written policy governing quality assurance culture in their universities, 95% (115 of the 120 respondents) acknowledged the presence of a rigorous and comprehensive coverage of evaluations which range from annual course monitoring at the departmental level, and from the faculty and academic board levels in their universities. Around 75% of the respondents indicated that students were involved in evaluating courses and teaching. Another 75% acknowledged that students' evaluations were communicated to all the lecturers. With these findings, the author seems to think that the involvement of the private sector in higher education in Ghana is a good foreboding for the future in which the bridge between universities and the labor market will be tighter.

Views from South Korea

South Korea is an emerging economy that has managed to develop its technology and electronics sector to a world class standard. Chae and Hong (2009) argued that higher education which is key to the research sector is globally important, particularly to emerging economies such as South Korea in transforming the economy. According to Chae & Hong (2009) even though both developed and developing countries have attempted to expand opportunities for access to higher education, an enrollment gap in higher education still persists between developed and developing economies (UNESCO, 2003). For example, while higher education enrollment rate in the United States rose significantly from 55% to 81%, between 1980 and 1995, the average enrollment rate in developing countries increased during the same period by only 4%, that is, from 5% to 9% (World Bank, 2002).

With the increasing role of higher education in producing qualified human resources, and yet with access to higher education being limited, privatization of higher education was embraced as a means to make higher education more easily accessible, particularly in developing countries where many governments are financially constrained and are still under severe pressure to meet various social demands (Johnstone et al., 1998). Furthermore, reforms based on "marketization, competitiveness, or globalization" that many countries have implemented since the 1980s have encouraged governments in developing countries to rely on private sources for funding higher education (Giroux, 2002; McCowan, 2004); in other words, they must privatize higher education, so that they have devoted additional resources to pressing social needs.

However, Chae and Hong (2009) argued that privatization of higher education means different things in different countries or in different contexts. For example, in European countries where higher education has been heavily subsidized by the governments, privatization means "charging tuition fees and introducing student loans" (Pritchard, 2004; Weiler, 2000). In the United States where private higher educational institutions are common, privatization takes the form of reducing state funding for public universities (Ehrenberg, 2006; Pick,

2006; Priest & John, 2006), and in developing countries, it generally means allowing the participation of the private sector in founding and running universities (see Levy, 1985; see also Patrinos, 1990; Welch, 2007). Thus, in developed countries the debate revolves around whether privatization damages the public nature of higher education (Ehrenberg, 2006; Lyall & Sell, 2006), while in developing countries where social demands for higher education have been unmet due to the presence of limited number of higher educational institutions, privatization generally means the expansion of private higher education institutions. Thus, the major issue for them is essentially whether privatization will negatively impact the equity and quality of higher education (Patrinos, 1990; Welch, 2007).

Against this background, Chae and Hong (2009) explored the role of the Korean government in expanding private higher education over time and examined the impact of such expansion on access to and equity in higher education by reviewing the related literature and statistics. The authors noted that the enrollment rate in Korean higher education increased by 80% during the past 60 years and attributed the phenomenal increase in enrollment to the rapid expansion of private universities which currently enroll about 80% of undergraduates and the Koreans' educational aspirations which is rooted in the cultural esteem for education. From the analyses, the authors concluded amongst other things that the government's role was paramount in the expansion by deregulating private universities. However, higher education expansion was led primarily by private resources with minimal government funding. Furthermore, the financial background of students determines their likelihood in enrolling one type of higher educational institution or the other. This is so because no government scholarship program was available for low-income families until 2005, and less than 10% of Korean college students were government student loan recipients. In view of these facts, the authors surmised that private sector expansion in Korea in actuality limited the access of students from low-income families to higher education in Korea.

On the bases of this evidence, Chae and Hong (2009) concluded that privatization of higher education in Korea resulted in educational inequity and noted that privatization of higher education in Korea was implemented through changes in the government's regulatory policies and supported by the Koreans' strong preferences for higher education, unlike in developed countries where privatization of higher education is driven by marketization and competitiveness. Thus, the Korean case should serve as a lesson for other developing economies that the government must maintain a "balanced role between acting as a regulator and promoter in the expansion of private higher education."

In short, according to Chae and Hong (2009), instead of privatization of higher education helping the poor, it ended up hurting the poor in Korea.

From South Korea, we will move on to Bangladesh.

Views from Bangladesh

Maintaining instructional quality in higher education in developing countries in the face of proliferation of private and for-profit universities is a question that has been often raised. Thus, it is not surprising that it has resonated in the context of Bangladesh also.

How is instructional quality maintained in higher education in developing Bangladesh with the proliferation of private and for-profit universities? To answer this question, Alam (2020) examined the Quality Assurance (QA) mechanism set up for the private higher education sector in

Bangladesh. In an interesting piece, the author traces the history of private higher education back to 970 in Cairo, Egypt, when the purpose of higher education was to train religious clerics (Altbach, 1999). According to the author, Europe later entered the field of provision of higher education through public means, but focused on medicine and sciences instead of religion (Clark, 2001).

However, the pendulum seemed to have shifted in the 1900s when the United States was thrusted into the limelight of higher education by providing simultaneously for public and private higher education institutions (Altbach & Knight, 2007). With this transformation, according to the author, it was realized that "every profession demands competent professionals to have a balanced development across all educational sectors for national development," and although the private sector plays a major role in United States' higher education, the basic aim and objectives of both the private and public higher education institutions are to help in national development.

According to Alam (2020), reasonable governance, participation of industries in research activities in universities, and alumni commitment help private higher education institutions in the United States to function in a desirable manner without compromising on instructional quality, syllabi, pedagogy, students' academics, and infrastructure (Brennan et al., 2004). However, this does not mean that the adoption of the United States' system in developing countries will necessarily work well for them also. With this acknowledgment, the author approached the examination of the Bangladeshi system by reviewing documents and secondary data, and by interviewing personnel from the Ministry of Education, the University Grants Commission, students, staff, and management from public and private universities using semistructured questionnaires.

The results of this study suggest that political considerations in which political leaders create an artificial demand for higher education by lowering the quality of education at the secondary level and other prerequisite qualifications required to qualify for higher education were relied upon, instead of market forces to ensure the survival of private universities. Relying on political considerations led to the mushrooming growth of private higher educational institutions in Bangladesh. Furthermore, the mechanism set up for quality assurance was yet to yield fruits. Meanwhile, the formal arrangements for the governance and regulatory control of private higher educational institutions in Bangladesh were neither sufficient nor up to date to help the sector function effectively. Ironically, what Alam (2020) reported of Bangladesh may not be an isolated case as far as developing private universities in many developing countries are concerned.

What Does Privatization of Higher Education Mean for Marketing Universities?

Having gained from the above readings, a panoramic view of the globalization of privatization of higher education, the logical question is what does it all mean for the marketing of higher education? Far from reducing the opportunities for the poor access higher universities as the case is in Korea according to Chae and Hong (2009), we think privatization of university education increases the opportunities for the poor as well as for many institutions to market themselves.

Privatization of higher education, more than anything else, has created the opportunity for many institutions in higher education to truly segment the market of higher education, select their target market, and position themselves accordingly. Universities and colleges can now more than ever position themselves to cater specifically to the needs of adult learners through unique strategies such as giving credits for real-life work experience, using distance learning technologies, flexible course schedules, and the like. Furthermore, many state universities can also form alliances or partnerships and joint programs with nonstate universities in which one university can enjoy the strengths of the other. Such relationships can be beneficial to the students and society in general, because it could produce better skilled workers as well as students who have been exposed to diverse viewpoints.

Summary

This chapter examines the theory privatization of higher education and the effect of translating the theory into real life around the globe. Besides showing that there is no universal interpretation of privatization of higher education around the globe, it specifically examined the literature on the role and the effect of private universities in Europe, Africa, Asia, and the Americas (United States and Latin America). The chapter shows that even though privatization of higher education frees up government resources to be channeled elsewhere, the effect of privatization is not the same around the globe. Nevertheless, privatization of universities creates a unique marketing opportunity for universities around the world to distinguish themselves and focus on segments in which they can excel in the delivery of their service.

Questions

1. Through which means can universities distinguish themselves?
2. What does "privatization of universities" mean?
3. Does "privatization of universities" expand or decrease marketing opportunities for universities?
4. What is the effect of privatization of universities in Malawi?
5. How is the effect of privatization of universities in South Korea different from those in Kenya?
6. What do you see as an advantage of privatization of universities in Bulgaria?
7. Why is privatization of universities in Bulgaria different from privatization of universities in Bangladesh?

Additional Questions

1. Which marketing strategies would you have pursued were you one of the administrators of a private university in Argentina?
2. Do you think public universities in Argentina also need to market themselves?
3. How would you market one of them?
4. What do you think you would have done in terms of marketing were you an administrator of one of the public universities in Bulgaria?
5. Would you have done the same thing were you an administrator in one of the private universities?
6. What would you have done differently?
7. Do you think it is all right for the government to contribute as much as 14% of the operating budget of private universities in Italy?

8. Should the government contribute more or less?
9. Do you think the government is doing the right thing in Tanzania by allowing private universities to operate?
10. Which marketing strategies would you use, if you were a senior member of administration in one of the private universities in Tanzania?
11. Can a university forge a relationship with a successful private company for financial support?
12. What are the implications of this type of arrangement?

References

Alam, G.M. (2020). Quality Assurance for Private Universities in Bangladesh: A Quest for Specialised Institutional Governance, Management and Regulatory Mechanism. *International Journal of Comparative Education and Development* 22 (1), 1–15.Altbach, P.G. (1999). Private Higher Education: Themes and Variation in Comparative Perspective. *Prospects* 29 (3), 311–323.

Altbach, P.G., & Knight, J. (2007). The Internationalization of Higher Education: Motivations and Realities. *Journal of Studies in International Education* 11 (3–4), 290–305.

Brennan, J., King, R., & Lebeau, Y. (2004). *The Role of Universities in Transforming Societies*. London: Open University.

Chae, J-E, & Hong, H.K. (2009). The Expansion of Higher Education Led by Private Universities in Korea. *Asia Pacific Journal of Education* 29 (3), 341–355.

Clark, B.R. (2001). *Issues in Higher Education: Creating Entrepreneurial Universities-Organisational Pathways of Transformation*. London: Emerald.

Ehrenberg, R.G. (2006). The Perfect Storm and the Privatization of Public Higher Education. *Change* 38 (1), 46–53.

Giroux, H.A. (2002). Neoliberalism, Corporate Culture, and the Promise of Higher Education: The University as a Democratic Public Sphere. *Harvard Educational Review* 72 (4), 425–463.

Hunter, F. (2010). Private Universities in a Public Framework: The Italian Experience. *International Higher Education* 59 (3), 25–27.

Ishengoma, J.M. (2007). The Debate on Quality and the Private Surge: A Status Review of Private Universities and Colleges in Tanzania. *Journal of Higher Education in Africa [Revue de l'enseignement supérieur en Afrique]* 5 (2–3), 85–109.

Johnstone, D.B., Arora, A., & Experton, H. (1998). The Financing and Management of Higher Education: A Status Report on Worldwide Reforms. Unpublished paper, World Bank.

Kajawo, S.C.R. (2019). Examining Performance and Challenges of Private Universities in Malawi. *International Journal of Research and Innovation in Social Science* 3 (6), 48–58.

Levy, D.C. (1985). Latin America's Private Universities: How Successful Are They? *Comparative Education Review* 29 (4), 440–459.

Levy, D.C. (2006). The Unanticipated Explosion: Private Higher Education's Global Surge. *Comparative Educational Review* 50 (2), 217–240.

Lyall, K.C., & Sell, K.R. (2006). *The True Genius of America at Risk: Are We Losing Our Public Universities to de facto Privatization?* Westport, CT: Praeger.

Malawi Government (2018). 2018 Population and Housing Census Main Report (PDF). *Malawi National Statistical Office*. Retrieved, August 13, 2021. https://malawi.unfpa.org/sites/default/files/resourcepdf/2018%20Malawi%20Population%20and%20Housing%20Census%20Main%20Report%20%281%29.pdf

Marcelo, R. (2012). Why the Argentine Private University Sector Continues to Lag. *International Higher Education* 66, 29–30.

McCowan, T. (2004). The Growth of Private Higher Education in Brazil: Implications for Equity and Quality. *Journal of Education Policy* 19 (4), 453–472.

Mwebi, B. (2012). Expansion of Private Universities in Kenya and Its Implication on Student Characteristics, Access Factors, Quality and Completion Rate. A Thesis Submitted in Partial Fulfilment of the Requirements for the Degree of Doctor of Philosophy in Planning and Economics of Education, Maseno University, Kenya.

Ntim, S. (2014). Embedding Quality Culture in Higher Education in Ghana: Quality Control and Assessment in Emerging Private Universities. *Higher Education* 68 (6), 837–849.

Okagaki, L., & Steinberg, R. (1993). Parental Beliefs and Children's School Performance. *Child Development* 64 (1), 36–56.

Patrinos, H. (1990). The Privatization of Higher Education in Columbia: Effects on Quality and Equity. *Higher Education* 20 (2), 161–173.

Pick, D. (2006). The Re-framing of Australian Higher Education. *Higher Education Quarterly* 60 (3), 229–241. Priest, D.M., & John, E.P.S. (2006). Privatization and Public Universities. Bloomington, IN: Indiana University Press.

Pritchard, R. (2004). Humboldtian Values in a Changing World: Staff and Students in German Universities. *Oxford Review of Higher Education* 20 (4), 509–528.

Slantcheva, S. (2005). The Private Universities of Bulgaria. *International Higher Education* 28, 11–13.

United Nations Educational, Scientific and Cultural Organization (UNESCCO). (2003). Synthesis Report on Trends and Developments in Higher Education since the World Conference on Higher Education (1998–2003). Retrieved June 7, 2006, from http://portal.unesco.org/education/en/ev.php-URL_ID¼42810&URL_DO¼DO_TOPIC&URL_SECTION¼201.html

Weckowicz, T.E. (1989). *Ludwig von Bertalanffy (1901–1972): A Pioneer of General Systems Theory.* Working Paper, February 1989. 2.

Weiler, H.N. (2000). States, Markets and University Funding: New Paradigms for the Reform of Higher Education in Europe. Compare 30 (3), 333–339.

Welch, A.R. (2007). Blurred Vision? Public and Private Higher Education in Indonesia. *Higher Education* 54 (5), 665–687.

World Bank (2002). *Constructing Knowledge Societies: New Challenges for Tertiary Education.* Washington, DC: World Bank.

World Bank (2003). *World Development Indicators.* Washington, DC: World Bank.

World Bank (2009). *Malawi Education Country Status Report: CSR 2008/09.* Malawi: World Bank.

World Bank (2012). New World Bank Report Finds 50 Percent Increase in Middle Class in Latin America and the Caribbean over Last Decade. World Bank at www.worldbank.org/en/news/press-release/2012/11/13/new-world-bank-report-finds-fifty-percent-increase-middle-class-latin-america-over-last-decade. Retrieved on September 10, 2021.

CASE #23 ZEE UNIVERSITY OF ENGINEERING

This case discusses a newly founded private university in a developing country, Ghana, West Africa. It shines more light on the question of whose interest is being served by some of the private universities that are mushrooming around the world in the wake of the deregulation of higher education.

The government of Ghana divested itself from being the sole operator of educational institutions at the tertiary level in the country in 1993 with the formation of a board to grant accreditation to private universities. Two privately owned and managed universities sprung up by 1999. However, Ghanaians are not known to shy away from an entrepreneurial opportunity as evidenced in the meteoric rise in the number of private universities from 2 in 1999 to 11 in 2006. However, running a private university is not exactly the same as running a chocolate factory or a retail bank. Even though the profit motive for the entrepreneur may remain the same, a university is a different entrepreneurial opportunity, and its journey towards profitability can sometimes lead to unintended consequences.

Zee University (fictitious name) is one of the private universities that was founded as a result of "deregulation." To differentiate it from the rest of the pack (other private universities) and market to an overlooked segment, Zee University positioned itself as a university of science and technology. Indeed, the school's background lends itself nicely to such differentiation strategy. It was built from a facility that was first used as a Royal Air Force (RAF) Training School during World War II and subsequently handed to the country's Cable and Wireless Department to train telecommunications technicians for British West African countries (i.e., Ghana, Nigeria, Sierra Leone, and the Gambia).

This Technical Training Centre with its facilities was rapidly upgraded under the government's deregulation and privatization policies to become a center to teach and certify telecommunications engineers for the government and other institutions in country and the region as a whole. In 2005, the institutions management again upgraded the infrastructure and equipment and converted the training center into a university that focuses on science, technology, engineering, and mathematics (STEM). Zee University was officially founded in November 2005, granted accreditation by the NAB in March, 2006. The school officially opened its doors in August 2006 and grew from a few hundred students in 2006 to about 8,000 students in 2020.

Like many private universities, Zee University pretty much depends on tuition fees to pay its faculty and staff and maintain utilities and develop infrastructure. Hence, the more students it admits the better its financial position, as such there is an economic incentive to increase its enrollment. This leads to many private universities, not only Zee, to admit cut corners and people who were not under normal circumstances qualified for admission into the public universities. The private universities admit some of these students under the guise of taking them into remedial programs and their admission into the university as full-fledged students depended on their performance in an examination at the end of the program. Since the exams are internally administered and evaluated, the outcome cannot be surprising.

An interview with a lecturer in engineering at the university gave us a little hope to be optimistic. He claimed that "it is impossible to train someone who could not pass basic mathematics at the high school level to become an electrical engineer. I think we are training people to go out and blow up the equipment," he ended with a chuckle. "In my days people with credit in additional mathematics were not even selected for electrical engineering in the country's only public engineering university."

In 2020 just prior to a new presidential election, Zee University was upgraded to the status of a full-fledged public university.

Questions

1. Do you think quality assurance can be a way for Zee University to distinguish itself?
2. Why do you think it is necessary for Zee University to position itself as a STEM university?

3. Is there another way that Zee University can signal the quality of its students to the public? (You can assume that there are no laws that prevent publishing students' names and grades).
4. What do you think constitutes an opportunistic behavior in this case?

CASE #24 PUBLIC-PRIVATE PARTNERSHIP IN UNIVERSITIES

This case discusses how some public universities in the United States such as Georgia State University, Atlanta, Georgia, are using the concept of public–private partnership to undertake projects that they could not have undertaken by themselves.

Many public universities in the United States, and perhaps, around many parts of the world, because of their age, have to rebuild or rehabilitate their old buildings and infrastructure in general in order to compete effectively with some relatively more modern private universities. Unfortunately, they have to do these with the ever dwindling public funding. Hence, amongst other things, public universities have to be resourceful to be successful in accomplishing their mission.

A resourceful way available that many public universities including Georgia State University have used is to engage Public–Private Partnership (3Ps) in some of their development projects.

Georgia State University (Georgia State, State, or GSU) founded in 1913 is a public research university in Atlanta, Georgia. It is one of the University System of Georgia's four research universities, and the state's largest with student population of over 540,000 including approximately 330,000 undergraduates. The university is located in downtown area in Atlanta and is classified among "R1: Doctoral Universities – Very High Research Activity." The university's over $200 million in research expenditures ranked it first for the third year in a row in the 2018 fiscal year among the nation's universities without an engineering, medical, or agricultural school.

GSU is the most comprehensive public institution in Georgia, offering more than 250 degree programs in over 100 fields of study spread across 10 academic colleges and schools. The school has several libraries which including the law school's library contains over 13 million holdings and serves as federal document depositories. The institution has a $2.5 billion economic impact in Georgia.

From its early days as a single-building night school, the school has developed occupying several blocks in the heart of urban Downtown Atlanta. GSU's nickname "the Concrete Campus" in the 1960s which used to be a "source of mild embarrassment" is now embraced by the university community and woven into their slogan which proclaims the school "a part of the city, not apart from the city" as it continually expands its downtown presence.

Strange as it may sound, the university did not have a residential facility until the mid-1990s. The university created its first 2,000-bed on-campus dormitories by acquiring the Olympic Village housing complex located at the southeast corner of Centennial Olympic

Park Drive (formerly Techwood Drive) and North Avenue that was used to house Olympic athletes during the 1996 Summer Olympics which were held in Atlanta, Georgia. A series of other residential facilities followed thereafter. For example, University Lofts in August 2002, the University Commons in 2007, Carl Patton Hall in 2009, Greek housing in 2010, etc. With the rapid growth in student enrollment, the demand for residential housing has exceeded the university's financial capacity, hence the need to think outside the box for a solution which led into the formation of a 3P with Corvias, Inc.

Corvias is a fully integrated development, construction, and property management firm, a private company that was originally founded in 1998 as Picerne Military Housing which was created to provide improved housing for America's service members and their families. Picerne Military Housing was under the umbrella of Picerne Real Estate Group, a Picerne family business founded in 1925. The partnership between the University System of Georgia (USG) and Corvias is a unique approach in student housing as it is the first time the USG has initiated the privatization of student housing through a portfolio of campuses. As part of the 40-year 9-university partnership, Corvias partnered with GSU to develop, construct, manage, and maintain student housing in the first phase of an unprecedented 3P. Working together with GSU, Corvias designed and built 1,152 beds in a new residence hall, Piedmont Central (Piedmont). The project comprises two-bedroom private and semiprivate suites. Piedmont also contains office and storage space, community kitchens, laundry rooms, state-of-the-art social spaces for group activities and collaboration, and a 15,239 square foot (SF) dining hall.

Corvias has one of the largest on-campus higher education partner portfolios in the United States. The company's website states that it has worked with more than 15 colleges across 6 states and the District of Columbia. The list of universities that the company has worked with includes Wayne State University in Detroit, Michigan, which the company partnered with in 2017 to solve a $38 million deferred maintenance issue.

Questions

1. What is 3P?
2. How does it represent an opportunity to market a university?
3. Do you think using a 3P route to expand the capacity of a public university is a viable option?
4. Can you come up with some other instances besides residence halls where the 3P option can be used?

13

REGULATORY ISSUES IN HIGHER EDUCATION

Introduction

Some people argue that no other businesses in the United States are more regulated than universities and healthcare providers/facilities. While we cannot ascertain the veracity of this statement, it is true that universities in their role as employers that employ individuals and as educational institutions that deal with students and their records in the United States operate under many layers of regulations – some of these regulations are from the federal government, others from the states in which they operate (particularly the public institutions), and some from their accreditation agencies. As in many cases, these regulations are necessary to protect the public and the individuals that have nexus with the institutions.

Some people argue that business regulations stifle innovation and often impose costly burden on business entities; however, others argue that regulations in general give consumers a peace of mind in knowing that opportunistic behavior on the part of business entities is primarily checked and that many business regulations simply guide. We do not take any side in this debate in this chapter, but simply discuss a few of the relevant regulations to educational institutions at federal level in the United States, and some common trends in the European Union. Covering all the federal regulations that educational institutions have to comply with could result in a book of its own – a law book, which is not our intention. Hence, the choice of the regulations covered here is arbitrary, but it is our hope that we chose regulations that are somewhat connected to the marketing and branding of universities.

Americans with Disabilities Act

The Americans with Disabilities Act (ADA) was signed into law in 1990. The ADA is a civil rights law that prohibits discrimination against individuals that have disabilities in all areas of public life, including jobs, schools, transportation, and all public and private places that are open to the general public. The law is intended to make sure that people with disabilities enjoy the same rights and opportunities as everyone else.

DOI: 10.4324/9781003160267-13

The ADA gives civil right protection to individuals with disabilities similar to those provided to individuals on the basis of race, color, sex, national origin, age, and religion. It guarantees equal opportunity for individuals with disabilities in public accommodations, employment, transportation, state and local government services, and telecommunications. The law is divided into five sections (titles) that relate to different areas of public life.

The ADA was amended in 2008 to become the Americans with Disabilities Act Amendments Act (ADAAA) which became effective on January 1, 2009. The ADAAA made a number of significant changes to the definition of "disability." The changes in the definition of disability in the ADAAA apply to all titles of the ADA, including Title I (employment practices of private employers with 15 or more employees, state and local governments, employment agencies, labor unions, agents of the employer and joint management labor committees); Title II (programs and activities of state and local government entities); and Title III (private entities that are considered places of public accommodation).

Some people might ask whether the ADA applies to higher educational institutions as well. The answer is yes, it does. In fact, Title II of the ADA covers publicly funded universities, community colleges, and vocational schools. All public or private schools that receive federal funding are required under Section 504 of the Rehabilitation Act to make their programs accessible to students with disabilities.

We offer a brief discussion of the five titles in the sections that follow.

Title I (Employment)

Equal Employment Opportunity for Individuals with Disabilities

This title (section) is intended to help people with disabilities access the same employment opportunities and benefits available to people without disabilities. Employers must provide reasonable accommodations to qualified applicants or employees. A reasonable accommodation is defined as any modification or adjustment to a job or the work environment that will enable an applicant or employee with a disability to participate in the application process or to perform essential job functions.

Title II (State and Local Government)

Nondiscrimination on the Basis of Disability in State and Local Government Services

Title II of the ADA prohibits discrimination against qualified individuals with disabilities in all programs, activities, and services of public entities. It applies to all state and local governments, their departments and agencies, and any other instrumentalities or special purpose districts of state or local governments. It clarifies the requirements of section 504 of the Rehabilitation Act of 1973, as amended, for public transportation systems that receive federal financial assistance, and extends coverage to all public entities that provide public transportation, whether or not they receive federal financial assistance. It establishes detailed standards for the operation of public transit systems, including commuter and intercity rail (e.g., AMTRAK).

This title outlines the administrative processes to be followed, including requirements for self-evaluation and planning; requirements for making reasonable modifications to policies, practices, and procedures where necessary to avoid discrimination; architectural barriers to be identified; and the need for effective communication with people with hearing, vision, and speech disabilities. This title is regulated and enforced by the US Department of Justice.

Title III (Public Accommodations)

Nondiscrimination on the Basis of Disability by Public Accommodations and in Commercial Facilities

This title (section) prohibits private places of public accommodation from discriminating against individuals with disabilities. Examples of public accommodations include privately owned, leased, or operated facilities like hotels, restaurants, retail merchants, doctor's offices, golf courses, private schools, day care centers, health clubs, sports stadiums, movie theaters, and so on. This title sets the minimum standards for accessibility for alterations to an existing facility/structure and new construction of facilities. It also requires public accommodations to remove barriers in existing buildings where it is easy to do so without much difficulty or expense. This title directs businesses to make "reasonable modifications" to their usual ways of doing things when serving people with disabilities. It also requires that they take the necessary steps to communicate effectively with customers with vision, hearing, and speech disabilities. This title is also regulated and enforced by the US Department of Justice.

Title IV (Telecommunications)

This title requires telephone and Internet companies to provide a nationwide system of inter-state and intrastate telecommunications relay services that allow individuals with hearing and speech disabilities to communicate over the telephone. This title also requires closed captioning of federally funded public service announcements. This title is regulated by the Federal Communication Commission

Title V (Miscellaneous Provisions)

The final title contains a variety of provisions relating to the ADA as a whole, including its relationship to other laws, state immunity, its impact on insurance providers and benefits, pro-hibition against retaliation and coercion, illegal use of drugs, and attorney's fees. This title also provides a list of certain conditions that are not to be considered as disabilities.

Age Discrimination in Employment Act

The Age Discrimination in Employment Act (ADEA) forbids age discrimination against people who are age 40 or older (Public Law 101–433). It does not protect workers under the age of 40, although some states have laws that protect younger workers from age discrimin-ation. It is not illegal for an employer or other covered entity to favor an older worker over a younger one, even if both workers are age 40 or older.

This bill was signed in 1967 and provides equal opportunity under conditions that were not explicitly covered in Title VII of the Civil Rights Act of 1964. Age discrimination involves treating an applicant or employee less favorably because of his or her age. It also applies to the standards for pensions and benefits provided by employers and requires that information concerning the needs of older workers be provided to the general public. In order not to be burdensome to really small businesses, the act applies to only employers who have 20 or more employees on regular basis within a calendar month.

Age discrimination can occur even when the victim and the person who inflicted the discrimination or the discriminatory act are both over 40. The ADEA protects US citizens working for US employers, including even those operating abroad except where it would violate the laws of the country in which they are operating.

Higher Education Act of 1965

The Higher Education Act of 1965 (HEA) was signed into law on November 8, 1965, "to strengthen the educational resources of our colleges and universities and to provide financial assistance for students in postsecondary and higher education." The HEA has been amended and reauthorized several times. The Obama-era amendment which inserted "gainful employment in a recognized occupation" clause in the act to prevent its exploitation by for-profit institutions has been recently challenged under Trump administration. Its inclusion caused a lot of debate as to whether it hurts or harms those that the act was originally intended to help.

Higher Education Opportunity Act of 2008

The Higher Education Opportunity Act (Public Law 110–315) (HEOA) was enacted on August 14, 2008, and reauthorized the HEA of 1965 as amended. HEOA was established to provide consumers with comparable information from all institutions of higher education. HEOA's required disclosures are mandated to give consumers easy access to information that can be used in making sound decisions about their education.

The mended bill includes many new reporting requirements for institutions, grant programs for colleges and students, and provisions designed to lower the cost of a college education. It addresses simplifying the federal aid application, developing campus safety plans, and rules regarding relationships between higher education institutions and student lenders. The law also mandates studies on 24 topics, including articulation agreements, nursing school capacity, and the impact of student loan debt on public service.

Title IX of the Education Amendments of 1972

Title IX of the Education Amendments of 1972 (Title IX) prohibits sex (including pregnancy, sexual orientation, and gender identity) discrimination in any education program or activity receiving federal financial assistance.

The bill states that "except for provided elsewhere in this part, no person shall, on the basis of, or be subjected to discrimination under any academic, extracurricular, research, occupational training, or other education program or activity operated by a recipient which receives… federal assistance." The bill goes on to provide some examples of sex discrimination, explains who is covered, and what should one do if one believes that they is discriminated against.

Title VI of the Civil Rights Act 42 U.S.C. 2000d et seq. ("Title VI")

Tile VI, 42 U.S.C. §2000d et seq., was passed as part of the landmark Civil Rights Act of 1964.

> Title VI prohibits discrimination on the basis of race, color, or national origin in any program or activity that receives Federal funds or other Federal financial assistance. Programs that receive Federal funds cannot distinguish among individuals on the basis of race, color or national origin, either directly or indirectly, in the types, quantity, quality or timeliness of program services, aids or benefits that they provide or the manner in which they provide them.

This prohibition applies to intentional discrimination as well as to procedures, criteria, or methods of administration that appear neutral but have a discriminatory effect on individuals because of their race, color, or national origin. Policies and practices that have such an effect must be eliminated unless a recipient can show that they were necessary to achieve a legitimate nondiscriminatory objective. Even if there is such a reason the practice cannot continue if there are alternatives that would achieve the same objectives but that would exclude fewer minorities. Persons with limited English proficiency must be afforded a meaningful opportunity to participate in programs that receive federal funds. Policies and practices may not deny or have the effect of denying persons with limited English proficiency equal access to federally funded programs for which such persons qualify (HHS.gov Civil Rights). The bill goes on to give examples of conducts that may violate the act.

Family Educational Rights and Privacy Act

The Family Educational Rights and Privacy Act (FERPA) is a federal law enacted in 1974 to protect the privacy of student education records. FERPA applies to any public or private elementary, secondary, or postsecondary school and any state or local education agency that receives funds under an applicable program of the US Department of Education. The Act is very important to students and serves two primary purposes because it gives parents or eligible students more control over their educational records, and it prohibits educational institutions from disclosing

> personally identifiable information in education records" without the written consent of an eligible student, or if the student is a minor, the student's parents (20 U.S.C.S. § 1232g(b)). An eligible student is one who has reached age 18 or attends a school beyond the high school level.
>
> *(www.cdc.gov/phlp/publications/topic/ferpa.html).*

The bill goes on to elaborate parents' and students' rights and remedies under the law regarding contested information. It is important to note that even though parents and students under the law have the right to review students' education records that are maintained by the institution, the institution is not required to provide copies of the records unless it is impossible for parents or eligible students to review the original records; for example, if they live too far away.

It is also important to note that FERPA is not "absolute" and that the bill allows schools to disclose information from a student's education record, without consent, to certain parties, for example, to a transferring school if the student is transferring and under certain conditions, for example, to "specified officials for audit or evaluation purposes.

The Freedom of Information Act

The Freedom of Information Act (FOIA) generally gives everyone the right to request access to any federal agency's records or information except in cases where the information being requested is protected from disclosure by any of the nine exemptions contained in the law or by one of three special law enforcement record exclusions.

Exemptions

The nine exemption categories that authorize government agencies to withhold information are:

1. Classified information for national defense or foreign policy.
2. Internal personnel rules and practices.
3. Information that is exempt under other laws.
4. Trade secrets and confidential business information.
5. Interagency or intra-agency memoranda or letters that are protected by legal privileges.
6. Personnel and medical files.
7. Law enforcement records or information.
8. Information concerning bank supervision.
9. Geological and geophysical information.

The Three Special Law Enforcement Record Exclusions:

1. Protects the existence of an ongoing criminal law enforcement investigation when the subject of the investigation is unaware that it is pending and disclosure could reasonably be expected to interfere with enforcement proceedings.
2. Limited to criminal law enforcement agencies and protects the existence of informant records when the informant's status has not been officially confirmed.
3. Limited to the Federal Bureau of Investigation (FBI) and protects the existence of foreign intelligence or counterintelligence, or international terrorism records when the existence of such records is classified.

Higher Education Gainful Employment Act

The 2011 amendment to the Higher Education Act discussed earlier inserted the gainful employment clause. This clause has had its share of checkered history. The gainful employment regulation is a requirement in the Higher Education Act that states that career education programs must "prepare students for gainful employment in a recognized occupation" in order to be eligible for federal student aid.

The Higher Education Act in its original form permitted the use of federal student aid funds at for-profit institutions for nondegree programs "of training to prepare students for gainful employment in a recognized occupation." However, what constitutes "gainful employment" was not defined in the statute or regulations. In 2009, the Department of Education initiated a negotiated rulemaking process to define the term "gainful employment." However, no consensus was reached by the negotiators, hence the Department of Education was not bound by any agreements reached during the negotiations.

The Department, in 2010, proposed two sets of regulations which dealt with the disclosure of information by institutions about their gainful employment programs and the student outcomes intended to establish whether students were gainfully employed after leaving their training programs. The disclosure requirements went into effect on July 1, 2011; however, most of the requirements related to student outcomes were overturned in a lawsuit brought by the Association of Private Sector Colleges and Universities, which represents for-profit schools.

The department again in 2013 under President Obama initiated a second round of negotiated rulemaking, but once again the negotiators failed to reach consensus. A new set of regulations on student outcomes was published in December 2014, but these regulations were challenged in court. This time, the regulations were upheld and went into effect on July 1, 2015. However, under President Trump, the Department of Education convened a new negotiated rulemaking panel in 2017 to begin the process of formally rescinding the Obama administration's gainful employment rules. Secretary Betty DeVos, under President Trump, formally terminated the Obama-era gainful employment regulations and reporting requirements in 2019. However, it is safe to guess that we have not seen the end of the "tinkering" of the gainful employment requirement.

Education Policies in the European Union

Developing a workable education framework that solves the different needs of several independent countries in the European Union can be challenging. In their 1996 study, de Villé, Martou, and Vanderberghe analyzed the European Union's education policies on student mobility in the Union. The authors acknowledged that European integration could benefit from more developed exchanges in education and training; however, this type of mobility could create problems and risks which could, in turn, impede its harmonious expansion.

To shine more light on the problem, the authors focused on creating a cost-benefit analyses structure that is implicated in student mobility programs. The authors acknowledged that developing such a structure poses a problem because the purpose of education is complex. Education is important not only for individuals, but also for society, hence a good analysis must combine these two elements. For European countries, it seemed each has made its own choice concerning higher education and it seems this choice favors state (public) funding of education because of its "social" benefits. However, state financing of higher education is based on national taxes, which are a "local" issue with budgetary constraints and fiscal competition problems.

Viewing the problem from these different angles, de Villé and his colleagues suggested that "the development of international student mobility, especially when asymmetrical, raises questions as to the direct and indirect financial impact on the host country. This asymmetry is also a problem for a country that sends students abroad" (de Villé et al., 1996, p. 205). Thus, it is not surprising that many countries have chosen to restrict access to certain disciplines to promote policies in various fields, such as health care. Student mobility therefore could be an obstacle, particularly because "collective interest is at stake at the level of the sending countries, the host countries, and of the supranational entity: the European Union."

In a further study on education in the European Union, Walkenhorst (2008) explores the evolution, expansion, and dynamics of EU education policies using the standard public policy analysis which examines context and process. The author concludes based on an examination of EU documents covering 1970–2006 that a shift from politico-economic to economic-functional goals has taken place and a strong indicator of the shift is a change in the method of policy-making, which has drifted back from a semicommunity approach to an inter-transgovernmental mode of policy-making. In other words, a shift in paradigm seemed to have occurred in policies which drifted away from pro-integrationist toward pro-market orientation. This new direction reflected the increased political and economic salience of education in the European Union and is characterized by what the author described as "flexibility but also by fragility."

Some EU Policies on Educational Issues

The Bologna Process

As indicated in the introduction to this chapter, higher education policies in the European Union are decided at the level of the individual member states. The European Union therefore performs only a supporting and coordinating role. The primary objectives of the Union action in the field of higher education are to encourage mobility of students and staff, foster mutual recognition of diplomas and periods of study, and promote cooperation between higher education institutions.

The continent of Europe which consists of 44 countries, according to the United Nations (see Worldometer, 2012), has a fractured educational system as many of the countries have had their own "unique" educational system that is shaped by their unique circumstances and history. However, we will attempt in the subsequent paragraphs to discuss the Bologna process and its associated policies that we think have a large impact on the education policies of the majority of the EU nations.

The wheels of the Bologna Process were set in Article 165(1), in Title XII of the Treaty of Lisbon which states:

> The Union shall contribute to the development of quality education by encouraging cooperation between Member States and, if necessary, by supporting and supplementing their action, while fully respecting the responsibility of the Member States for the content of teaching and the organization of education systems and their cultural and linguistic diversity.
>
> *(European Union, 2021, p. 1)*

The **Bologna Process** therefore created the European Higher Education Area under the Lisbon Recognition Convention as a result of a series of ministerial meetings and agreements between European countries to ensure comparability in the standards and quality of higher educational qualifications. The Bologna Process got its name from the University of Bologna where in 1999 the Bologna declaration was signed by education ministers from 29 European countries. The process was opened to other European countries in the European Cultural Convention through a series of meetings.

The basic education framework agreed upon in 2005 amongst the ministers of the participating counties at the Bergen meeting in Norway are the qualifications produced through the three cycles of higher education. The cycles are described using the European Credit Transfer and Accumulation System (ECTS) as outlined here:

1. First cycle: typically 180–240 ECTS credits (a minimum of 60 credits per academic year). This usually leads to the award of the bachelor's degree. The European Higher Education Area did not introduce the bachelor-with-honors program, which allows graduates to receive a "BA hons." degree (e.g., in the United Kingdom, Australia, New Zealand, and Canada, such degrees are awarded). The "BA hons" or "B.Sc. hons" degrees in the United Kingdom, Australia, and New Zealand may enable graduates (the holders of such degrees) to begin doctoral studies without first obtaining a master's degree.
2. Second cycle: typically 60–120 ECTS credits (a minimum of 60 ECTS per academic year) usually leads to the award of the master's degree.
3. Third cycle (doctoral degree): There is no concrete ECTS range, since the disciplines vary in length and comprehensiveness. However, some countries have minimum credit weight requirements on doctoral degrees. Those country-level requirements typically require 120–420 ECTS of study.

In most cases, it would take three to four years to earn a bachelor's degree and another one or two years for a master's degree. Doctoral degrees usually require another two to four years of specialization, primarily individual research under a mentor. The degree names, under the agreement, may vary by country; however, one academic year normally corresponds to 60 ECTS credits, the equivalent to 1,500–1,800 hours of study.

These changes can be appreciated in light of the fact previously there was no bachelor's degree equivalent in such countries as Poland, Bulgaria, Romania etc. who were formerly a part of the USSR where the first university degree takes five to six years and therefore was approximated to be equivalent to the master's degree in such countries as the United Kingdom or the United States.

Is the Bologna Process a Binding Agreement?

The simple answer is no. An intergovernmental agreement between EU and non-EU countries does not have the status of EU legislation. Since the Bologna Declaration is not a treaty or convention, there are no legal obligations for the signatory states; thus, participation and cooperation are strictly voluntary. However, some countries introduced the ECTS and have discussed their degree structures, qualifications, financing, and management of higher education and mobility programs at the intercountry level.

Integrating Migrants and Refugees

It is impossible during the past few years to turn on the news and not see or hear anything about refugees on the borders of some countries in Europe or United States. Streitwieser et al. (2019) noted that the global refugee population increased by 65% in the past five years (i.e., till 2017), and according to the United Nations High Commissioner for Refugees (UNHCR, 2017) about 25.4 million refugees worldwide had been displaced by 2017, the largest in the agency's history since the end of World War II.

Securing shelter and safety are the primary concerns of refugees; however, according to Ager and Strang (2008), beginning or resuming education is generally an important next step for successful integration of refugees. Being able to return to the routine required by studying in an institution is part of the process of providing pathways for integration into the host community. It also serves as a counterweight to the trauma of forced migration (Crea, 2016). With renewed educational perspectives, refugees have been found to be resilient and ambitious learners (Mangan & Winter, 2017) even while facing extraordinary challenges (Stevenson & Willott, 2007; Zeus, 2011).

In their recent studies Streitwieser et al. (2019) examined current interventions that are aimed at reducing barriers to access higher education for refugees in North America and Europe. The authors analyzed a range of interventions organized by host governments, higher education institutions, foundations, nongovernmental organizations, and individuals. On the basis of review of the literature, the authors classified the current interventions into six categories which differed in size, delivery method, focus, extent of support, and range from a single language course or limited online learning opportunity to fully accredited higher education programs. The authors concluded on the basis of their study that though the current interventions programs are well-intended, significant problems still hamper the efficacy of the methods.

Streitwieser et al. (2019) further analyzed providers' rationale for providing refugees with education using Knight and De Wit's (1995) argument for internationalization of higher education. This argument was later reconceptualized into the following four interrelated groups of rationales – academic, political, economic, and sociocultural, and proposed adding a fifth category which they called "humanism." To expand opportunities for refugees to participate in higher education, the authors suggested that policy-makers and administrators adopt a "longer-term perspective, increase transparency, and use evidence-based approaches to develop and evaluate refugee programming."

Promoting Inclusion and Fundamental Values

Concerned about intolerance and discrimination, the EU education ministers adopted the Paris Declaration on March 17, 2015. This declaration was aimed at promoting citizenship and the common values of freedom, tolerance, and nondiscrimination through education. It calls on the education sector to be mobilized in promoting inclusion and fundamental values. The declaration established a list of concrete objectives that should be pursued at national and local levels and defines four overarching priorities for cooperation at EU level (Colloquium-leaflet_promoting-inclusion-and-fundamental-values.pdf. 2017). These are:

1. Ensuring young people acquire social, civic, and intercultural competences by promoting democratic values and fundamental rights, social inclusion and nondiscrimination, as well as active citizenship.
2. Enhancing critical thinking and media literacy, particularly in the use of the Internet and social media, so as to develop resistance to discrimination and indoctrination.
3. Fostering the education of disadvantaged children and young people, by ensuring that our education and training systems address their needs.
4. Promoting intercultural dialogue through all forms of learning in cooperation with other relevant policies and stakeholders. (European Commission on Education and Training, Colloquium-leaflet_promoting-inclusion-and-fundamental-values.pdf, p. 1).

Following the Paris declaration, six key priority areas in the field of education and training (ET2020 framework) have been identified for cooperation between the member states and the European Commission. Concrete steps are to be taken in the following key areas:

1. Mobilizing funding – make more than €400 million available for transnational partnerships to develop innovative policy approaches and practices at grassroots level.
2. Better knowledge and policy support – "The Commission will create a better knowledge base, reinforce the collection of evidence at EU level, and provide reinforced policy support related to inclusive education as well as to the teaching of social and civic competences."
3. Teachers and schools – allow schools to be in a position where they can make a major contribution to inclusion and better prospects in life.
4. Higher education – recognize the fact that students and staff of higher education institutions can play an important role in engaging with their communities through institutional and grassroots initiatives and by providing spaces for discussion.
5. Youth work, volunteering, and virtual exchanges – acknowledge that youth work is a powerful tool that can reach out to the most vulnerable young people and bridge the gap between society and individuals in need of support.
6. Sport – participating in sport can be an effective way of integrating into a community and developing a sense of belonging.

Through these pillars, European Union hoped that tolerance and inclusiveness in society at large could be promoted using youth programs and schools.

Higher Education Attainment (Erasmus+ and Horizon 2020)

EU member states have realized that higher education and its links with research and innovation will play a key role in individual and societal development. It also recognized that education is key in providing the highly skilled human capital and the engaged citizens that Europe needs to create jobs that will ensure economic growth and prosperity. To this end, higher education institutions are "crucial partners in delivering the European Union's strategy to drive forward and maintain sustainable growth." It is against this backdrop that the Europe 2020 strategy set a target that by 2020 40% of young Europeans would have acquired a higher education qualification (Grove, 2013).

To attain its educational objectives to create new opportunities for people in higher education to learn from one another across national borders, to work together on joint projects to develop good learning and teaching, and to undertake excellent research and promote innovation, the European Union through its Erasmus+ and Horizon 2020 programs supports international exchanges for students, academic staff, and researchers, as well as structured cooperation between higher education institutions and public authorities in different countries.

Marketing Opportunities

The question one can easily ask is what is the meaning of all these laws? Our answer is to govern, but that would be too easy an answer. The most important thing is to look for the marketing opportunities that the laws and agreements have created. In other words, how can one educational institution use the laws and regulations to its marketing advantage? If you are a university in Europe, participating in the Erasmus project could easily be used to one's advantage. For example, what about going abroad to study for a semester and paying the same home tuition fees? In the United States, using the Universal Design (UD) approach to complying with the ADA could also present some interesting marketing opportunities – we can easily see Hope University developing a slogan such as "At Hope we see only possibilities not disabilities"!

Summary

This chapter attempts to draw attention to some important regulatory issues that concern education in the United States and the European Union. It also shows the difference in the approaches through which the governments in the United States and European Union influence activities in higher educational institutions. Whereas the United States uses the law, the European Union uses agreements. The most important thing in this chapter though is to understand the intent, the objectives, and origins of certain laws and agreements, and appreciation will follow. With appreciation, we believe marketing opportunities will be developed.

Questions

1. What is the relevance of the Higher Education Act of 1965?
2. What is the relevance of the ADA in schools?
3. Can you see some marketing opportunities for an institution with these acts?
4. How important is the Freedom of Information Acts?
5. What is the relevance of the Bologna Process in the European Union?
6. Why did EU education ministers see it necessary to adopt the Paris Declaration on March 17, 2015?
7. What is Erasmus+ about?

Additional Questions

1. Would these laws have made any difference to you when you were applying for admission into the university?
2. Can you think about how you or someone you know used the rights protected under FERPA?

References

Ager, A., & Strang, A. (2008). Understanding Integration: A Conceptual Framework. *Journal of Refugee Studies* 21 (2), 166–191.

Crea, T.M. (2016). Refugee Higher Education: Contextual Challenges and Implications for Program Design, Delivery, and Accompaniment. *International Journal of Educational Development* 46 (A1–A2), 12–22.

de Villé, P., Martou, F., & Vanderberghe, V. (1996). Cost-Benefit Analysis and Regulatory Issues of Student Mobility in the EU. *European Journal of Education* 31 (2), 205–222.

European Union (2021). Fact Sheets on the European Union – 20211www.europarl.europa.eu/factsheets/en. Retrieved on November 10, 2021

Grove, J. (2013). Horizon 2020 and Erasmus Budgets Approved at www.timeshighereducation.com/news/horizon-2020-and-erasmus-budgets-approved/2009234.article. Retrieved on October 21, 2021.

Knight, J., & De Wit, H. (1995). Strategies for Internationalization of Higher Education: Historical and Conceptual Perspectives. In H. De Wit (Ed.), *Strategies for Internationalization of Higher Education: A Comparative Study of Australia, Canada, Europe and the United States of America*, pp. 5–33. Amsterdam, The Netherlands: European Association for International Education.

Mangan, D., & Winter, L.A. (2017). (In)validation and (Mis)recognition in Higher Education: The Experiences of Students from Refugee Backgrounds. *International Journal of Lifelong Education* 36 (4), 486–502.

Stevenson, J., & Willott, J. (2007). The Aspiration and Access to Higher Education of Teenage Refugees in the UK. *Compare: A Journal of Comparative and International Education* 37 (5), 671–687.

Streitwieser, B., Loo, B., Ohorodnik, M., & Jeong, J. (2019). Access for Refugees into Higher Education: A Review of Interventions in North America and Europe. *Journal of Studies in International Education* 2019 23 (4), 473–496.

United Nations High Commissioner for Refugees (UNHCR) (2017). Global Trends: Forced Displacement in 2017. Geneva, Switzerland: UNHCR. Retrieved from www.unhcr. org/en-us/statistics/unhcrstats/5b27be547/unhcr-global-trends-2017.html.

Walkenhorst, H. (2008). Explaining Change in EU Education Policy. *Journal of European Public Policy* 15 (4), 567–587.

Worldometer (2021). www.worldometers.info/geography/how-many-countries-in-europe. Retrieved on October 12, 2021.

Zeus, B. (2011). Exploring Barriers to Higher Education in Protracted Refugee Situations: The Case of Burmese Refugees in Thailand. *Journal of Refugee Studies* 24 (2), 256–276.

CASE #25 SUCCESS SHOULD NOT BE RATIONED

This case discusses why and how Martin University (a fictitious name) transitions to the UD approach to handling disability issues to comply with Section 504 of the ADA.

As indicated at the beginning of this chapter in the review of Section 504 of the ADA, the act has been in effect for about three decades now. It has during this time undoubtedly given hope to and has allowed a growing number of Americans with challenges of one form or the other (which are generally referred to as disabilities) not only access to higher education, but on a broader scale, a social promise to promote equal access and full participation in all aspects of the US society. It is not surprising that recent statistics have estimated that about 19% of undergraduates and 12% of graduate students have disabilities. If access to higher education allows for upward mobility as evidenced in many studies, can you imagine the number of people whose lives would have been much harder had the act not been passed?

The literature on how schools have adapted to the ADA shows that two approaches have been primarily used: (1) the provision of accommodations to students and (2) the use of UD to structure campus environments, policies, and practices. Accommodation strategies are often seen as retroactive or specialized case-by-case approach completed by the personnel in the office of disability services on campus, as reasonable accommodations are covered by the ADA and Section 504. Accommodations for the learning disabled are individualized and intended to respond to specific contexts and individual circumstances. There are many different kinds of accommodations, with the most common for students with learning disabilities being specialized tutoring, recorded/audiobooks, class notetakers, preferential seating, lecture notes, or study guides to prepare for exams.

Research on access to higher education has noted several barriers to the provision of accommodation. For example, many accommodations are based on physician recommendations and are often not evidence-based nor are they responsive to the individual contexts of students with disabilities. Other barriers include lack of faculty knowledge regarding federal regulations, "ambivalent attitudes" about supporting students with disabilities, as well as perceived ethical implications of accommodations. Some faculty cite ethical concerns, where there is a perceived dilemma between providing the same experience for students while also equalizing opportunities, or levelling the playing field for students who may need accommodation. The misperception of accommodation as special treatment rather than equal access is a common educational barrier for students with disabilities. On the contrary, instead of individual accommodation, a UD perspective suggests that changes should be made to the overall environment to increase access for everyone, which includes addressing the potential inaccessibility of many campus programs. Access under UD therefore means proactive, inclusive, and sustainable development.

Martin University (fictitious name) decided ten years ago, based on faculty feedback, to transition from a policy in which it made specific accommodation to disabled students to a policy of actively using UD to enable everyone. This transition was necessitated by a survey which showed that about 25% of the faculty seemed to have misunderstood the school's policy for accommodating disabled students, and instead felt that the disabled students were actually being advantaged over the abled students. With funding from a group of generous donors, the university took a number of steps to address these perceived inequities by replacing every door on campus with automatic self-opening doors, and by redesigning classrooms to have flexible work spaces for students. This includes spaces for quiet individual work, small and large group work, and group instruction. Also, the office of student disabilities on campus purchased several laptops that students with disabilities can borrow for classes. These computers were especially equipped to be used by students with disabilities. Furthermore, the faculty also was advised to:

1.   Attend four computerized training sessions on disability rights and issues each year.
2.   Attend a workshop each year on UD.
3.   Use as much as possible class materials that are accessible for all types of learners. Students have many options for reading, including print, digital, text-to-speech and audiobooks. For digital text, there are also options for text enlargement, along with choices for screen color and contrast. Videos have captions, and there are transcripts for audio.
4.   Flexibility is encouraged as much as possible in the choice of formats for evaluating assignments and testing students. Instead of the traditional essay or worksheet format, the faculty was asked to consider multiple options. For instance, it should be possible for students to demonstrate their mastery of course materials through podcasts or videos instead of the traditional essays or multiple-choice examinations that are used for student assessment.

Questions

1. Does complying with the ADA offer any marketing opportunities to a university?
2. How can Martin University use its approach to complying with the ADA to market the university without alienating some people?
3. Discuss the ethical ramifications in complying with the ADA.
4. Why was the ADA enacted?

CASE #26 FOR-PROFIT OR TO EDUCATE: THE CASE OF SALLY CAREER COLLEGE

This case discusses how some unethical admission counselors have been taking advantage of naïve, uninformed, and vulnerable segments of the population to swell their enrollment numbers.

With the amendment in HEA which made federal financial aid, federal student loans, and military educational benefits available to be used in vocational and career colleges, some entrepreneurs saw the opportunity to sell "dreams" to many receptive audiences including military veterans by establishing career colleges and vocational educational institutions. Many of the students who ended up going to these schools would have, for financial reasons, stayed away from them, but with enticing ads about better jobs, availability of financial and excellent "salesmanship" by admission counselors, many students found themselves enrolling in some of these schools unwittingly. Some of the graduates of these schools have ended up with good jobs that they would not have otherwise had; however, anecdotal stories indicate that many of them ended up being worse off – still with their original jobs, if any, and yet with thousands of dollars in debt.

Ali was a young teenager who migrated to the United States at 17, soon after graduating high school in one of the English-speaking Caribbean Islands. Ali's parents were divorced. She was brought to the United States by her father who remarried a year after Ali's arrival in the United States and moved to another state with his new wife without Ali. At 18, Ali was forced by circumstances to live on her own. She worked full-time as a waitress in a restaurant for minimum wage out of which she had to pay her rent, utility bills, and buy food. It was undoubtedly hard for her to make ends meet.

From the Caribbean where the importance of getting higher education was emphasized, Ali knew that her current job was not going to get her the American dream, and that the most likely route for her to the middle class was through getting higher education. She actively searched for a way by which she could obtain higher education. Being only a permanent resident at the time, she knew that she was not qualified for many financial assistance and scholarship opportunities and that it would be financially impossible for her at the time to go to college. Then something interesting happened! She stumbled upon an ad for Sally Career College.

The ad struck her with four things that resonated with her: (1) affordability – the ad stated that the tuition was affordable and arrangements could be made for flexible payment; (2) convenience – the school attaches importance to students' convenience in terms of scheduling of classes; (3) speed – the ad emphasized the fact that many programs take only ten months to complete and make students eligible to take national certification exams; (4) hands-on experience – the school provides a supporting and caring environment and emphasizes hands-on approach to teaching and learning whereby students actually learn by doing instead of memorizing theories. The school also bragged about having ongoing enrollment which meant that a student could enroll at any time. As an icing on the cake, Sally Career College was only five miles from where Ali lived.

Excited about her discovery, Ali made appointment over the phone to meet an admission's counselor, in-person, on campus the following day. The admission counselor went over the application process with her and helped her to fill the application for admission, and a student loan application form. The loan was for $10,000.00 for the ten-month course in medical billing and coding. Ali was told that she could reduce the outstanding loan amount by making small payments while still going to school while she was working and that after completion of the program she could get a job that paid around $30, and could therefore quickly finish paying off the loan in about two years after completing the program. From earning $2.00 per hour plus tips (which was the going rate that many restaurants paid) to hearing that she could easily make, at the least, $30.00 per hour was like music to Ali's ears.

She enrolled in school the following week in the medical office management and billing and coding program. Thoroughly enchanted about what she thought was her good fortune and the beginning of a turn in her life for the better, she approached her classes with enthusiasm. She attended classes during the day, and worked in the restaurant in the night. In addition, she made periodic payments of about $150.00 toward the student loan. Ten months after Ali enrolled in the program, she graduated; in the meantime the market was saturated with people looking for billing and coding jobs. The course was by that time available at far cheaper cost at several other venues. The entire course was even available online for $250.00. Ten years after graduating from the program and continuing to make monthly payment of $150.00, Ali still owed over $8,000.00 on the student loan. The wonderful jobs she was told that she could find after the program were nonexistent and she tells everyone who would listen that the promise of a great job after graduating was like a fantasyland that did not exist in reality.

In the meantime, an investigative journalist revealed that some admission counselors in some of the career colleges were compensated based on the number of students they were able to recruit, hence the tendency to embellish and exaggerate job prospects and the like were not uncommon. So what Ali thought was a ticket to the American dream was more a ticket into a quicksand of never-ending debt.

Questions

1. Discuss Obama era's "gainful employment in a recognized occupation" clause or the requirement that career colleges provide student outcomes intended to establish whether students were gainfully employed after leaving their training programs based on your understanding of the case on Sally Career College.
2. Do you think there are too many regulations that higher educational institutions have to follow? Why?
3. If there are few bad apples in the for-profit college industry, how do you think they can be stopped from taking advantage of people like Ali?
4. What are the marketing opportunities presented in this case to for-profit schools that operate within the confines of the law?

NAME INDEX

SUBJECT INDEX